This England's Book

BRITISH DANCE BANDS

from the Twenties to the Fifties

This England acknowledges the help and assistance of the following enthusiasts, without whom it would have been impossible to compile and check the enormous amount of material contained in this book:-
David Ades, Percy Bickerdyke, Eric Holmes, Arthur Jackson, Nigel Ogden, Ray Pallett, Brian Rust, Edward Towler, Edmund Whitehouse, Don Wicks, and Doug Wilkins.
In addition, *This England* is pleased to recognise the staff production and design team whose hard work made it possible to piece everything together:-
Ann Augur, Keren Bowers, Maureen Compton, Sally Hunt, Paul Makepeace, Christine Manifold, Susan Beaty, and Peter Worsley.

Published in July 1999 by This England Books,
Alma House, 73 Rodney Road, Cheltenham,
Gloucestershire GL50 1HT. Tel: 01242-577775

Printed in Great Britain by Polestar Wheatons Ltd., Exeter

ISBN 0 906324 25 4

Contents

Above (left to right): Maurice Winnick, Billy Cotton, Jack Jackson, Sydney Lipton, Lloyd Shakespeare, Marius B. Winter, Nat Gonella, Joe Loss, Lou Preager.

Introduction

It is hard to appreciate the insularity and parochialism of the early Edwardian period, especially for a generation which now has instant access to almost everything — anywhere in the world. Most people never left their village or town, and entertainment, such as it was, was confined largely to public concerts at the local parish hall, or private *soirées* around the family piano in the drawing room. Some urban folk were lucky enough to visit a theatre, music hall, or even a new-fangled picture palace which screened silent movies but, for many, especially in rural areas, it was almost a noiseless world, punctuated only by the sounds of nature and passing railway trains. Motor car horns were rarer than electric trams, and everyone knew and understood their place in life. Society was well stratified, with music very much in keeping with a person's social class.

Yet across the sea in North America, things were very different. Unlike the staid and stately dance customs in this country, a new branch of music was taking shape. Based on the Negro folk traditions of the Deep South, jazz was beginning to spread outwards, and was destined to make a major impact across the globe. But owing to the fact that there were few commercial records, no wireless, and no quick means of transport across the Atlantic, Britain would probably have remained largely ignorant of this contemporary American popular music scene for several more years. However . . .

In 1914 everything changed dramatically. Within three years of the start of the First World War (or Great War as it was known at the time), huge numbers of young American servicemen were thronging Europe. They could not fail to make an impact and, after hostilities ceased, it was an all-white American group called the Original Dixieland Jazz Band (totally misnamed but new to Britain), which created

an absolute sensation. Appearing at the London Palladium, and Hippodrome, but most famously at the Hammersmith Palais (a converted roller skating rink and redundant aircraft factory), the "ODJB" turned British popular music on its head. Out went the strict tempo "old time" dance routines, to be replaced by a syncopated extrovert brand of music which had young couples flocking in their thousands to listen and dance to it. Instead of being just part of the musical background, the bands now became entertainment in themselves.

The Roaring Twenties set everybody going. With the advent of national wireless stations; mass produced cheap but good quality records (especially after the first electrical recordings were pressed in 1925); talkies at the cinema; motor cars; and an increasingly accessible telephone system . . . life was buzzing. Efficient mass public transportation systems now existed in all large urban areas, and people were able to move about freely. The world was shrinking and American musicians began appearing here in increasingly large numbers. The old order had been swept away — and there would be no turning back.

Unfortunately, the booming western world economy crashed at the end of the decade, and many people suffered great social deprivation. Nevertheless, the popular music industry had become so well-established that it could not be derailed and, with few other distractions around, by the early Thirties the golden period of the British Dance Bands was firmly consolidated.

The rich and famous dined out in London's West End clubs and restaurants, followed by late night dancing to one of the country's top bands. Not to be outdone, all the posh hotels also engaged resident orchestras, following the lead of the previously sedate Savoy which, in

Above (left to right): Ambrose, Sydney Kyte, Jack Hylton, Carroll Gibbons, Roy Fox, Lew Stone, Herman Darewski, Harry Roy, Charlie Kunz, Geraldo.

what proved to be a hugely successful business venture, had been persuaded to give the new music a try during the early Twenties. Meanwhile, the middle classes flocked to watch famous bands on tour, while the less well-off found solace in listening to their primitive radio, or wind-up gramophone. Dance band music was popular everywhere in the land — enlivening the spirits of the well-to-do, and banishing the blues of those less fortunate.

With the wireless in its prime, and television not even a distant glow on a cathode ray tube, 78 rpm records sold in their tens of thousands. Dance bands appeared at every appropriate venue in the country, and also as star turns in between films at large cinemas. So popular were they that police were sometimes called to control noisy crowds anxious to see their favourite stars in person, many of whom commanded appearance money which still seems large by today's standards. Economic depression or not, the Roaring Twenties, at least as far as most dance bands were concerned, moved smoothly into the Thriving Thirties.

All was never quite what it appeared on the surface, of course, and regular disputes between American and British musicians' unions resulted in restrictive practices and much friction. In 1935 the BBC banned the word "hot" and instructed band leaders henceforth to call their music "bright" or "swing". Also, allegedly in response to some listeners' complaints, it tried to ban "scat" singing at the same time. First popularised by Louis Armstrong, this involved unintelligible vocal noises replacing the words — but the prohibition proved short-lived because the sound was invariably melodic and most listeners enjoyed it. Other short-sighted and short-lived BBC edicts, such as refusing to name tune titles over the air, annoyed several musicians, but their own in-house dance orchestras, notably Jack Payne and Henry Hall, did much to popularise and fortify the dance band genre from John O'Groats to Land's End. Almost everyone was a winner. Then ...

In 1939 it happened all over again. During the next five years the Second World War deprived the country of a great deal, including most of its top dance orchestras — although many fine new Service bands sprang up in unexpected places. The wartime years were effectively ones of "make do and mend", with the unsatisfactory situation inevitably continuing into post-war austerity — accompanied by a rapid decline of traditional dance band and cinema-going audiences. In little more than two glorious decades the magnificent spectacle of colourful, uniformly-attired bandsmen, led by an immaculate baton-wielding leader in lush and glamorous surroundings, gave way to smaller groups of musicians in civvies, eking out an existence wherever anyone would pay to listen to them.

All too soon wall-to-wall television finished off the ailing local palais, theatre, music hall, and cinema. It was not uncommon in the mid-Fifties to walk down a deserted early-evening suburban street, and witness a flickering silver screen shining out from the front room of every home. Falling box-office revenues resulted in a spiral of higher prices, and going out for a musical evening became an extremely expensive affair. Live performances simply could not compete with an increasingly mobile population, which now had so many cheaper options that it never quite knew what to do next. The writing was no longer on the wall ... because the wall had already collapsed.

In the following pages we learn all about the golden era of British dance band music; who played where, when, and with whom; which bands adapted successfully to change; and which ones disappeared into oblivion. Many famous names moved from wireless into television and enhanced their popularity, but others died in poverty and obscurity. Whatever their epitaph, however, they all contributed richly to that part of our musical heritage which we now lovingly refer to as *"The Dance Band Days"*.

EDMUND WHITEHOUSE

Henry Hall

(1898-1989)

Listeners to the wireless in the early Thirties were terribly disappointed when Jack Payne, easily Britain's most popular dance band leader, announced he was giving up his job as head of the BBC Dance Orchestra. Under his baton, every weekday afternoon at 5.15 the orchestra had broadcast its lively music over the expanding air waves to a public which for a period of four years, from 1928 to 1932, had grown to love the band's bright and breezy tunes as much as the cultured if clipped tones of Jack Payne himself. So you can imagine the feeling of intense dismay when Jack decided to go off the air and take his orchestra on tour as a showband. But the public's unhappiness at the prospect turned to near outrage when his successor was named. For instead of a carbon copy of the suave and polished Jack Payne, the BBC brought in his almost complete opposite — a shy, quietly spoken, gangling young fellow with a hesitant way of talking. His name was Henry Hall ... and what's more, he came from the Salvation Army!

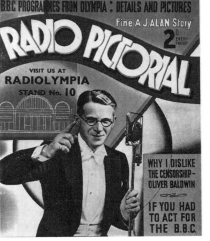

△ *Henry Hall featured on the front cover of "Radio Pictorial" in August 1934.*

Most dance band leaders, though popular with the fox-trotting public, were regarded as "Flash Harrys" by Britain's sober social establishment. Their black patent-leather shoes, slicked-down hair, jazzy suit and a permanent glitzy smile, all contributed to an archetypal image which had spread here from across the Atlantic. So when young Henry, blinking through horn-rimmed glasses and wearing a dark pin-striped suit, appeared in front of a band in public, they looked and listened — and couldn't believe it. But they liked his music, and so they warmed to him in typical British fashion of supporting the underdog. When he later

stood in front of a BBC microphone and announced his band's dance numbers in quiet, hesitant tones, his popularity soared even further. Indeed, who can ever forget the deliberate way he said those memorable few words to introduce his programmes:

"This *is* Henry Hall speaking ... and tonight is my Guest Night."

Hardly a dynamic choice of words, or delivery — but it won the hearts of millions of people who disliked the pushy style of most other dance band leaders. From that moment on, Henry Hall became a legend who lived on in the public's heart and mind for over 30 years, well into the age of television.

Henry Robert Hall was born in Peckham, south-east London, in May 1898, the son of a blacksmith turned greengrocer. Both his parents were members of the Salvation Army and it seemed only natural that they wanted their lad to learn music and play in the local Salvation Army band based at nearby Nunhead, between Peckham and Lewisham. He learned to play the cornet and concertina, but his soft voice was never strong enough to put over the gospel message at Salvation Army open-air meetings in the London suburbs before the First World War.

"I was no infant prodigy", he wrote later in his autobiography. "I was no Mozart creeping downstairs in my nightshirt to compose sonatas. I was just plain Henry Hall, the grocer's son, who had a bit of an ear for music".

On leaving school at 14, Henry worked as a page boy at the National Health Insurance Commission and became very impressed by his bosses, whom he regarded as very important

The B.B.C. Dance Orchestra

"Here's to the Next Time"

Burton Gillis
Jack Halsall
Eddie Cromar
Freddy Williams
Bert Read
Les Allen
Cyril Hellier
HENRY HALL
George Dickinson
Jack Hitchenor
T. Farrar
A. E. Williams
Frankie Wilson
Len Bermon
Bill Mulraney

△ *A contemporary 1934 cartoon of Henry Hall's band.*

people. It was while there, earning nine shillings a week, that he got the ambition to be big and famous himself one day. He trod his first rung on the long ladder when he was barely a year older, for he joined the Salvation Army's music department at Judd Street, King's Cross, under Colonel Richard Slater, a fine musician and composer who had a clear concept of musical excellence.

Although he began his new job typing letters and copying out music scores by hand, he had a go at writing marches for "the Army" in his spare time . . . and he learned a lot from Colonel Slater, who corrected his scores and encouraged his budding talent for composing and arranging. The great Christian soldier General William Booth, founder of the Salvation Army, always urged his followers to play cheerful music, but he could hardly have expected how much one of his youngest adherents would take that message to heart and spread it far and wide. For among young Henry's earliest compositions was a simple, bright and breezy piece called *The Sunshine March*. If you heard it today you'd immediately recognize it as the basis for Henry Hall's famous signature tune *Here's To The Next Time*. If, as Catherine Booth (the General's grand-daughter) once supposed, the Salvation Army's own newspaper *The War Cry* was "published in heaven", then their tunes were composed by angels for they brought a rousing lift into the drab lives of down-trodden folk in our

city streets. Henry's sister Edna remained a Salvationist all her life, becoming a senior officer, but fame proved too strong a magnet for her illustrious brother, although even at the height of his popularity with the BBC he sometimes telephoned the Army's London headquarters to enquire about friends and to catch up on news.

Still in his early teens, Henry later claimed he was glad to have done his basic training in the Salvation Army, rather than amidst the seedier parts of Tin Pan Alley. In his autobiography *Here's To The Next Time*, Henry stated: "I myself was never deeply religious, nor felt any sort of vocation for its work, but the Salvation Army did leave me with a code of musical honesty and an over-riding independence of thought."

When war came, young Henry volunteered for the other Army on his 18th birthday, but his musical skills meant he stayed in Britain, playing in a military band. When the war was over he went on the stage as a variety turn playing the concertina, but quickly formed a three-piece musical act called "The Variety Three". It soon failed and by 1920 he was back as a soloist, this time playing the piano for silent films in a cinema at Notting Hill Gate. The work bored him after a while and he felt that the audience didn't really mind what he played as they sat with their eyes glued to the flickering screen in front of them. So for a bit of fun he tried out some of the classic piano pieces

△ *A rare picture of "The Henry Hall Trio" in 1934 — but it never broadcast. Henry enjoyed playing music with his daughter Betty, then aged nine, and Michael, six, at their London home.*

he had been learning at Trinity College and the Guildhall School of Music. As Rudolph Valentino flashed his piercing eyes, and Buster Keaton romped with the Keystone Cops, Henry Hall sitting at the cinema piano gave them snatches of Chopin and Debussy! What's more — nobody seemed to notice!

Cinema work soon proved too monotonous for young Henry and just before Christmas 1922 a friend persuaded him to take a fortnight's temporary stint deputising for the regular pianist in a dance band at the Midland Hotel, Manchester. "It was madness", Henry wrote later — "but luckily I was mad!".

However, Henry's Salvation Army music background hardly fitted him for the role of ragtime pianist for Manchester's trendy quick-steppers, and it seemed he would soon be heading back to the cinema stool again. But, as so often happens, fate intervened in a peculiar way. It was New Year's Eve 1922, and as part of the hotel's gala festivities for the night there was to be an exhibition of the latest dance steps by two professionals, man and woman. This entailed them switching from waltz to the latest foxtrot — and that meant a change of costume for the lady partner. It would take her just 60 seconds backstage to slip out of one dress and into another — but who could keep the audience's attention from straying for that vital minute? Inevitably, the manager's eye fell on the pianist — and young Henry was told to "play something, quick!".

Instead of a bouncy new number by a popular composer of the time, sober-sided Henry Hall jumped up and played an intricate classical piece by Chopin, called *The Butterfly*. He had just one minute ... but when he finished the whole ballroom erupted with applause. As young Henry blushed, one man in a dinner jacket called the Head Waiter over and whispered a few words. It was Arthur Towle, boss of the Midland hotel group, part of the LMS railway conglomerate (London, Midland and Scottish). Mr. Towle's whispered verdict on Henry's one minute of glory was: "Who's that boy? — we must keep him!" And he did — within a month Henry was leader of Manchester's top hotel band at the tender age of 24.

Within a year he had married, bought a smart new Rover saloon car, and was in charge of five hotel bands for the LMS group. Not bad going for the former page-boy from the Salvation Army! His marriage makes an interesting pointer to Henry's supposedly self-effacing and shy personality. While holidaying with friends in Devon in September 1923, he met a girl called Margery — and proposed 48 hours later! They were married in January 1924 and had two children, Betty and Michael. Commenting on such a quick courtship, Henry stated in his autobiography: "Marry in haste, repent at leisure? — Nonsense! Not when you were as sure of yourselves as Margery and I were". They eventually celebrated their Golden Wedding in 1974!

The following year (1924) Henry transferred his band from Manchester to the latest star hotel in the LMS crown — the Gleneagles in Perthshire, Scotland, and hit on the bright idea of having the opening night broadcast on the new "wireless" system. So in June 1924, for the first time outside the Savoy Hotel, London, the BBC featured a dance band from faraway Scotland. For the next eight years Henry Hall broadcast regularly from Gleneagles, plus the Midland hotels in Manchester and Liverpool. By this time he was in charge of all the LMS group's 32 dance bands.

The "wireless" was just beginning to develop in the early 1920s, through a network of town and city-based stations of somewhat modest output. Dance bands, linked with night-clubs or restaurants, were welcomed into the programme schedule, although the BBC Year Book for 1933 left little doubt as to the relatively poor acoustics of those live broadcast relay sites. Indeed, the creation of a BBC Dance Orchestra under Jack Payne in 1928 was partly motivated by the possibility of securing a better quality broadcast sound, under controlled studio conditions. There was also the matter of Corporation policy: the BBC, which came into being on 1st January 1927, after operating as a limited company since November 1922, had a morbid fear of "song plugging" and even employed staff to make sure that none of it was being done.

Despite his youth, and the relatively small size (six players) of the LMS ensemble, Henry quickly took to the new medium of radio, and was especially fortunate in his Manchester broadcasts, the Northern Region being second only to London in its variety of programming.

The next turning point in his career came in January 1932 when he was invited down to London to a meeting at the BBC's Savoy Hill headquarters. Henry thought it was to discuss more broadcasts from the north, but he was told that Jack Payne was leaving the Corporation to go into show business. Would Henry like to succeed him?

Modest, unassuming, quietly-spoken Henry Hall hesitated. The BBC bosses wanted an answer that day — and when Henry finally said "yes" his stairway to stardom was all ready and waiting. The next day he gave up his job with the LMS hotel group, dined with Jack Payne at the Savoy Hotel, and signed a recording contract with Columbia.

Still only 33, the world was his oyster. On 15th March, 1932, the New BBC Dance Orchestra under the direction of Henry Hall went on the air for the first time, coinciding with the opening of Broadcasting House in London, from where the technical quality of the broadcasts was much superior to the "relays" that came from faraway hotels.

Beginning at 5.15 and lasting for 45 minutes, five nights a week, listeners to the "wireless" tuned in and heard the latest rhythms, dance tunes, and novelty numbers ... for Henry Hall was well aware that, at that time in the early evening (before the 6 o'clock News) many children would be listening, so he always included a song or two for them — *The Teddy Bears' Picnic* being an especial favourite. Although first published in 1908, without words, Henry wrote a new arrangement with lyrics by Jimmy Kennedy, and it sold a million records — 78rpm of course. For years it was used as a test piece by BBC sound engineers, because of its extraordinary wide range of notes from the high xylophone down to the bass sax. He also included Enid Blyton-type characters Rusty and Dusty Brown to amuse the youngsters in between popular tunes. Within a couple of months Henry Hall had become a household name, and he and the band were given a tumultuous reception by fans at Radiolympia in 1932.

The original 1932 BBC Dance Orchestra under Henry's baton was a 13-member ensemble — trumpet, trombone, four saxophones (all doubling with clarinet), two violins, oboe, guitar, double bass, piano and drums (including percussion and "effects"). There was also a vocalist although, as the 1930s proceeded, "crooners" also doubled as instrumentalists, moving to the microphone only when required. These included drummer George Elrick who later had his own band and was also a popular "Housewives Choice" presenter in the 1950s. One of his best numbers with Henry Hall was the popular 1936 hit song *The Music Goes Round and Round*.

Among other vocalists who worked with Henry Hall were some of the best known of the time — Val Rosing, son of a Russian operatic tenor, who disliked the description "crooner" and was hardly one of the type as developed in America; Les Allen, from Canada, who recorded with "The Canadian Bachelors" on the Columbia label, and was very popular indeed; Dan Donovan, the band's baritone saxophone player; Bob Mallin, who specialised in cowboy

▽ *Dan Donovan was best known as a crooner, but he also played the saxophone, and later became a band leader in his own right.*

ballads, and even Flanagan and Allen who recorded their famous *Wanderer* song with Henry Hall in 1932.

The following year (1933) Henry went to America where he was impressed by the way that radio announcers set the scene when introducing band shows. Up till that time, announcements on his BBC programmes had been made by a studio manager, but Henry decided that in future he would do them himself ... and the public loved his soft English voice and his almost stumbling way with words. He made it his own distinctive style.

But there was another big milestone to come. At mid-morning on St. Patrick's Day (17th March) in 1934, Henry and the band were in the HMV studios at Abbey Road, London, making several new recordings. Also there, for other records, were Anona Winn, Elsie and Doris Waters, Flanagan and Allen and Lupino Lane. On the spur of the moment, while they all chatted, Henry invited them to join him on his regular BBC programme later that day. From this informal gathering of well-known personalities sprang the famous "Guest Night" series of programmes, and many believe it gave rise to what we now call television chat shows.

The programme was so popular that a week later such stars of the time as Layton and Johnstone, Leslie Sarony and Ronald Frankau, appeared on what by then was called "Henry Hall's Guest Night". It quickly became the week's most popular radio show and almost every big name in the Thirties' entertainment scene appeared on it.

In 1935, Henry Hall made a short film "Music Hath Charms" for British International Pictures, intended to give some idea of the behind-the-microphone life of the band, but the public seemed to prefer gangster dramas and epics. Henry Hall and the band also appeared on television, but the originally London-based audience was small compared to his national following on radio.

Henry was invited to be guest conductor and lead the dance band in the first-class saloon on board the liner *Queen Mary* when she made her maiden voyage to America on 27th May, 1936. During the four-day voyage Henry and the band made 14 separate broadcasts from mid-Atlantic — another first for the BBC. While Henry was in the USA, one of the BBC's staff announcers had spoken the opening words to introduce the "Guest Night" programme to listeners in Britain. So when the man himself came back to London he emphasised his actual presence by saying: "This *is* Henry Hall speaking and tonight is my Guest Night" — the accent on the first "is" then became a literal Hall-mark which he had to repeat every week to satisfy his now world-wide army of fans, and it is still one of the oddities by which most older people remember him.

When Jack Payne led the BBC Dance Orchestra he created a precedent by starting each programme at 5.15 with the same song — *Say It With Music* — which became his signature tune. But when Henry took over the band he had to think of something different, so he sat down and wrote the letters B-B-C which he then played as notes on the piano — and out came the tune for *Five-Fifteen* with which he briefly introduced each programme.

Most if not all dance bands have a signature tune — but Henry Hall is renowned for having two! He always began his broadcasts with *It's Just The Time For Dancing*, a song written especially for Henry and the band by a BBC producer (Roger Eckersley) who worked at Savoy Hill. It was so distinctively associated with Henry Hall that no other band ever recorded it. Henry always closed his programme with *Here's To The Next Time*, based on the march he himself had composed as a 16-year-old in the Salvation Army. That song endeared itself to his massive audience because it pre-supposed there would be a "next time", not just for the band but the listeners too. And in the Thirties,

▽ *Les Allen released hundreds of records including, in 1934, "Little Man, You've Had a Busy Day". Assisted by his wife, Anne, and small son, Norman, and accompanied by Sidney Torch on the organ of the Regal Cinema, Edmonton, the record was so successful that it launched Les on a solo career.*

with Adolf ranting away in Berlin, our to-morrows were by no means certain.

In 1937, after five years as top bandleader at the BBC, Henry thought it was time for another change. Like Jack Payne before him, he took the band on tour in variety shows throughout the country, eventually topping the bill at the London Palladium. His last official BBC programme was on Saturday, 25th September, 1937, at 10.40 pm till midnight. Appropriately it was called "Here's To The Next Time" and consisted of the orchestra's most-requested numbers.

Gracie Fields came over from her show at the Palladium to sing the final number: *You've Got To Smile When You Say Goodbye*. It must have been a tearful occasion. When the Second World War started, however, all theatres were closed for an initial period and Henry was unable to work, so he returned to the BBC and broadcast his "Guest Night" from the Colston Hall in Bristol which, by coincidence, had been the venue for many Salvation Army rallies in previous years.

A number of BBC radio programmes had already moved to Bristol. "Garrison Theatre", with Jack Warner and Joan Winters, was broadcast from Clifton Parish Hall, whilst the studios at Whiteladies Road in the city gave a war-time home to radio shows including "Monday Night at Eight" and "Strange to Relate". Colston Hall had a seating capacity of 2,000 and "Henry Hall's Guest Night" was broadcast on Thursday evenings. Binnie Hale was an early guest.

During the war, Henry Hall was involved in the presentation of Services entertainment and that unforgettable tonic for civilians, "Music While You Work". Like Vic Oliver (of "This is Show Business" fame) Henry Hall presented live and televised entertainment in the 1950s, but new public tastes in pop were looming, including rock and roll, as well as "heavy metal", so-called for its visual and audio similarity to life in a scrapyard. In recent years, however, there has been a sturdy revival of interest in the great British dance bands of the past.

Henry Hall, awarded an OBE in 1970, died aged 91 after a pleasant retirement at Eastbourne, Sussex, on 28th October, 1989. It was indeed cheerfully appropriate that he lived to see so many of his 1930s recordings reissued as LPs. His broadcasting career finally ended in 1964, though he continued with his many other business interests.

But in his retirement he was always glad to see old friends. And in a very real sense, Henry Hall had millions of them.   □

Charlie Kunz
(1896-1958)

△ *"Clap Hands, Here Comes Charlie" was the instantly recognizable signature tune for rhythmic pianist, Charlie Kunz. Sadly, he died aged 61 after several debilitating illnesses.*

Charlie Kunz was born at Allentown, Pennsylvania, on 18th August, 1896, the son of a French horn player, and grew up surrounded by an atmosphere of classical music. He began learning the piano when he was six, and by the age of 11 he was already good enough to play the organ at services in his local church. Some indication of his progress from then on can be gained from the fact that by the time he reached his 19th birthday — in the same month that the First World War started — he was already leading a dance band in his home town.

When America entered the war in 1917, Charlie took a job in a munitions factory, working day shifts while leading his band at dances

△ *The famous picture that shocked London in the Twenties — Santos Casani and a "flapper" with a gramophone at their feet, dancing the "Charleston" on top of a taxi as it drove down Kingsway.*

in the evening. Although he was turned down by the Army for military service, due to asthma, most of his fellow musicians were drafted in, leaving Charlie with no bandsmen to lead. So he became resident pianist at a local hotel, dovetailing the late hours his new job required with that of an early morning milkman. Thus he would sometimes have to slip off the piano stool in the wee small hours, and glide straight into the driving seat of his milk float, delivering pints on the doorstep while still in his evening clothes!

It was 1922 when he heard about an audition being held in New York to find an American pianist to play at the Trocadero club in London. Charlie, who by then had developed a unique soft-pedal playing style which delighted all who heard him, got the job and sailed over here. It was a contract for 16 weeks only — but after mixing with the people of London he liked Britain so much that he stayed here for the rest of his life. When his stint at the Trocadero was over he took piano solo spots at several other venues, and then led the resident band at the Chez Henri nightclub in Long Acre for seven years from 1926, making several records on the way. But his big moment came in the early Thirties with the "explosion" of British ballroom dancing.

At that time, one of the world's leading dancing teachers was Santos Casani, a former pilot in the Royal Flying Corps, who opened a dancing school at Hyde Park Corner after the war. Santos had roared to fame in the Twenties after being photographed dancing the Charleston with a girl while balancing on top of a London taxi as it drove slowly down Kingsway! In March 1933, Santos leased the mezzanine floor of Imperial House in Regent Street and opened the Casani Club, featuring fashionable dancing to strict tempo music, and invited Charlie Kunz to form and lead the orchestra. For the next four years this quietly-spoken, exceedingly modest American achieved great acclaim as a bandleader, broadcasting regularly from the club to an ever-increasing and highly appreciative radio audience, also making several hundred records. From 1934 onwards he also appeared regularly as a solo pianist on stage at music halls including the Holborn Empire and the London Palladium, always beginning his act with his famous signature tune *Clap Hands, Here Comes Charlie*.

Many of London's best-known vocalists sang with Charlie Kunz at the Casani Club, including Harry Bentley who fell seriously ill in 1935 and died, aged just 36; the glamorous Eve Becke, and Aberdeen-born George Barclay whose voice was regarded as Britain's answer to Bing Crosby. But there was one hopeful teenage crooner who was to be eternally grateful to Charlie for boosting her early career. He invited her to sing with the Casani Club band during one of its regular Saturday night broadcasts in August 1935. Though virtually unknown to the general public, she was an instant success and recorded a dozen songs with the band over the next eighteen months, just the start of what became a glittering career. She was, of course, "Sweetheart of the Forces" Vera Lynn, then only 18 years old. Charlie also put Vera into his Sunday concerts, paying her the princely sum of £5 for a brief performance — that was equivalent to a full week's wage at the time for a girl vocalist with other bands.

In her biography *Vocal Refrain*, Dame Vera wrote:

> What stays clearly in my memory is that Charlie Kunz, for all his great popularity, was a genuinely shy man. He'd come to fame with a piano style that was as gentle as he was, very easy on the ear, and simple enough to make his listeners feel that with a spot of practice they could do it too. Charlie's broadcasts attracted huge audiences, and his records sold well. By the standards of show business he was entitled to a swollen head, but he wasn't the sort.

▷ *George Barclay, the bespectacled farmer's boy (born 1911) from Aberdeen who went to London in the 1930s and became a crooner, singing with many top bands, including Charlie Kunz, Billy Thorburn, Mantovani, Felix Mendelssohn, Victor Silvester, Bert Firman, and Harry Leader.*

After Charlie left the club in March 1937, and the band dispersed, he continued with his solo work, also accompanying singers on his regular broadcast "Cadbury Calling", sponsored by the famous British chocolate company, on Tuesdays over Radio Luxembourg, and undertaking exhausting tours of Variety theatres up and down the land. His wife — one of his first fans whom he got to know soon after arriving in Britain — died in 1938, leaving him with two children to bring up. He remained a widower throughout the war, eventually marrying the actress Patricia Ball and settling at Middleton-on-Sea in Sussex.

In the depths of the war, from February 1941 until September 1942, he began recording for Decca using the title "Charlie Kunz and his Ballroom Orchestra", which was a change from some of the many pseudonyms that other record companies had used for him during the Casani Club years, for then he was variously given the title of Al Gold and his Band, Billy Fredericks and his Band, Harold Cox and his Serenaders, the Eddie Walters Dance Band, Ben Fields and his Band, and even The Twelve Cavaliers — all of which titles were Charlie Kunz and his men in disguise.

It was at this time that a rumour began to circulate that Charlie was a German spy who sent morse-coded messages to the Nazis by tapping out certain notes on the piano during his broadcasts! It was later realised that this story had been given credence because of an earlier spy film which featured an actress communicating with U-boats through her piano programmes on the radio. Good-natured Charlie, and the rest of the country, just laughed that one away.

It was in 1940 that Charlie first showed signs of suffering arthritis in his talented hands. Perhaps it had its origins in an accident 20 years earlier when, working a wire-stapling machine at a ladies' clothing factory in the USA, he had inadvertently stitched two of his own fingers together. As he got older the pain in his hands grew worse and the public never knew that when recording his famous piano medleys he had to stop playing every now and again to dip his hands into a bowl of warm wax to bring some feeling back into them.

Matters were made worse by a bout of spinal tuberculosis in 1945 which left him with a "spur" on his backbone, making it difficult for him to walk on stage while touring Variety theatres after the war. So, with the curtains closed, he was carried to the piano and the audience's first view of him was when the tabs were pulled back and they saw him already seated on the stool playing his famous signature tune *Clap Hands, Here Comes Charlie*. At the end of every performance, of course, he delighted them with a snatch of his closing theme *Pink Elephants*.

Charlie endured several operations on his hands but finally had to give up playing altogether, spending the last few months of his life enjoying his favourite hobby — gardening at his home on the Sussex coast. He died peacefully in his sleep on March 17th, 1958, aged only 61. But the legacy of records he left behind is a treasure trove for the mature majority who can rightly clap hands as they continue to listen to and enjoy the many medleys and dance band tunes of Charlie Kunz, a true gentleman of music. Absolutely unmistakable in style, Charlie's playing, especially when backed by light rhythmic percussion, compels the listener to join in the melody, either by humming our loud, or silently in the mind. Few musicians have such an effect on their public. □

Jack Hylton

(1892-1965)

Jack Hylton was not just a musician but a showman through and through. There could be no greater contrast in the style and presentation than the sight of the immaculate Mr. Hylton conducting his well-groomed orchestra of top musicians on stage in the Thirties, and today's pop-music scene. Then it was all about music ... today it's all about money.

Jack Hylton made a speciality of stage shows and earned a well-deserved reputation for leading Britain's best show band before the war, touring many countries on the Continent and being the first British band to broadcast from here to radio audiences in America. The slogan "Jack's Back" became a sort of trademark association with his appearances at shows up and down the country, for he conducted his bandsmen in the grand and traditional style, with his back to the audience — hence the pun.

His success was based not only on the quality of his superb musicians — and Jack only hired the best — but also the brilliance of his band arrangements which set a new standard on this side of the Atlantic. Listening today to the Hylton magic, it is hardly believable that the exciting numbers his band produced are so old.

But, as with many jewels in the crown of British popular music masters, Jack Hylton's story began amid the tawdry streets of working-class England. He was born Jackson Greenhalgh Hylton on July 2nd, 1892, in the Great Lever district of Bolton, Lancashire, the son of a cotton mill hand. But Hylton senior was determined to better his lot, and became a trade union "shop steward" at the mill before delighting his employers by leaving to take over as landlord of a public house in Rochdale. Young Jack's early piano lessons began to bear fruit when he started playing and singing in his father's pub to draw in the customers ... but hopefully not the police, for he was only 12 years old!

Talent, perhaps driven by sheer necessity, must have abounded in the back streets of Rochdale in those days, for near to the pub where Jack was entertaining, another Lancashire phenomenon was just emerging. Little Grace Stansfield, then aged seven, used to sing at the top of her voice while scrubbing out backyard toilets in Baron Street (for threepence a week). A passing music hall artist heard her and arranged a stage debut ... and so began the career of Lancashire's unforgettable superstar, Gracie Fields.

So well did the young Jack Hylton progress that at 13 he made his professional debut playing piano for a seaside concert party in Rhyl, North Wales, followed by a spell on stage as "The Singing Mill Boy". At seventeen, with no previous experience, he became conductor for a touring pantomime at the princely sum of 45 shillings a week, paving the way for his eventual role as a bandleader. His next step was as organist at a cinema in Stoke Newington, which gave Jack a foothold in London and led to his acting as relief pianist in Stroud Haxton's dance band at the "400 Club" in Bond Street. When the club closed at the start of the First World War, Jack — then 22 — joined the 20th

This rare photo was taken from the first issue of "Radio Magazine" in February 1934. Published monthly, and one of a number of similar popular music-oriented periodicals, the cover price of sixpence was quite expensive for the time.

Hussars and later became musical director in the Army's entertainments division.

After the war, calling himself "Jackson Hylton", he was conductor of a review entitled "Shanghai", where he met and worked with the great comedian Tommy Handley — though long before his ITMA days — appearing with him again in a concert party at Bognor Regis. They decided to team up as "Two Entertainers & a Piano", trying out the art at the Bedford Music Hall in Camden Town, then at Lyon's Popular Café in Piccadilly where, sad to say, they were a flop due to their inexperience of cabaret. Next, Jack wrote the music for a burlesque called "Seasoned to Taste" starring Tommy Handley and Bobby Howes, which opened at the Metropolitan, Edgware Road, in December 1919, running till early in 1920.

Jack then left Handley and Howes to get on with their careers as comics while he concentrated on music as deputy pianist with the band at the Queen's Hall Roof ballroom in Langham Place. But when records by the nine-piece Paul Whiteman Orchestra arrived in this country from America, Jack was the only one in the band capable of transcribing the musical arrangements, the first attempts to orchestrate dance music and jazz. HMV, Britain's top recording company, were quick to capitalize on this, and on 28th May, 1921, the seven-piece Queen's Dance Orchestra recorded four long-forgotten songs arranged by their pianist ... Jack

△ Creator of Britain's first show band, Jack Hylton (right) was a master of publicity and went on to become a highly successful show business entrepreneur.

Hylton! When they returned to the studio six weeks later Jack claimed an extra fee as arranger, but neither HMV nor his colleagues would agree. However, he *was* allowed to have his name credited on the label in lieu, so these sides were issued as "Jack Hylton's Jazz Band". A year later it had grown into an 11-piece known as Jack Hylton and His Orchestra for their HMV releases, also recording for Zonophone as The Grosvenor Dance Orchestra, The Metro-Gnomes, and Hylton's Brighter London Band. By 1929 the sales of Hylton records were running into millions, aided by the band's broadcasts from the Piccadilly Hotel and the Kit-Cat Club, plus personal appearances.

In 1927, Jack Hylton made news headlines with a song that became known as "the 3,000-miles a second hit". It happened when songwriter Lawrence Wright was crossing the Atlantic on board the ss *Majestic*. A tune came into his head, which he quickly wrote down, and on arrival in New York he used the new transatlantic telephone service to ring Jack Hylton, then rehearsing at the Alhambra Theatre in London. Lawrie (who composed under the name of "Horatio Nicholls") sang the song over the phone to Jack, who quickly took it down in music notation and had his band play it in that night's show! The song not only

15

Singer Ennis Parkes
became Mrs. Jack Hylton,
and later led a band of her
own.

Sam Costa, the comedian,
began his broadcasting
career as a crooner with
Hylton.

Pat O'Malley, the band's
principal vocalist in the
early 30s.

Shep-herd of the Hills,_____ I hear you call - ing_____

made news because of it's novel form of transmission, but also became a popular world-wide hit:

Shepherd of the hills I hear you calling
Shepherd of the hills, when twilight falls
I seem to picture the black sheep returning,
I miss the fold, and my sad heart is yearning
For the daffodils and crimson clover,
By the rocks and rills, I long to roam
To the near ones and dear ones who love me,
Shepherd of the hills, I'm coming home.

Ever the showman, Jack took a few members of his band up in an aircraft to fly round Blackpool Tower in 1927, dropping leaflets on the seaside crowds to advertise his latest hit song *Me and Jane in a Plane*, which was currently being sung on the promenade below by young men in striped blazers, crooning though megaphones.

This stunt proved to be a useful forerunner for another hit that swept the country a couple of years later. When Amy Johnson, a plucky lass from Hull, took off from Croydon on her solo flight to Australia in a tiny bi-plane, her name was on everybody's lips. The year was 1930, the Depression had begun, Germany was rumbling with arrogance, and the British people were once again looking for a lift. It took a brave girl to light the touch-paper . . . a wave of national pride and patriotic feeling swept the country, centered on Amy Johnson's heroism, and popular composers of the day vied with

each other to bring out a song that would capture the moment. Once again it was Horatio Nicholls who did the trick, and Jack Hylton scored yet another triumph with his arrangement of the song that had all Britain singing: *Amy, Wonderful Amy*. The record even had the sound of Amy Johnson's aeroplane dubbed in the background.

In 1931 Hylton left His Master's Voice for the newly-formed Decca company, but soon realised that the sound quality was not as good, so he quit at the end of 1933 and made no records until rejoining HMV in 1935, when he found great success with hits from his show at the London Palladium, entitled "Life Begins at Oxford Circus".

In all, Jack Hylton made something like 1,700 recordings in 19 years, from orthodox dance music to concert arrangements, Sousa marches to Gilbert & Sullivan selections, light classics to comic songs, and dozens of musical comedy medleys, even making records in Berlin, Paris and Milan. In addition to his own vocalists, Hylton accompanied other singers like Paul Robeson, Webster Booth, Peter Dawson and Olive Groves, while popular artistes such as Maurice Chevalier, George Formby, Stanley Holloway and Leslie Sarony lent their talents to the orchestra's recording sessions.

Peter Yorke and Billy Ternent are just two of the many famous names in dance music who perfected their arranging and conducting skills in the Jack Hylton orchestra. Others included Billy Thorburn, who became a top-liner in Variety as well as leading "The Organ, The

Dance Band & Me". Jack Jackson, Paul Fenoulhet and Woolf Phillips all graduated from the brass section to lead their own bands, and Cyril Stapleton was among Jack's violinists. Other embryo leader/arrangers were Percival Mackey, Spike Hughes and Phil Cardew. Xylophonists Jack Simpson and Rudy Starita went on to form their own small groups, Sid Millward to lead his "Nitwits" comedy band, and Chappie d'Amato, Freddy Bretherton and Sonny Farrar acted as deputy leaders when Hylton and Billy Ternent were otherwise engaged, as when they visited America to tour with a band of American musicians in 1935-6.

Many other famous names passed through the Hylton ranks ... E.O.'Poggy' Pogson, Monia Liter, Joe Crossman, Billy Munn ... the list is endless and reads like a "Who's Who" of British music. Even the classical influence was there with early arrangements by conductor/composer Leighton Lucas and a string section comprising at various times Alfredo Campoli, Jean Pougnet and Hugo Rignold, together with harpist Sidonie Goossens. Clearly Jack Hylton had no ordinary dance band, and was no ordinary leader. His presence on the stage, even at rehearsals, seemed to electrify and inspire musicians who always made just that much more effort when the boss was on hand.

Singers? There was Ennis Parkes, who had married Jack in their concert party days, sang with the band from 1928, and later took her own outfit on tour as "Mrs. Jack Hylton and Her Boys". Jack also used guest vocalists such as 16-year old Ella Logan who later went on to Broadway and Hollywood stardom, Jack Plant, Peggy Dell, Eve Becke, Brian Lawrance, Phyllis Robins and Denny Dennis. After Sam Browne vacated his 17-month residency in 1930, the majority of Hylton vocals for the next six years featured Pat O'Malley until he too, took off for Hollywood and Broadway as an actor. Hylton himself was no mean vocalist and in the final years had a girl singer named Dolly Elsie (who just happened to be his sister!) at which time he also had teenagers Pat Kirkwood and Celia Lipton, with male vocals by his double bass player, a young baritone named Bruce Trent, who eventually dispensed with his instrument and became a star of musical comedy and operetta instead.

Jack Hylton really did it all — 16 prestigious European tours during which he was created a *Chevalier du Legion d'Honneur* and an *Officier de l'Instruction Publique*; a film built around the band and his musicians, "She Shall Have Music"; and many sell-out music-hall tours which confirmed his reputation as "The British Paul Whiteman". Then in 1939 he made his farewell in the film and stage versions of the radio show "Band Waggon".

When war broke out the Jack Hylton Orchestra was split in two, one for stage work conducted by Freddie Bretherton, and one dispatched to the BBC for war time broadcasting from Bristol under the direction of Billy Ternent. The last activities under the Jack Hylton name were recording sessions in March 1940 and a visit to the Paris Opera House a month later, before the Nazis moved in. But it was too much to expect that a showman like Hylton would retire, and it was soon plain to see that this was the furthest thing from his mind.

Early in the war he sent the London Philharmonic Orchestra on a tour of provincial music halls and theatres under Sir Malcolm Sargent and Basil Cameron. This was the start of a new career as an impressario in which he earned a name for presenting artistes as diverse as Gigli and the San Carlo Opera Company at Covent Garden, the Crazy Gang at the Victoria Palace, international ballet companies, Arthur Askey at the Palace Theatre and the Harringay Music Festival with the likes of José Iturbi, Lily Pons, Eileen Joyce, Andre Kostelanetz, Yehudi Menuhin, Kirsten Flagstad and Artur Rodzinski. He also put on two circuses at Earl's Court, Ingrid Bergman in "St Joan at the Stake", big musicals like "Kiss Me Kate", "Pal Joey", "Kismet", "Call Me Madam", "Salad Days" and "Paint Your Waggon". Oh, and naturally he was one of the first into commercial television!

The last time a band played under the personal baton of Jack Hylton was in 1950 when the old maestro got together a special orchestra of top musicians for the Royal Command Performance at the Palladium — a fitting and triumphant finale for Britain's best-known showband.

Over the years, the Hylton empire expanded until it employed more than 500 people and controlled or owned many London West End theatres. The last venture for which Jack was personally responsible was the Drury Lane production of "Camelot" in August 1964. It ran for 518 performances, but Jack Hylton did not live to see the end of what may well have been his most spectacular triumph, for he died in the London Clinic on 29th January, 1965 only five months into the run. He had achieved more than most men in his lifetime, but to many of us his finest hours were those heralded by the familiar signature tune *Oh Listen To The Band* when we could really enjoy saying "Jack's Back".   □

Ambrose

(1897-1971)

Bert Ambrose was a legend in his own lifetime, for his was the sort of rags-to-riches story that dreams and Hollywood scripts are made of. Born in the abject poverty of London's East End in 1897, the son of a humble rag-and-bone merchant, he rose to become the doyen of British dance band leaders in the Thirties, the immaculately attired friend of royalty, the rich and famous. None of them knew that a few years earlier, his father could have been seen pushing a handcart round the dingy back streets of Whitechapel collecting wool and cloth cuttings from the many tailors' workshops in the area, which he then sold on to the mills for the making of "stuffing". Such a background taught Bert an early lesson in thrift and the value of money which he never forgot throughout his life.

A rare picture of Ambrose in 1937 playing his violin.

In common with all other caring parents, young Albert's mother and father wanted him to get on in life — and that meant always being able to earn a living, no matter what disaster or hardship may befall. Jewish families, ever mindful that prejudice might flare up and force them to move away at a moment's notice, usually taught their children a trade or skill which they could carry with them if they were compelled to pack up and leave in a hurry — such as tailoring, diamond dealing, or music. And the latter talent was best served by learning an instrument that could be easily tucked under your arm. The humble fiddle was ideal for this purpose, hence many of the world's top violinists were of Jewish origin (Heifetz, Menuhin, etc.). Not that young Bert ever aspired to such heights, for he remained only a moderate player throughout his life. But it was enough to get him started.

Unlike so many pre-war bandleaders, Ambrose was never a mere figurehead but an accomplished orchestra leader in every sense of the word. Himself a man of no outstanding musical talent (he neither composed, nor arranged) his genius was as a musical director and catalyst, a man who brought together the best playing and writing talents available, plus the ability to control them. He was a strict disciplinarian with the saving grace of having a cutting sense of humour.

"Ammie", as he was known to his friends (nobody ever called him Bert!), knew the value of his band and his own name, and set a minimum price for engagements below which he would not drop. This was less a sign of personal avarice than a recognition that he employed only the finest musicians in his orchestra, including such bandleaders of the future as Ted Heath, Sid Phillips, Sydney Lipton, George Melachrino, Reginald Pursglove, Lew Stone and Stanley Black. The reputation of Ambrose and his Orchestra was such that they played at only the best venues — the Embassy Club, the Mayfair Hotel, Ciro's Club (which he eventually owned), and the Café de Paris. Ammie's idea of a summer season was not Butlin's or Blackpool, but to take the band to Monte Carlo, Biarritz, or Cannes where the money was even greater. Money which, regrettably, Ammie all too often left on the casino tables; he would literally lose a fortune on the turn of a card.

Whether in London or one of the plush Continental resorts, the orchestra fulfilled the function of a society band playing sweet music

△ *The Ambrose orchestra was rightly regarded as one of the finest in the business.*

for often musically illiterate dancers. At Monte Carlo, Ambrose once said: "If I can't hear the surf, we're playing too loud"! At the Mayfair his criterion in the matter of volume was to hear the shuffle of the dancers' feet. But for his Saturday night broadcasts from the Mayfair, and at other times in Decca's recording studios, his musicians were allowed to show listeners and record buyers alike just what a top band could do.

Ambrose had achieved much since starting violin lessons at the age of five. He had gone to New York while still in his teens and played with Emil Coleman and his Orchestra, then went on to play sixth fiddle at the Palais Royal on Broadway. Six months later, at the age of only 20, he was conducting the band there! Returning to London in 1920, the elegant young man took his first band into the Embassy Club in New Bond Street, but went back to New York in 1922 to form a band of American musicians. He put his bandleading experience to good use when he returned to London's Embassy Club with some key musicians from his New York band, only to transfer to the Mayfair Hotel when it opened in March 1927, staying there for eight years. His band starred in the film *Soft Lights and Sweet Music* and made hundreds of records, including *When Day Is Done*, the famous Ambrose signature tune, with its fine vocal by Sam Browne (died 1972).

Others of note were *You've Got Me Crying Again* and *The Clouds Will Soon Roll By* by Elsie Carlisle who, with Sam Browne and later Jack Cooper, Evelyn Dall and 20-year old Vera Lynn, ensured that however strong the band was instrumentally it was equally well served by its vocal team.

For most people, however, the Ambrose orchestra's main strength lay in its immaculate musicianship and sense of rhythm. Listening to Ambrose today, though his most memorable recordings are all pre-war, is like plugging in to the magical atmosphere of those dancing days of the Thirties. The bands didn't just play repetitive series of the same rhythms, they varied them to suit the occasion — there would be quick-steps, foxtrots and slow waltzes mixed with a variety of numbers including comedy songs, often with the whole band providing a

19

chorus background. Ambrose was a past master at pleasing his dancers and listeners. He never played anything vulgar or noisy, and as a result he built up a reputation for quality dance music which was never surpassed on either side of the Atlantic during his spell at the top.

By the end of the Thirties, Ambrose was at his peak, but on the outbreak of war many of his musicians joined the RAF to form the nucleus of the great Squadronaires Dance Orchestra. During those early war years an Ambrose Octette was taken round the halls with Norman Hackforth leading the brilliant blind pianist George Shearing, Carl Barriteau (alto sax) and trumpeter Teddy Foster, while Ambrose himself carried on at the Mayfair during the Blitz. He also maintained a prodigious recording programme for Decca all through the war, adding a string section to his orchestra which now had the benefit of vocals by the teenage Anne Shelton, who left school to join the Ambrose band in 1940. Her suprisingly mature voice added greatly to the band's attraction.

For a while after the war Ambrose led a young band at the Nightingale Restaurant in Berkeley Square, but he belonged to another era than youngsters like Johnny Dankworth and Ronnie Scott, with whom he had little rapport. In the late Fifties he lent his name to a large concert orchestra arranged and conducted by Laurie Johnson for MGM Records at the same time that he was himself leading a sextet at the Café de Paris, scene of his former triumphs. It was difficult to recognize in this small, bald and insignificant figure, the sleek

△ Although trained for opera, Cavan O'Connor (1899-1997) became famous as "The Strolling Vagabond", singing with many top dance bands including Ambrose, Bertini, Geraldo and Mantovani.

sophisticated maestro who had dominated the West End scene some 20 years previously.

A year later, while appearing at Ilford Palais, he discovered singer Kathy Kirby, and thereafter managed her career with great success. It was fitting that when Ambrose died — still a bachelor in June 1971 — he was at work in a TV studio, but ironic that it was in Leeds, a whole world away from his glittering career in London, New York and the South of France. But it is that career which has become a byword in British music. And those glorious "Dance Band Days" in Britain would not have been quite the same without Bert Ambrose. □

▽ Sam Browne, who made a large number of records during a lengthy career.

▽ Elsie Carlisle, a familiar voice with all dance band followers.

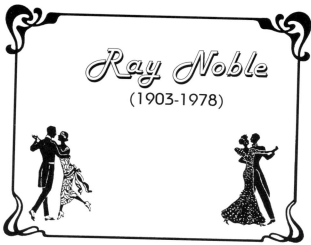

Ray Noble
(1903-1978)

Picture the scene — a Saturday night "hop" at the local Palais de Danse in Wimbledon which, in late 1925, was still a fairly quiet Surrey village on the outskirts of London. A suburban band was providing the music for the couples on the dance floor, jigging to a jazzy piano number which had come over from America. Among the crowd near the band's rostrum stood a young but elegant English gentleman, listening and watching the pianist intently. The syncopating style of playing, he confessed later, "electrified" him ... and it charted the rest of his career and brought new higher standards to the world of popular music for decades to come. For that tall and elegant young man was Sussex-born Ray Noble who went on to climb the ladder of success and became a top composer and bandleader on both sides of the Atlantic.

Raymond Stanley Noble was born at Brighton on 17th December, 1903, the son of a wealthy London surgeon who had rightly expected his son to follow in his footsteps and carve out a distinguished career in medicine. But although Ray had done well at Dulwich College and later at Cambridge, he had a compulsive love of classical music. He was far happier playing Chopin than studying pathology, so he switched from medical school to attend the Royal Academy of Music, intending to become a classical pianist. And so it would have been but for that chance visit to the Wimbledon Palais when he was not quite 22. Ray was so fascinated by the piano number that he just had to discover its title. So he climbed round the back of the bandstand to have a look at the sheet music. It was called *Kitten on the Keys*.

Next morning, Ray bought a copy of the music, locked himself in the parlour of his parents' London home and played the piano all afternoon until he had mastered it! He later admitted that the "Kitten" gave him his first real interest in popular music of the day, and he bought every song sheet he could lay his hands on, eventually joining up with another amateur musician to form a small six-piece band which played for local hops in the dance halls of South London ... much to his father's disgust!

Ray wrote and arranged several little numbers for this band and as a result caught the eye of one of Britain's best-known music publishers, Lawrence Wright, who was perhaps better known to the public as a songwriter under the pseudonym of Horatio Nicholls. In 1926, Ray joined the Lawrence Wright music publishing company in Denmark Street, London, working as an arranger. The following year, by which time the American grip on British dance music was stronger than ever, young Ray entered for a competition advertised in the *Melody Maker*, a music magazine founded by his boss, Lawrence Wright. The competition was launched to find the best British dance band orchestrator ... and Ray won it.

The following year the BBC bowed to public pressure for more popular music on the wireless and formed its own resident dance band under the direction of Jack Payne. Ray Noble became one of the band's staff arrangers and began writing songs of his own instead of just orchestrating the music of other composers. But as often happens, success didn't come easily, for his first published song, *Nobody's Fault But Your Own* (1928) made no impact and he had to wait another three years before he wrote his first hit.

▽ *Ray Noble was expected to become a doctor, like his father, but he preferred popular music.*

Ray was unlike most of the people in popular music — he was well educated, charming, and had a posh accent. In the early days, his suave and sophisticated manner led to a few snide remarks from other musicians. But Ray had talent as well as poise and he converted them all with his brilliance at composing and arranging. In 1929 he was made musical director at the EMI recording studios and led the house band that made His Master's Voice records. It was called the New Mayfair Dance Orchestra, but it had nothing to do with the plush Mayfair Hotel. The band had been formed by HMV's previous musical director, Carroll Gibbons, purely for recording purposes. In those affluent days it even included polo-playing horsemen who would arrive for a recording session in jodhpurs after riding in Hyde Park! Ray felt that was classy but much too casual, so he began hiring all-star musicians from a variety of top London bands to come to the studio during the day for a recording session, later returning to their regular jobs at fashionable London night clubs and hotel restaurants.

Playing mainly his own orchestral arrangements, Ray Noble gradually built up a high reputation for the quality of his recording work and HMV gained an enviable name in the booming world of dance band discs. Among the big names that Ray invited to "sit in" with his orchestra were such eventual top-liners as Nat Gonella on trumpet, violinists Reg Leopold and Reg Pursglove, Freddy Gardner on alto-saxophone, and Bill Harty on drums. They were paid £1 an hour for studio work which helped to swell the average £18 wage they earned playing with their regular band on six nights a week.

Early vocalists included Pat O'Malley, Cavan O'Connor and Jack Plant, but in 1930 — by which time the studio band had been re-billed as "Ray Noble and his Orchestra" — they were joined by a new "crooner" who had been so impoverished by the Depression that he had been driven to singing for theatre queues. His name was Al Bowlly. Drummer Bill Harty heard the young South African singing and brought him round to the studio for a personal audition with Ray Noble. The maestro liked what he heard and gave Al a job — and another legend was born. In the following April (1931) Ray introduced a song which he had just composed and got Al Bowlly to sing it on the latest HMV record. It turned out to be one of the biggest dance band hits of all time:

▽ *Almost entirely a recording group, Ray Noble's band was never seen live in Europe, apart from a brief appearance in Holland, before touring America. Packed with fine artists the band is pictured here arriving on Dutch soil in 1933. Left to right: Tiny Winters, Nat Gonella, Al Bowlly, Mrs. Noble, Ray Noble, Harry Berly, Lew Davis, Bob Wise, Mrs. Gardner, Freddy Gardner, and Alfie Noakes.*

GOODNIGHT SWEETHEART

Goodnight, Sweetheart,
All my prayers are for you,
Goodnight, Sweetheart,
I'll be watching o'er you
Tears and parting may make us forlorn
But with the dawn
A new day is born (So I'll say)
Goodnight, Sweetheart,
Sleep will banish sorrow,
Goodnight, Sweetheart,
Till we meet tomorrow,
Dreams enfold you,
In them, dear, I'll hold you
Goodnight, Sweetheart, Goodnight!

△ *South African-born Al Bowlly became a legend in his own lifetime, singing with many bands in England and Europe from the late Twenties onwards. His unfortunate demise came in his own London flat when, without leaving any apparent injuries on his body, he was killed instantly by a bomb blast during an air raid in April 1941.*

Ray Noble wrote the song in collaboration with Jimmy Campbell and Reg Connelly, and it became an instant success as the song which ended most dance evenings, when the ballroom lights were shaded down and partners clung together, gliding along in a slow fox-trot as they whispered their fond farewells.

Ray brought in some other well-known vocalists too, like Sam Browne and Elsie Carlisle. Gracie Fields made a record with him, as did Anona Winn who, although later thought of as a TV panellist ("What's My Line?") was at one time a songwriter and singer. Soon afterwards he wrote the words and music of what many people still regard as his finest song:

Love is the sweetest thing
What else on earth could ever bring.

By 1932, Ray's name was at the top of the record-selling charts, but the public didn't know the face behind the name for his work was almost entirely done in the HMV studios at Abbey Road, London. In his autobiography, Noel Coward recalls meeting Ray Noble, then still only 28, and couldn't believe that this "skinny young man with sticking-up hair" was HMV's Light Music Director. But he was later to afford Noble the greatest respect for resisting the invasion of Afro-American ragtime and jazz, and offering the public something more refined and elegant.

Ray Noble gave the world a new, sentimental sound of English sweetness which captured the hearts of romantics the world over. In 1934 the former medical student trotted out yet another world-beating hit song which eventually became his signature tune, opening his many orchestral concerts on stage and radio. Originally sung by Al Bowlly it was eventually recorded by Bing Crosby and many other famous names.

The very thought of you,
And I forget to do,
The little ordinary things that ev'ryone ought
to do;
I'm living in a kind of day-dream,
I'm happy as a king
And foolish though it may seem,
To me that's ev'rything . . .
The mere idea of you,
The longing here for you,
You'll never know, how slow, the moments go
Till I'm near to you.
I see your face in ev'ry flower;
Your eyes in the stars above,
It's just the thought of you
The very thought of you, my love.

With that song alone making him a world name, Ray Noble toured Europe with his band to rapturous applause, and with such a following the American music barons couldn't afford to wait any longer. Although they thought that the best songwriters, bands and vocalists came only from the USA, they were forced to admit that Ray Noble was something special. His records were selling well in Depression-hit America so later in 1934 accompanied by Al Bowlly and drummer Bill Harty, who by this time had become Ray's manager, he sailed off to take up a lucrative appointment as leader of the band in New York's Rainbow Room, a restaurant and night club on the 65th floor of the RCA building at Radio City. First he had to overcome a lengthy protest by American musicians' unions who didn't like the idea of an Englishman taking over the top spot, but they relented when it was agreed that only Americans would form the rest of the band, apart from Bowlly and Harty. So an orchestra of hand-picked musicians was chosen for Ray by an up-and-coming young trombonist called Glenn Miller, who was soon to form his own top show band, reigning supreme in the world of popular music until his mysterious death in 1944 when the aircraft taking him from Britain to France vanished without trace.

When the Rainbow Room contract ended in 1936, the band — which included such future big names as Tommy Dorsey and Glenn Miller on trombone, Charlie Spivak (trumpet) and George van Eps on guitar — went on a year-long tour of America where, as a result of his weekly broadcasts, the name of Ray Noble was on everybody's lips.

Despite making a couple of return trips to Britain just before the war, Ray decided to take up the offer of work in Hollywood, where he became musical director for many top radio shows, including George Burns and Gracie Allen, and then for 13 years with the inimitable Charlie McCarthy, a ventriloquist's dummy brought to life for Americans every week by Edgar Bergen. In both cases, Ray played a speaking part in the shows and many listeners wondered how he had got his English accent, unaware that he wasn't an American! The ventriloquist show transferred vey well to television after the war and when it finally ended in the mid-50s Ray Noble and his British born wife Gladys retired to their home in Santa Barbara, California. But despite a quarter of a century in the USA, the pull of the Old Country was still strong in them both, and Mr. and Mrs. Noble returned this side of the Atlantic, seeking retirement in the land of their birth. For reasons of climate, and perhaps also to save a little tax, they went to live in the Channel Islands for 10 years until, on the 2nd April 1978, Ray died in a London hospital, aged 74. ☐

Lew Stone
(1898-1969)

In the early Thirties, the BBC was slow to realise the value of the wireless to Britain's dance-band enthusiasts. Most of them could never hope to patronise the swish London hotels and restaurants where the big names played, and so they relied on the late-night programme that the BBC eventually — nay, reluctantly — reserved for dance music. The top bands all had their own special night, week in week out, and on Tuesdays from 10.30pm until the chimes of Big Ben rang out the midnight hour, the airwaves carried the sound of one of the most brilliant musicians of the pre-war era. He built his reputation on sheer talent — as a player, composer, arranger and director of stage musicals. Even today, dance-band afficionados nod their heads in agreement that this man and the players that he led were at the top of Britain's musical tree. He was a soft-spoken Cockney called Lew Stone.

▽ *Lew Stone with his bride Joyce — a former Cheltenham Ladies' College girl — pictured after their wedding in 1937.*

△ *Lew Stone and his band at the Monseigneur Restaurant in Jermyn Street, London, in 1933.*

Unlike many big names in the dance band business, Lew was never just a figurehead. He was a composer, musical director of some 50 films and West End shows, a talented and creative arranger who formed the styles of three famous bands, and who wrote the definitive book on orchestration. But to the public at large he was a band leader who epitomised the best of the BBC's late-night dance music. Everything he did was in the best possible taste, like the man himself. This great all-rounder was, like so many others of the era, a London East Ender, born Louis Steinberg in May 1898 at Bethnal Green. He had three brothers, only one of whom survived the First World War, after which the family — Jewish refugees from Eastern Europe — changed their name by deed poll to Stone.

As a boy Lew was mad about football and cricket, more than piano lessons which he dropped when he was ten. Although diminutive in stature, he later played half-back for the Corinthians and Casuals, joining a musicians' team alongside Billy Ternent and Tiny Winters, with brother Fred and Jack Hylton as officials! This single-minded love of sport lasted until he was 13 when, on a visit to the Proms, he was inspired to return to music. His interest had been purely classical, but he was influenced in another direction by a visit to the Hippodrome revue "Hello Ragtime" in 1912. Now he wanted to find out more about this new syncopation, and haunted Lyons' Strand Corner House to

pick up what he could from Percy Cowell's band.

His father had a timber business in Shoreditch, and was storing some pianos which young Lew tried out. Next door was Lipman's cardboard box factory, and hearing that Lipman's eldest son had ambitions as a ragtime pianist, Lew asked him to come and try the pianos, hoping to pick up more hints. Young Lipman was later known as Syd Roy and his young brother turned into Harry Roy.

Lew's first professional work was with a quintet called The London Lyrics Band, before joining the Aeolians at Newcastle in 1925. The following year he was playing piano at London's Cosmo Club when he had an offer to join Bert Ralton's famous Savoy Havana Band on tour. Just before the band's ill-fated visit to South Africa, where Ralton died on safari, they were asked to record four numbers for Columbia. The band had no arranger on tour so Ralton asked Lew if he could handle the work. By dint of burning much midnight oil, Stone came up with the scores, and word soon got round the profession about this new arranger, who promptly opened an office in Denmark Street — London's "Tin Pan Alley" — to supply scores for all and sundry. His first assignment was for a 12" HMV record by Carroll Gibbons and the Savoy Orpheans, a selection from "Lido Lady", the Rodgers & Hart show at the Gaiety Theatre with Jack Hulbert, Cicely Courtneidge and Phyllis Dare. He went on to do scores for George Fisher's Rhythm Band at the Kit-Cat Club, and for leaders like Jay

Whidden, John Firman, Howard Godfrey, Debroy Somers, Percival Mackey and the Starita brothers (Al, Ray, Rudy) and their bands.

Concurrent with this freelance work Lew Stone was creating the style of the new Ambrose Orchestra which he joined as resident arranger, producing 80 scores for the band from 1927-31, and between these he found time to accompany Sophie Tucker on piano on her 1928 double-sided Columbia record of *My Yiddishe Momma*.

In 1930 Roy Fox arrived in this country with an American band for a date at the Café de Paris. They were not well received, and Roy Fox replaced the Americans with a band of British musicians that Lew Stone formed for him including Nat Gonella, Lew Davis, Billy Amstell, Jack Jackson, Bill Harty on drums and Al Bowlly as vocalist. The band opened the new Monseigneur Restaurant, broadcasting from there every Tuesday night, building Lew's reputation as a deputy leader and arranger. When Roy Fox collapsed in October 1931 he was ordered to a Swiss sanatorium for six months, leaving the band in Lew Stone's capable hands.

While Roy Fox was recuperating in Switzerland, Lew Stone was not only leading the band and making Decca recordings, but also using some of the players under the name of the "Durium Dance Band". Durium flexible records were pressed on brown cellulose with a cardboard backing, which Boots the Chemists sold for sixpence.

When Roy Fox returned in April 1932, fit again and raring to go, it was to find that his band had become a nationwide success under Lew's leadership. The Monseigneur management later fell out with Fox and it was little surprise when they asked Lew Stone to carry on under his own name. At this time, Lew was also acting as musical director for British and Dominion Films, scoring and conducting 26 movies from 1931-35, including most of the Aldwych farces and Herbert Wilcox productions like "Goodnight Vienna" and "Bitter Sweet" for which he engaged Ray Noble to write *What More Can I Ask?* and *Brighter Than The Sun*. Lew was also musical director of "Say It With Music", built around Jack Payne's band, and again commissioned Ray Noble to write his immortal *Love Is The Sweetest Thing*.

Meanwhile, Lew was also one of the best-known bandleaders on radio and records, and when the Monseigneur closed down to become a news cinema he took the opportunity to go on tour and meet his radio fans.

In 1934, when drummer Bill Harty and Al

Bowlly went to New York with Ray Noble, Lew opened at London's Hollywood Restaurant with his usual team of Nat Gonella, Alfie Noakes, Lew Davis, Monia Liter, Tiny Winters, Don Barrigo, Stanley Black etc., and Alan Kane replacing Bowlly. It says much for the regard in which Lew Stone was held by his men that so many of them were with him for years ... 36 in the case of saxophonist Joe Crossman. The band toured again in 1936, then went into the Café de Paris.

This was a momentous period in Lew's personal life also, for he had met a young lady called Joyce Newman when he played for her 21st birthday party at the Monseigneur. This young pianist, a Gold Medallist and LRAM, was increasingly attracted to Lew Stone's music and eventually to the man himself. They were married three years later, in June 1937, and thus began a life-long partnership in which they were ideally matched in every way, musically as well as emotionally. Joyce's knowledge of music made her invaluable to Lew as a copyist of orchestral parts when he had arrangements and film scores to write.

He made his debut as a stage musical director in February 1937 when he conducted the first of 123 performances of Rodgers and Hart's "On Your Toes" at the Palace Theatre starring Jack Whiting and Vera Zorina. He also did films for British National, like "Melody and Romance" starring Arthur Tracy and Margaret Lockwood, and "Kicking The Moon Around" with the Ambrose orchestra. Lew continued to double band leading with the theatre when he conducted Vivian Ellis's "Hide and Seek", the songs from which, including the well-remembered *She's My Lovely*, were recorded by the stars Bobby Howes and Cicely Courtneidge with Lew and the London Hippodrome Orchestra.

▽ *Known universally as "The Street Singer", Arthur Tracy was a familiar figure both pre- and post-war.*

On the outbreak of war, Lew followed the same pattern of work, conducting the revue "Orchids and Onions" at the Comedy Theatre while working at the Dorchester Hotel with a seven-piece band which he led from the Novachord, a sort of electronic piano with an individual organ-like tone. He augmented to a full-sized band for recording with such men (later to become leaders themselves) as Ted Heath, Carl Barriteau, Frank Weir, Leslie 'Jiver' Hutchinson, Kenny Baker, George Evans, Woolf Phillips and members of the Squadronaires moonlighting from their RAF duties. Like any other society leader, Lew was limited by the musical taste (or lack of it) of the clientele who patronised the West End venues. They wanted sweet music for dancing, and this Lew gave them — probably much better than they deserved or were able to appreciate! He was at his best with good, commercial, standard tunes, such as the well-remembered Al Bowlly vocals on *Music Maestro Please* and *Little Lady Make-Believe*.

Returning to the wartime scene, however, Lew Stone and His Stonecrackers were a nine-piece band that recorded a dozen righteous jazz titles at the same time as his Concert Orchestra performed light classics and Russian folk songs for Decca — confirming the point that he was a man of many parts. For the rest of the war he toured the music halls and service camps. At one of the latter, an RAF station, he was warned not to be surprised if some of his audience walked out. Sure enough, some airmen did — including Wing Commander Guy Gibson who gave up an evening with Britain's top band to lead his Dambusters in bombing the Möhne Dam ... an event which led to him winning the VC.

The war over, Lew on Novachord fronted a small group he called the Novatones, firstly at the Royal Court Hotel, Southampton, then back on the West End scene again at the Embassy Club. He left there, intending to have a long, leisurely holiday at Minehead (Somerset), but on the first day he received an offer from the impresario Emile Littler to go back to London as a conductor of a new American show to be presented by Rodgers & Hammerstein. He was never to regret sacrificing his holiday, for the show was Irving Berlin's "Annie Get Your Gun", and for the next two years or more Lew Stone had the job of welding together a 28-piece orchestra, a large vocal chorus and a ballet company. It was the highlight of his career and anything following that could only be an anti-climax. While all this was going on he also returned to radio with a big band for the BBC

△ George Evans became leader of a post-war big band with a large saxophone section.

and Radio Luxembourg. After "Annie" finished, Lew took his band to the newly-opened Pigalle Restaurant in Piccadilly, supervising the cabaret as well as catering for dancing. Then he celebrated his 60th year, perversely enough, by taking a band round the Mecca ballroom circuit as a sort of farewell tour, and by forming a sextet for "Music While You Work" broadcasts. After this he retired from active music-making, but ran an entertainment service to supply bands for society functions and private parties, until his death on 13th February, 1969 ... aged 70.

The supremacy of Lew Stone as a tasteful and discriminating music master was assured long ago and cannot be denied, but he wasn't too well-known as a composer, for he never pushed his own work at the expense of others. Yet he did collaborate with Hoagy Carmichael on *Give Me Tonight* and with Vivian Ellis on *Apple Pie*, and recorded some of his own instrumental pieces such as *Canadian Pacific*, *Clockmaker's Nightmare*, and *Hello Mike*, etc.

Lew Stone was not ashamed of his childhood background and he never forgot the little Jewish boy, Louis Steinberg. His widow Joyce Stone, a product of the Cotswolds and Cheltenham Ladies' College, said: "My background was very different in childhood from his, but I never heard him say he had ever been unhappy or hungry. He was a genuine Cockney with the real Cockney wit, and sometimes on a summer evening we would drive down to the East End, where Lew would take me on a tour of all the places he had lived in (Stepney Green, Hoxton, etc.) and show me his infant school, playgrounds, etc. Lovely evenings to look back on with great nostalgia". ☐

Jack Payne

(1899-1969)

Like many veterans of the Royal Flying Corps, Jack Payne could have carved out a career as a pilot when the embryo airline business took off after the First World War ended in 1918. Yet again, he might have become a successful farmer, for agriculture and a love of the countryside was forever in his blood. But instead this many-talented man used his musical ability to built up Britain's most versatile and successful popular orchestra, known and loved by millions via the early days of "wireless" as the leader of the BBC's first official dance band.

John Wesley Vivian Payne, to give him his full name, was born at Royal Leamington Spa in Warwickshire on 22nd August, 1899, though the Payne family soon moved the 23 miles to Birmingham where young Jack attended the Rookery Road council school, going on to Handsworth Grammar as a day boy until March 1915. Academically, he failed to impress his headmaster — but he stood head and shoulders above his chums in two other fields — the school's cadet corps, and music.

Jack's mother was a soprano in local amateur circles and his father (John Edwin Payne) was the manager of a music publisher's warehouse, so it is not surprising that he became quite an accomplished pianist by the age of 12. He sang in the school choir and also excelled in "square bashing", which all college boys under-

△ Jack Payne at home in the 1950s playing a duet with his second wife, the talented Peggy Cochrane, a pianist who became the BBC's "Tune-a-Minute Girl" in the Thirties, playing 15 songs non-stop in 15 minutes.

took in those war-torn days as part of the Officer Training Corps. Jack rose to the rank of sergeant in the school's OTC and in 1917 he volunteered for the Royal Flying Corps, won his wings and became Lieutenant John Payne while still only 18.

It was in the officers' mess at Scampton, Lincolnshire, that Jack got the idea of forming a little dance band. Now that the USA had joined in the war, the station had acquired a few American air mechanics, two of whom played saxophones. With buglers converted to trumpeters, and Jack belting out the latest song hits on the piano, this little combo entertained at social functions during off-duty hours. After the war, when the RFC became the RAF, Jack took demob instead of hanging on for a Service career, and spent some time on a Worcestershire farm training for a life on the land. But the finances of buying and stocking his own farm proved too formidable, and so he fell back on his music. Correctly forecasting the growing popularity of ballroom dancing, he formed a local band in the Birmingham area in 1919, and in 1920 began promoting his own dancing events and Saturday-night "hops".

Once again, however, he lacked the capital to beat the big boys who opened a huge *Palais de Danse* in the city, forcing Jack to give up promoting dances and returning to playing for

△ Jack Payne on tour with his band in the mid-Thirties

◁ The band-leader with his first wife (Doris Pengree) who died in 1939.

▷ Two of Jack Payne's regular vocalists — (right) Billy Scott-Coomber, and (above) Ronnie Genarder.

them instead. He formed his own band of local musicians and they played all over the Midlands, including a regular Saturday night stint at the Royal Hotel in his home-town of Leamington. He followed this in 1923 with one-night stands in various parts of Britain, including a summer season at the Grand Hotel, Folkestone, before going to London (still aged only 24) and convincing the owners of the luxurious Hotel Cecil in the Strand that what they needed to capture the spirit of the jazz age, and the growing upsurge in modern dance music, was a young and vigorous orchestra. And he was just the fellow to do it for them! Despite some misgivings, the hotel's conservative owners gave him a four-week trial and he opened his seven-piece band there on 13th February, 1924, proving so popular with the bright young things of those days (the Charleston didn't arrive till 1925) that he stayed on for four exciting years! During that time he established a demand for top quality dance music, plus a varied menu of semi-classics and comedy numbers (known as "variety novelties") which he began recording in 1925, first on Zonophone, followed by a short flirtation with the ill-fated Duophone Unbreakable Record label, and then on to Regal records (a subsidiary of Columbia).

The BBC was rather grudging with its time devoted to dance music, and the few slots they did allow were generally given to bands broadcasting from the snooty Savoy Hotel, situated quite close to the Cecil. But Jack persisted with the BBC until, on Boxing Day 1925, they gave him his first chance — as "Uncle Jack Payne" on the famous "Children's Hour" programme! His big break, however, came in March 1928 when the BBC decided to appoint a resident dance band of its own. Up to that time, the only regular orchestra the corporation could call on was the London Radio Dance Band, directed by Sidney Firman. After some soul-searching, the directors of the BBC invited Jack Payne to form and become leader of the new dance band venture, which meant broadcasting every weekday from 5pm till the 6 o'clock news. And as a result his popularity soared in line with his radio and recording output.

In the following four years, Jack's slightly crusty voice became very familar to the growing army of listeners throughout Britain, for he did his own compering. On many of the vocal numbers for the programme he sang the refrains himself, often helped by other instrumentalists in his band, and from 1930 by Val Rosing, Elsie Carlisle, Ella Logan, and latterly by Billy Scott-Coomber, a trained singer who became the band's principal crooner for the last two years of Payne's leadership at the BBC. When he relinquished that position in 1932 to Henry Hall, Jack Payne took his band touring this country and the Continent.

This was the line-up of top musicians who took to the road with him in 1932: *trumpets* — Jack Jackson and Tommy Anderson; *trombones* — Ben Oakley and Jesse Fuller; *saxophones* — E.O. (Poggy) Pogson, Frank Johnson, Bob Easson and Dave Roberts; *strings* — Eric Siday, Reg Leopold, Herbert Powell (violins); Dick Escott (double bass); Steve Gauner (guitar); *tuba* — Charlie Asplin; *drums* — Bob Manning (plus occasional vocals); *pianos* — Bob Busby and Billy Thorburn; *vocalist* — Billy Scott-Coomber.

Jack Jackson and Billy Thorburn later formed their own bands, and Reg Leopold became a leader of light music in the Palm Court tradition which the BBC went on to establish with its famous "Grand Hotel" series of programmes.

On leaving the BBC, Jack Payne signed a contract with Imperial records, a quality product which sold for 1s 6d (7½p today), half the price of expensive, three-shilling Columbias. Also, the Imperial labels bore Jack's portrait and a facsimile of his signature in gold ink — collectors' items now! In 1934 Imperial records were discontinued in favour of the new Rex label which sold even more cheaply without any loss of quality.

Jack Payne's arranger in the early years at the BBC was a young man named Ray Noble. He went on to become one of the best-known bandleaders in Britain, but he never had a band outside the recording studio until he went to America in the autumn of 1934, invited there on the strength of his records that had sold well despite the economic blizzard that had almost killed the American record industry. Ray Noble

▽ *Scottish singer Ella Logan pictured in 1939.*

also wrote the score for the 1932 film which featured Jack Payne and his band — "Say It With Music" — the same title as Jack's signature tune. It proved immensely popular, with one song scoring a world-wide smash hit, Noble's immortal *Love Is The Sweetest Thing*.

Much was made of the coming of so-called "Swing" music in 1935, but for the most part it was just a big band — five brass, four saxophones and four rhythm (piano, guitar, string bass and drums) — playing smart, often tricky arrangements, allowing space for improvised solos from such members of the sections as could play them. Yet that is exactly what Jack Payne and his band had been doing for over five years, before anyone had heard of Benny Goodman, Glenn Miller or any of the other idolized "Kings of Swing".

Jack's first record for Imperial was *Hot Coffee*, a tune devised by Billy Scott-Coomber and pianist Billy Thorburn as they sat drinking hot coffee in a roadside café for drivers (and itinerant overnight dance band musicians, en route between one-night stands). It shows the vitality of the band had not diminished in the slightest in the changeover from BBC residence to nationwide travel.

After touring South Africa in 1936, Jack retired from the dance band business to attend to his constant love of farming interests, but the lure of music proved too strong and he reappeared in 1939 with a new band, in time to make some records for Decca soon after the outbreak of the Second World War. The end of hostilities found him on HMV records, briefly, after which he gave up bandleading again and devoted his time to being a disc-jockey, a television presenter, and even running a wine shop. This last venture, however, was not a success; it was a case of a square peg in a round hole, and his health began to cause anxiety.

In 1923, with his wordly wealth totalling a meagre £9, Jack had eloped with an Army colonel's daughter (Doris Pengree). She died in 1939 and a year later he married the talented pianist Peggy Cochrane, who was also an occasional vocalist with the band. Jack Payne's last known appearance on record was as the anonymous sound effects man who said the words "S-s-s-steam Heat" in Peggy Cochrane's piano medley of tunes from the 1954 musical "The Pajama Game". Jack retired to his country home at Tonbridge in Kent and it was there on 6th December, 1969, that he died... after a lifetime spent "saying it with music." ☐

Carroll Gibbons
(1903-1954)

England's premier hotel — the Savoy just off the Strand in London — faced a dilemma in the early Twenties. The awful memory of the First World War was just beginning to fade and there was a growing mood of gaiety around. For decades the Savoy had catered for the élite of English society, as well as visiting foreigners, and inside its hallowed portals you could be sure that patrons would behave impeccably and dress with extreme good taste. Sedate couples on the dance floor would enjoy waltzing to the "Veleta" and "Destiny", with perhaps an occasional two-step in between ... but times they were a-changing.

New jazz music had recently arrived from America to replace the earlier ragtime, and with it came a whole new genre of dances including the "Charleston" and the "Black Bottom". In lower quality hotels up and down the country,

△ Carroll Gibbons at the Savoy Hotel piano.

gentlemen were wearing lounge suits instead of the usual dinner jacket, black tie, and patent leather shoes; and frizzy-haired girls were hitching up their skirts, kicking off their shoes, and jigging the night away while grandma slept. By today's standards, of course, they were as pure as the driven snow, but this was the early Twenties when even the thought of an unchaperoned daughter dancing the new fox-trot in a calf-length skirt was enough to bring mother out in a cold sweat.

Hence the Savoy's dilemma ... should they stick to their guns in the ballroom, ignore the new trend in syncopation, and continue with old-fashioned music and dancing that had gone down so well since Edwardian times, or ought

they to relax their rigid (some said frigid) style, let their hair down and up the tempo to accommodate the growing number of Britain's bright young things?

In effect they did neither. Instead of standing still, or importing a well-known jazz band, under the guidance and leadership of W.F. de Mornys (*q.v.*) they developed their own sophisticated sound with a new orchestra, the Savoy Havana Band in 1922, which provided syncopation without losing style. The following year they launched a second ensemble called the Savoy Orpheans under the baton of 33-year-old Debroy Somers, who was always impeccably attired in evening dress. But both bands were soon in desperate need of more quality musicians. So the following year the hotel management sent banjo player Joe Brannelly back to his native America to seek new talent.

While there, Joe met two clean-cut young men who were studying at the New England Conservatory of Music at Boston — Carroll Gibbons, a quietly-spoken piano player then aged 21, and his bright-eyed chum Rudy Vallee (1901-1986), a budding saxophonist who was later to make a big name for himself as a vo-de-oh-do crooner with a megaphone. Brannelly was fascinated by the music they both made and cabled the news of his find back to London, only to receive this succinct reply from the Savoy: "Bring Vallee. Not Gibbons".

The hotel bosses thought the saxophone would be just right to add glamour to their band, whereas London was already full of talented piano players. But their reply came too late. Joe

△ *Carroll Gibbons and the Savoy Hotel Orpheans as they appeared in the 1937 film "Calling All Stars".*

had already bought tickets for the musical pair to cross the Atlantic on the *Olympic* and he didn't have the heart to tell Carroll that he was not wanted. On their arrival, Rudy went straight into the Savoy Havanas, and the shy, bespectacled Carroll Gibbons swallowed his pride and enrolled for yet more piano lessons at the Royal Academy of Music. It was there that he developed his "velvet touch", coupled with a distinctive and stylish back-tenth with his left hand, which became the envy of lesser piano syncopators and was to thrill music lovers for the next 30 years.

After a short time Carroll got a part-time job at the Berkeley Hotel in Piccadilly, playing the piano when the regular band left the stage for a "supper break". But the diners and dancers liked what they heard, so he was taken on full-time as main pianist in the hotel band. In 1926 he moved down the Strand to play with the Savoy Orpheans and when conductor Debroy Somers left in 1927 Carroll was offered the baton as leader. The clientele at the world's most famous hotel quickly warmed to the quiet American with that unforgettable slow drawl — the result of speech therapy to cover up a childhood stammer. As it turned out, they regarded his slight stutter when talking from the piano as an added attraction. Many of today's older generation can perhaps recall his ultra-relaxed voice saying "Hello Everybody" while sitting at the piano at the start of his many regular broadcasts. Among the latter who had Carroll to thank for helping them rise to prominence, were George Melachrino (clarinet, sax and vocalist), Paul Fenoulhet (trombonist and arranger), Reg Leopold (violin), Bert Thomas (guitar), Howard

Jacobs (saxophone) and Rudy Starita (drums and xylophone). Early vocalists with Carroll at the Savoy included Al Bowlly, Les Allen, Brian Lawrance, Jack Plant, Maurice Elwin and Harry Bentley — all men, for there were very few female vocalists in those days.

That all changed in the autumn of 1934 when, after finishing his stint at the Savoy Hotel, Carroll walked into Murrays — a club in the West End — with a party of friends and was enchanted by the voice of a young girl singing to the late-night patrons through a megaphone. He discovered she was called Anne Lenner, one of six talented sisters from Leicester. Carroll asked her to come to the Columbia studios next day to make a record with the Orpheans, and she then signed a contract on the spot.

Anne became the first female crooner to sing from the august stage at the Savoy — through a microphone this time — and she set a trend that soon saw girl singers appearing in ball-rooms all over Britain. Unlike some of them, however, Anne Lenner retained her English accent, refusing to adopt the pseudo-American twang that affected most others.

As a result, she was just perfect for the Savoy and she remained with the Orpheans from then on until the outbreak of the war.

Anne retained many fond memories of her years singing with Carroll Gibbons and the Orpheans at the Savoy. Among the celebrities who used to frequent the ballroom at the hotel was Winston Churchill whom she remembered in the mid-Thirties playing a game of ping-pong with off-duty members of the band in a recreation room at the hotel!

Carroll composed his own signature tune in 1932 and he always opened his Savoy Hotel broadcasts with it: *On The Air*. Harry Bentley sang the vocal on the record the Orpheans made, but Carroll would often "sing" it himself when opening his programme at the Savoy ballroom each evening, his drawling voice becoming almost a trade-mark for the hotel's top-drawer image. He had earlier composed another great hit — *Garden in the Rain* — which was recorded in 1928 by singer George Metaxa, a Rumanian diplomat who went on to become a musical comedy star.

The Savoy Orpheans made many tunes famous in the Thirties and Forties, while under the direction of Carroll Gibbons, most particularly *As Time Goes By* sung by Jack Plant in February 1932, ten years before it soared to fame in the Humphrey Bogart and Ingrid Bergman classic film "Casablanca"; *When Did You Leave Heaven*, recorded with a vocal by George Melachrino in 1936 (after Carroll had paid for him to have singing lessons!) and two Eric Maschwitz numbers — *A Nightingale Sang in Berkeley Square* (1940), and *Room Five Hundred and Four* (1941), both sung by Anne Lenner.

Since America was officially neutral for the first two years of the Second World War, Carroll Gibbons could have chosen to return to the USA to live, but he refused. He was actually in America on holiday in September 1939, but immediately war broke out he scrambled to get back to Britain, which had become his adopted home. His regular broadcasts from the Savoy during the Blitz became tremendous morale-boosters. On one occasion when a bomb fell close to the hotel, he and his musicians were blown off the stage. While Carroll groped around looking for his glasses, a famous personality jumped onto the rostrum and began playing the piano to cheer everyone up . . . it was Noel Coward.

So Carroll Gibbons stayed in London throughout the bombing and in 1943 he played and sang a song which seemed to epitomise the spirit of the nation during those dark days — *I'm Going to Get Lit-Up When the Lights Go Up in London*. It was written and composed by Hubert Gregg, the radio and television personality who also gave us *Maybe It's Because I'm a Londoner*.

Just after the war, Carroll was asked to conduct the orchestra at the Winter Gardens, Drury Lane, for Leslie Henson's troop show "Gaieties" which had been on a tour in France and the Low Countries. In the show was a young dancer

△ *One of six singing sisters, Anne Lenner was closely associated with the Carroll Gibbons orchestra.*

called Joan Alexis who had the added talent of being a piano-accordionist. This fascinated Carroll and the two became good friends, eventually marrying. But four years after their wedding, he died at his London home.

Carroll was a great favourite with the Royal Family, often being asked to play for private functions at Buckingham Palace, and particularly to celebrate the Silver Wedding of King George VI and Queen Elizabeth in 1948. But it was at the Savoy that he endeared himself to the British public, and a gold-plated plaque is still to be found on one of the hotel's grands, stating simply:

Carroll Gibbons played at this piano 1926 to 1954.

That final date refers to the year that Carroll Gibbons died, at the early age of 51. In a tribute to him, the well-known music author Brian Rust wrote: "All who had been entertained by his music for so long felt they had lost a valued friend — an American who wasn't the brash, loud-mouthed type that some Transatlantic visitors had been, but one who came to entertain, to cheer and sustain his British friends".

That perfectly sums up the quiet, gentlemanly charm of Carroll Gibbons. Those Savoy Hotel patrons still fortunate enough to enjoy its many lavish facilities could be excused for dipping into reverie as they sip their late-night cocktails. If they are old enough, and if they care enough about style and sophisticated music, they may just be able to hear a piano tinkling from far away. Maybe they will pick out those broken-tenths in the bass, the rippling runs of syncopating melody — and even a drawling, hesitant voice saying from somewhere: "Hello Everybody . . ." □

Billy Cotton

(1899-1969)

Ask most people today if they recall band leader Billy Cotton and they will immediately think of the Cockney-voiced comedian in charge of a famous radio programme which livened up our Sunday lunchtime listening in the 1950s with that rousing call: "Wakey-Wakey!" This was the prelude to a noisy chorus of *Somebody Stole My Gal*, his signature tune, followed by a few knockabout comedy turns and tunes which meant that the "Billy Cotton Band Show" was on the air again. But the rotund and bespectacled band leader's musical prowess went back much further than that, for he had once been among Britain's top-name dance bands — for 40 years in fact, from the Twenties to the late Sixties.

William Edward Cotton, to give him his full name, had begun his musical career as a 12-year-old Boy Scout bugler in the 1st City of Westminster troop, which met close to Smith Square, London, where he was born on 6th May, 1899, the youngest of 10 children. William's father worked as a waterman at the local fire station at a

△ *Billy Cotton as a drummer boy during the Great War.*

time when the brigade answered emergency calls by charging through London's streets clinging to horse-drawn carriages while frantically ringing a brass bell. All the Cotton children were taught early to go out into the world and earn their own living, and this was one of the reasons why young Billy joined the Army in August 1914 as soon as the First World War broke out. He became a drummer-bugler in the London Regiment (Royal Fusiliers) at the age of 15, later denying that he lied about his age to get into uniform. "They never asked me", he said with a wink and that cheeky grin of his.

He hadn't even started shaving by the time he waded ashore with his regiment to take part in the fatal Gallipoli landings of 1915, and he only left the battle zone many months later when a general evacuation was ordered. Back in Britain, he joined the Royal Flying Corps and managed to get his pilot's wings when still only 18, but was badly injured when his fighter plane crashed, causing him to spend the remaining few months of the war in hospital.

After the Armistice, Billy took on a variety of jobs — he became an acrobat in a circus, tried his luck as a boxer with London Polytechnic, and played soccer as an amateur for Brentford in the Third Division of the Football League, later switching to Wimbledon. Amid all this he even found time to get married just before Christmas 1921 to Mabel Gregory, a local butcher's daughter whom he had met while roller-skating at Cricklewood. This meant he had to get a steady job and was eventually taken on as a bus conductor for London Transport, based at Cricklewood. Even though hard-up, he managed to save something from his wages every week to buy a huge drum kit, complete with a set of bells, for use when playing (part-time) with local bands at the Ealing Palais de Danse and at the great Wembley Exhibition which opened in 1924.

By the beginning of 1925 Billy had formed his first band, a musical grouping that he called the London Savannahs, and they were offered a contract to play at the Regent, Brighton, which was part cinema, part dance hall. Billy went down to live at the Sussex coastal resort with his wife and first son, Ted, but three months later moved his band and family up to

△ Billy was a regular at Brooklands race track in Surrey.

Lancashire to play at the Southport Palais dance hall. It was while playing there that he was joined by three former wartime pals — singer-trombonist Joe Ferrie, violinist Sydney Lipton who went on to become a band leader in his own right, and pianist Clem Bernard, a stunted Scot who suffered from a severe hunched back. Though always preferring to stay in the background, the shy little man became Cotton's right-hand man for the next 33 years, acting as musician, arranger, and deputy conductor until he collapsed while rehearsing for a TV broadcast in 1958, and died in Billy's arms. It was Clem who had turned the London Savannahs into a strict-tempo dance band. He it was who had listened to short-wave broadcasts of dance music coming from America, enabling Billy's band to introduce new dances to Britain. These included the saucy "Black Bottom" which had London's high society, plus most of the country's grandmas, tut-tutting in the Twenties.

After a spell at the Liverpool Rialto, Billy and the band moved back to London in the Spring of 1928 where his second son, Bill junior — later to become a BBC executive — was born. A week after that happy event, Billy and the band opened at the Astoria Ballroom in Charing Cross Road and soon began making records. Billy then moved to Ciro's — the posh nightclub in the West End, from where he began regularly broadcasting for the BBC in 1929. Ciro's was a favourite haunt of the Prince of Wales (later King Edward VIII) who would sometimes get up from his table and join the band to play the drums — much to Billy's ill-concealed annoyance. However, Ciro's provided the platform for Billy Cotton's band to earn the affection of Britain's growing late-night radio audiences and there were occasions when it was on the air every night of the week — except Sundays, of course.

During the Thirties, the band included such later top names as trumpeter and singer Nat Gonella, saxophone and clarinet player Mick Burberry and the amazing black trombonist Ellis Jackson, who became renowned not only for his brilliant musical skills, but also his impromptu tap-dancing routines performed in front of the band, to the delight of musicians and onlookers alike. Jackson, born in America, came to Britain as a child in 1907 and loved life here so much that he never returned to his native USA.

Probably the best-known personality in the Billy Cotton band, and a firm favourite with radio listeners, was singer Alan Breeze whose father was a member of the original D'Oyly Carte Opera company. Young Alan, born in 1909, was also destined for an operatic career and had broadcast as a boy soprano from station 2LO at Savoy Hill, long before the BBC came into being. "Breezy", as he became known, was heard singing off-stage in a film that the Cotton band was making at Wembley Studios in 1932. Billy invited him to join the band as a regular vocalist and he remained for almost four decades until the band eventually broke up in the Spring of 1969. Not many people knew that young Alan had a speech impediment, so that he often stuttered when he spoke — though this defect left him when he was singing. Nevertheless, he became a major star with the band and was its principal vocalist for almost four decades, cheerfully acting as the butt of Billy Cotton's extrovert humour...

▽ A loyal servant to the Billy Cotton band for almost 40 years, Alan Breeze had an instantly recognisable voice.

△ *Ever the showman, Billy Cotton became a household name via his radio and television "Band Show".*

Recalling his many years with the band, Alan Breeze remarked: "It was like being part of one big happy family. There was a marvellous spirit in the band — very seldom was there a quarrel or bad feeling. We were always playing jokes on each other and Billy was as bad as the rest of us."

Among the other vocalists who recorded regularly with the band were trumpeters Teddy Foster and Sid Buckman, Doreen Stephens, Sam Browne, Dolly Elsie (Jack Hylton's sister), Elsie Carlisle (the "Radio Sweetheart" from Manchester), Kathy Kay, and the Western Brothers, famed as the drawling cads with their monocles and old school ties. One singer who Billy Cotton took on in 1935 was Vera Lynn, then a budding crooner, though still a teenager. But after three days he sacked her, deciding that in his opinion she would never be a popular vocalist!

In addition to regular broadcasts and record-making, the band travelled around Britain's theatrical circuit in the Thirties as a kind of Music Hall show and during wartime joined ENSA for a series of tours to Service bases at home and overseas. Among its many broadcasting successes was the "Billy Cotton Song Shop", a twice weekly series which began in January 1944 on the General Forces Programme of the BBC. This later developed into the well-remembered "Billy Cotton Band Show" which broadcast for half an hour every Sunday from February 1949 until switching to tele-

vision in 1957. The band show continued until October 1968, and included guest appearances from many leading singers and entertainers of the day, including Bob Hope, Vanessa Lee, Arthur Askey, Alma Cogan, Max Bygraves and Cilla Black, etc. — the only stipulation being that all of them needed to have a strong sense of humour, for much of the comedy was spontaneous and unscripted.

Billy continued to lead his band for a quarter of a century after the war, when (apart from Joe Loss) most other big bands had long since disbanded. He appeared at five Royal Command Variety performances and continued working until well after his official retirement age. He suffered a stroke in 1962, but despite all the dire predictions that he would never be able to frolic in front of his band again, he walked out of the hospital after ten days and straight back to work. At Christmas 1968 he began the long-delayed task of writing his autobiography — eventually published under the title *I Did It My Way* — which he finished during the afternoon of March 25th, 1969. Always a keen sports fan, he went to Wembley Stadium that night to watch a boxing match — but while sitting at the ringside he suffered a heart attack and died, aged 69.

Billy Cotton's funeral took place at the famous church of St. Margaret's, by the Houses of Parliament at Westminster where, some 60 years earlier, he had been a choirboy.   □

36

Debroy Somers
(1890-1952)

Debroy Somers looked to be everybody's idea of an upper-crust Englishman. He spoke with a BBC accent, had a posh name, was always immaculately dressed, had a centre parting in his crinkly hair and sported a fashionably thin moustache. Yet despite all that he was, in fact, an Irishman called "Bill"!

Among fellow musicians — whether engaged in dance bands, symphony ensembles, or theatre orchestras — he was always known as "Bill" because he was born William Debroy Somers, in Dublin, on 11th April, 1890. He was the son of an Army bandmaster and perhaps because of that, plus some expert tuition at the Royal Irish Academy of Music, he could play virtually every instrument in an orchestra — including piano, harp, oboe, cor anglais, trumpet, xylophone, clarinet and saxophone. He also studied musical composition and orchestration, and it was this aspect of his learning that later served to make him one of the most popular dance band leaders in the London of the Twenties and Thirties.

After three years, the Savoy management decided to increase the scope of the hotel's music policy and asked Debroy Somers to form a larger band to be known as The Savoy Orpheans. The only problem was that they wanted him to *conduct* the band, which he was reluctant to do. He was really only interested in the classics as a performer, and was content to remain behind the scenes as far as dance music was concerned. He eventually agreed, however, and as a result brought a degree of class to dance music, evident not only in the music itself and his presentation of it, but also in his own appearance and attitude.

He was a tall, distinguished figure, with dark wavy hair, gleaming teeth, and a black moustache, all of which gave him a decidedly military appearance, so that in white tie and tails he cut a most impressive figure in front of an orchestra ... but no mere figurehead! As a leader, Somers was a musical *director* in every sense. In 1923 the Orpheans made the first broadcast from the studios of 2LO at Savoy Hill, next door to the hotel, recording for Columbia under their own name but also for His Masters Voice as The Albany Dance Orchestra and The Romaine Orchestra. This early band included Al and Ray Starita on saxophones, Reginald Batten, Cyril Ramon Newton and Sydney Kyte (violins), Carroll Gibbons and Billy Thorburn on pianos ... even Ray Noble was there in some unspecified capacity before he joined Lawrence Wright Publishing. So we see that even as early as 1923 Debroy Somers was, in effect, running a "nursery" for embryo band leaders.

The Savoy Orpheans made their stage debut at the London Hippodrome in their first year, and on 10th March 1925 joined forces with the Havana Band and other musicians as The Savoy Orpheans Augmented Symphonic Orchestra in a concert of symphonic jazz at the Queens Hall, in emulation of American bandleader Paul Whiteman's 1924 concert that introduced *Rhapsody In Blue*. Radio added to the popularity of Debroy Somers, who had received no credit for his Savoy work, and so he decided to capitalise on the high reputation he had built up inside the profession by forming his own band independently of the Savoy.

△ *Always debonair and very English in appearance, Debroy Somers was actually born in Dublin.*

Thus did the name "Debroy Somers and His Orchestra" come into being, leaving the Orpheans to carry on under other leaders including Reg Batten, Cyril Ramon Newton, and finally with Carroll Gibbons fronting the band with his own unique piano style. This first Somers orchestra included his brother R.G. 'Bobby' Somers on oboe, Jean Pougnet (violin), Dan Donovan (baritone sax and vocals), Ronnie Munro and Arthur Sandford on pianos, Harry Robbins and Tommy Blades handling xylophone, drums and percussion. Hotel and night-club work came to an end after he relinquished his tenure at Ciro's Club in 1927, and he embarked on a new career as a conductor of West End musicals, beginning with "That's A Good Girl" in 1928, starring Jack Buchanan and Elsie Randolph.

After a South African tour in 1931, Somers conducted the band for Vivian Ellis's show "Out of the Bottle" (1932), did a season of cine-variety at London's Plaza Cinema in 1933 and conducted a series of Leslie Henson's Gaiety Theatre shows, from "Lucky Break" in 1934 to "Going Greek" in 1937, selections from which he recorded. The band's personnel remained remarkably constant for both stage work and recording (not too many musicians had steady employment, after all) and Somers took them into the film studios to appear in "Aunt Sally" and "Music Hall" (1934), "Stars On Parade" (1936), and a special feature called "Royal Cavalcade" to celebrate the Silver Jubilee of King George V and Queen Mary.

Debroy Somers was active on Radio Luxembourg before the war as musical director for several shows including the well-remembered "Ovaltineys". BBC listeners and Merchant Navy men alike will also remember Somers in charge of "Shipmates Ashore", the popular war-time programme featuring Doris Hare. He returned to the West End theatre to take up the baton for the big hit of 1943, "The Lisbon Story" at the Hippodrome, then worked for George Black at the Palladium.

Ill-health curtailed his activities in the late Forties, but he came back for a summer show at the Blackpool Hippodrome. Then once again his formidable presence was felt in "Latin Quarter" at the London Casino in 1949 where he was in overall charge for all the music, on-stage and even in the foyer. His last work was for George Formby's "Zip Goes A Million" at the Palace Theatre in 1951, but he collapsed during the run of the show and died on 27th May, 1952, at the early age of 62. ☐

Fred Elizalde
(1908-1979)

Dance band leaders in Britain during the Twenties were sceptical of many of the new sounds being spawned by musicians across the Atlantic. Ragtime had come and gone leaving a legacy of wild rhythms which only the "bright young things" enjoyed, much to the disdain of mature dancers. "Jazz" seemed to be yet another craze emanating from the black population of the southern USA until a Cambridge undergraduate — a classical pianist and composer — formed a new student dance band with his brother in the university town and began playing the new music in 1926. Suddenly, dance band leaders and instrumentalists all over Britain sat up and took notice of this "white man's jazz" and something else he was playing called "the Blues".

By the end of the following year, the 19-year-old was invited to lead a band at the top spot in British dance band music — the ballroom at the Savoy Hotel in London! The effect was astounding, but the new jazzman's reign was short-lived for he soon returned to his first love, classical music. However, his impact on the dance band scene in this country was to prove long-lasting and profound. Even so, few people nowadays have even heard the name of Fred Elizalde the talented youngster who pioneered a new era in music.

The Savoy was the world's top hotel, based on its high-class accommodation, fabulous restaurants, and renowned standards of service. Throughout the Twenties, it had set the new dance music trend with its famed Havana bands and later the Savoy Orpheans led by Debroy Somers until 1926, and then by Carroll Gibbons, who provided the late-night clientele with sophisticated music. So it must have come as something of a culture shock to the Savoy's regulars in December 1927 when, in addition to

△ *Fred Elizalde at the piano, surrounded by his eager young Savoy Band.*

the sweet society music played by the Orpheans, they were invited to jig around the hotel's elegant dance floor to jazzy tunes from a band led by a 20-year-old Cambridge undergraduate!

The leader of this revolutionary sound at the Savoy was Fred Elizalde, an unknown university student. But within a year he had earned the respect and admiration of instrumentalists and listeners alike, stamping an indelible mark on the popular music scene of late-Twenties Britain. Yet, even now, after this daring experiment by the Savoy's ultra-conservative management, not many of today's jazz enthusiasts have even heard of his name.

Fred Elizalde came from a wealthy Spanish family who had settled in the Philippines, where they owned large sugar-cane plantations and processing factories in the early years of this century. Fred (real name Federico) was born at Manila in December 1907 and studied the pianoforte, seemingly intent on pursuing a career in classical orchestral music. However, as a teenager, he and his brother Manuel (always called "Lizz") were sent to Stanford University in California to study law, but instead they cultivated a liking for jazz music, until then regarded as a preserve of America's black population. Lizz played saxophone and he encouraged Fred to switch from the classical brilliance of Chopin to the foot-tapping style of Jelly Roll Morton and Duke Ellington.

Predictably, however, their parents did not approve and so in 1925 they packed them off to England to complete their studies in the hope that the revered college halls of Cambridge would help to mould their minds and put them on the road to a worthwhile career in the legal profession. But music was embedded in their souls, and shortly after arriving in the university town Fred and his brother formed a "hot" band — known as "The Quinquaginta Ramblers" — to play for student dances and also Cambridge's annual "Footlights Revue" (1926).

One member of this band of undergraduates was Maurice Allom, the future Surrey and England bowler who would later earn his place in the cricket record books by taking four New Zealand wickets in five consecutive balls during his 1930 Test debut at Christchurch. In his student days, Allom played tenor and baritone saxophone and is listed among the personnel of "Fred Elizalde and His Cambridge Undergraduates" when the band made its first few recordings in June 1927. Also playing in that 10-piece band were students with typical English public school names like John D'Arcy Hildyard (trumpet) and J. Eric Saunders (drums).

Fred was also composing tunes of his own as well as producing dance music arrangements for other bands, and as a result his style and talents came to the notice of such big names as Bert Ambrose, playing at the Mayfair Hotel, and Reggie Batten who was leader of the Savoy Orpheans at the time. Ambrose was so impressed with Fred Elizalde's work that he urged Brunswick Records to offer him a contract, and when they did so he decided to lend the talented youngster several of his own musicians for the recording sessions to augment the poverty-stricken student band.

Among the dozen or so records Fred and his band made in the summer of 1927 was one of his own composition *Stomp Your Feet*, which

△ *Fred Elizalde (right) and his brother Manuel, known as "Lizz". Their parents tried unsuccessfully to dissuade them from playing jazz in both America and Britain.*

included trumpeter Jack Jackson borrowed from the Jack Hylton band. These early records excited young people at the time and the Savoy's directors, sensing an opportunity, decided to jump straight in and capitalize on what was seen as a new trend in dance music. But they then shocked the dinner-jacketed world of big bands by inviting Fred and his musicians to take over as the second band at the Savoy's elegant ballroom, while still keeping the genteel Orpheans on hand for more sedate and traditional dancing.

Once the contract was signed in October 1927, Fred sent his brother over to the USA to sign up several well-known American jazz instrumentalists to replace some of his lesser experienced fellow students, and when this all-star band opened two months later, during Christmas week, the hotel's party-goers could hardly believe their ears and eyes — for the sound was something they'd never heard before, and the leader of the band was only just out of his teens!

After that opening night, dance music in Britain was never to be the same again. The band — all wearing formal evening dress, which was *de rigeur* at the Savoy — were placed on a turreted platform made to look like a mediaeval castle. Their music stands were painted in scarlet, silver and gold — the Savoy always did things in style! Then instead of dancing to the Veleta or an old-time waltz, the sophisticated diners found themselves swinging and swaying to something called the "Blues", or strutting to an up-market version of the "Black Bottom"! Suddenly, alice bands and bead-fringed skirts became respectable, and bright young things began saying "boo-boop-ee-doop" in a posh accent.

Perhaps because of his upper-class back-

ground, and his impeccable manners, Fred became the darling of London society and brought a new following to the Savoy. Mrs. Louis Oppenheimer, wife of the millionaire diamond magnate, threw a dinner party there for 120 guests and garlanded young Fred with laurel wreaths as a sign of his success and acceptance into the circle of the capital's well-heeled upper-crust. Within a week, somebody important must have pulled strings inside the BBC (well known for its entrenched opposition to all forms of dance music) for on New Year's Eve the Elizalde band was featured in an unscheduled late-night broadcast ... and thus its fame spread far and wide.

Throughout 1928, Fred Elizalde — noted for interspersing his own dazzling piano solos within the band's performances — continued broadcasting and making records, but even though he came top in a poll conducted by the musical magazine *Melody Maker* to name Britain's best-liked dance-band that year, not all the Savoy's staid customers were pleased with his music, or convinced that it was here to stay. Some older ones said it was too difficult to dance to, and radio audiences complained that they couldn't recognise their favourite old tunes when served up in such a peppy fashion. However, musicians throughout the land loved the happy new sound that Elizalde pioneered at the Savoy and it prompted many of them to change their own style of playing.

In an era when jazz music was supposed to be purely instrumental (i.e. non-vocal) Fred got his banjo player Dick Maxwell to stand up and sing a few numbers. Then, he introduced a near-penniless young crooner to the "mike" — the South African singer Al Bowlly, who later joined

Ray Noble and became a legend in his own right.

Among Fred Elizalde's more unusual musical innovations can be heard in his recording of *Tiger Rag* made in January 1928, three weeks after opening at the Savoy. When the record was issued in the following April, *Melody Maker* held a competition asking its readers to guess how the slapping effect in the number was produced. Only three entrants got it right — the drummer (Ronald Gubertini) did it by drumming on his overcoat wrapped in a newspaper!

The Savoy, stung by criticism that it was pandering to the young and the avant-garde instead of the older, more solid (and better-paying) clientele, terminated Fred's contract in 1929 and, after a three-week stint at the London Palladium where the *hoi-polloi* could see and hear him, he took his band on a tour of dance halls in Scotland, with disastrous results. His music was greeted with incomprehension north of the border, as many kilted members of his audiences couldn't understand why he never played an Eightsome Reel!

Fred made a few more sides for the Decca and HMV labels, but although he reluctantly played the occasional old-style dance (*Diane* is one of only three waltzes he is known to have ever recorded) his band and his music was still too far ahead of its time for many folk and he grew increasingly discouraged at the slow pace of change. Facing near bankruptcy, and with his university course beyond recall, he disbanded his orchestra and left for Spain in 1932.

Thereupon, the dispirited young man who had done more than anyone else to introduce pleasurable jazz to Britain virtually gave up on modern music and instead retraced his steps to the classics, studying at Granada and the Madrid conservatoire under the great Spanish composer Manuel de Falla (*Ritual Fire Dance*), and also in Paris under Maurice Ravel (1875-1937), famed for his *Bolero*. Later on, he returned to his native Manila where he became head of the Philippines broadcasting network, returning to Britain occasionally to conduct classical concerts. But by that time few people over here connected him with the dashing young man who had introduced the first wave of "white man's jazz" to England, via the elegant portals of the Savoy Hotel.

Fred Elizalde died at Manila in January 1979, aged 71, but for all who enjoy music from the golden era of Britain's dance band days, he deserves to be remembered with affection for having initiated new musical ideas with the vision and vigour of youth.   ☐

Maurice Winnick
(1902-1962)

Maurice Winnick is best remembered by dancing enthusiasts in Britain for playing *The Sweetest Music This Side of Heaven*, his signature tune. Not many people realised, however, that he had more than one string to his bow because immediately after the war he became a successful impresario and the brains behind a number of radio and television shows. Remember the following . . . ?

"And now . . . over to the mystery voice."
"And the next object is . . . "
"Animal, vegetable or mineral?"

These familiar phrases are all from the famous post-war radio programme "Twenty Questions", which Maurice Winnick personally imported from America, together with the shorter-running "Ignorance is Bliss" and the favourite 1950s television programme "What's My Line?" All three programmes employed well-known personalities, including Anona Winn and Norman Hackforth, both of whom, like Winnick, were part of the

▽ *Like Jack Jackson, Maurice Winnick began a completely new career after the war.*

rapidly changing popular music scene. Other panellists included Jack Train — from ITMA — Stewart Macpherson, Richard Dimbleby, Joy Adamson and the crusty Gilbert Harding. Although an extremely varied group of individuals, thanks to Winnick's show business flair they soon became a highly effective and unified team.

As a pioneer dance band leader, the young Winnick always kept one eye on what pleased the public and his flourishing career bore testimony to his intuition. Born in Manchester on March 28th, 1902, he studied violin at the local Royal College of Music before making his professional debut as a cinema pianist. Still in his teens he then led a band on a trans-Atlantic liner, also taking the opportunity to study the saxophone in the USA. Returning to England in 1922 he played with various bands before leading his own eight-piece combination at Manchester's Plaza Dance Hall.

His potential was quickly spotted and in 1928 he made his way via Nottingham to lead a dance band at the famous Hammersmith Palais in London. From there he progressed to the Piccadilly Hotel where, in 1931, he made his first radio broadcast. Like most bands of the period he frequently moved venues and also appeared at both the Carlton Hotel and Ciro's Club, where one of his violinists was Max Jaffa, later to find fame as the popular leader of the Palm Court Orchestra on the radio programme "Grand Hotel". Maurice Winnick's was also the first British band to appear in a talking film, subsequently appearing in more movies than any other.

His early signature tune was the lively but traditional *Lend Me Your Ears*, but on moving to the San Marco Restaurant, Mayfair, in 1934, he decided to transform his conventional image

▽ *A child prodigy, Maurice Winnick trained at the Royal Manchester College of Music.*

and remodelled the band on Guy Lombardo and his Royal Canadians, who were renowned for playing *The Sweetest Music This Side of Heaven*. Maurice adopted this song as his signature tune, a romantic piece written by Cliff Friend and Guy Lombardo's sentimental saxophone-playing brother, Carmen. It provided a stylish new focus for the band, but not all music aficionados liked the new ultra-sweet style. The public loved it, however, and from then on Winnick never looked back.

In 1936 he succeeded Harry Roy's energetic band at the Mayfair Hotel, engaging Sam Costa as pianist/crooner and Judy Shirley as vocalist. After three years he then moved the short distance to the Dorchester Hotel, producing a cabaret entitled the "Dorchester Follies" and stayed until 1940 when, against the wishes of the management, he expanded the size of the band. Amongst his new members was a fine trombonist who later became a celebrated band leader, Ted Heath. However, the hotel was not prepared to foot the increased wage bill so he took his musicians off on a national tour instead. In 1944 he supported ENSA by leading the whole company to Italy, and also entertained troops in Palestine, Egypt and Syria.

In addition to the early sounds of Sam Costa and Judy Shirley, Winnick's later vocalists included a teenage Vera Lynn, Joe Leigh, Dorothy Carless, Jack Plant, Ronnie O'Dell, Hughie Diamond and Al Bowlly. The band's recordings sold well throughout the 1930s but when war intervened the music world was turned upside down and, despite his popularity, Winnick's last commercial records were made in 1940.

Although he continued as an occasional band leader for another ten years, the would-be businessman recognised the rapidly changing market and decided to embark on a new career. When hostilities ceased in 1945 he joined the BBC and, as a popular impresario, continued to work enthusiastically and effectively right up until his death on 29th May, 1962.

Always in tune with the popular mood, just like Jack Jackson, Maurice Winnick is now remembered by two separate generations, firstly as a dance band leader and latterly as a show business personality. Virtually every adult in the land tuned in at some point to "Twenty Questions" or "What's My Line?", programmes which became an integral part of post-war Britain and, thanks to their British innovator, set the standards and pattern for all later panel-game broadcasting. □

Felix Mendelssohn

(1911-1952)

The crowd stood and stared. Was it really a famous dance band leader, riding on top of an elephant across London's Oxford Circus? It was, in fact, just one of many publicity stunts organised for band leader Harry Roy by an entertainment entrepreneur called Felix Mendelssohn who claimed to be a descendant of the illustrious 19th century composer. The diminutive Harry Roy made an excellent *mahout* (elephant driver) and the crowds flocked to the London Palladium to see him take part in his latest show.

Felix Bartholdy Mendelssohn, unlike his better-known namesake, was born in England, at Brondesbury Park, London, on 19th September 1911. He began work at his father's office on the Stock Exchange but left to join the Merchant Navy when he was 17. Inspired by visits to faraway places, he vowed one day to form his own Hawaiian ensemble and introduce South Sea island music to British dancers. After leaving the sea, he took up acting and toured the country before settling in the West End, where he opened the Club Felix. This venue soon became a favourite haunt for many stage personalities, so Felix decided to enter show business as a publicity agent.

With such a famous name, it was not long before he came to wider public attention and in the late 1930s formed a quality dance band, usually playing without a vocalist, although Al Bowlly and George Barclay were occasionally to be found crooning into the microphone. It was in 1940 that Felix fulfilled his early ambition by forming his "Hawaiian Serenaders", a group which was to make dozens of records through-

△ Felix Mendelssohn was a great sshowman — but could not play any musical instrument!

out the war years. Their style and dress was modelled on the colourful South Sea islands, both flamboyant and exotic, and brightened up an otherwise drab period of the nation's history. The public loved it and bought his records in vast quantities.

Mendelssohn broadcast over 1,000 times, both at home and overseas, and took part in no fewer than 43 films. Nearly a million people accepted the invitation to "dance the Hula" with his South Sea Lovelies, a troupe of girls from Arabia, Hawaii, Spain, Africa, China — and Golders Green! His signature tune was *Song of the Islands*, after which he named his wartime radio programme. His signing off tune was *Aloha Oe* ("Farewell to Thee"), a typically warm piece which reflected the friendly style of the Polynesian people.

Always an excellent entertainer, Felix Mendelssohn both created and filled a niche in the dance band market. Although he had never visited Hawaii himself, and could not play a musical instrument, he was a popular member of the show business fraternity and provided an unusual style of steel guitar music, which was always well received. Unfortunately, just like his namesake, his prolific output was cut short in its prime. Felix Mendelssohn the elder, who made frequent visits to this country, died aged 38, while returning to the Continent from England in 1847. His Hawaiian music-loving namesake lasted only a little longer, dying prematurely in 1952, at the age of only 41. It was sad, both for them and for music lovers generally, that neither man lived long enough to fulfil his true potential. □

Harry Roy

(1900-1971)

There were many top-line dance bands in Britain during the "Golden Age of Popular Music" before the war, each renowned for its particular style of playing, and a high-profile leader conducting a glittering array of well-known musicians. But there was one band that stole the limelight not so much for its musical prowess as for the unpredictable antics and bubbling personality of the man in front — Harry Roy. He delighted late-night diners at London's swish Mayfair Hotel in the mid-Thirties with his unusual vocals, and in 1935 he made headline news by marrying a "Princess" from the jungles of Sarawak. Broadcasting regularly on the BBC and from Continental stations, he was also known to his many fans as "the Little Hotcha-Ma-Cha-Cha"!

Harry wasn't just a band leader turned vocalist — he was a cabaret all by himself! For this small man with the big, wide eyes had more talent in his little finger than many musical stars of today. And for over 40 years he kept the British public's feet tapping to

△ *The effervescent Harry Roy.*

some of the liveliest tunes and the best arrangements to be heard on record and the airwaves from the Twenties to the Sixties. For Harry Roy's life not only spanned but overlapped the decades that have come to be known as the "Golden Age of Dance Music".

He was born Harold Lipman in Stamford Hill, London, on 12th January 1900, and although his father ran a cardboard box factory, music was definitely in the family's blood, for Harry's elder brother Syd had started his own small dance band at the end of the First World War after service with the Royal Flying Corps. When the war started, many innocent people with German-sounding names then living in Britain suffered at the hands of thugs who vented their hatred of the Hun on them, even though most had fled as refugees from the anti-Jewish pogroms in Europe. The Lipmans of Bishopsgate, London, were one of those families who feared reprisals because of their surname, so they changed it to Roy. Their three children — Sydney, Harry and sister Sadie — followed in father's footsteps by working in the carton factory at Shoreditch.

Young Harry seemed destined for a career in business, even though he hated office work, so when his family's firm went bust due to material shortages and low sales during the war he was forced to look elsewhere for a living. In this case, for him at least, bankruptcy proved to be a blessing in disguise.

Harry had begun learning the piano at the age of seven, but he was fascinated by all musical instruments and as he grew up he tried his hand at playing most of them, including the banjo, violin, double bass and trumpet in his brother's band. But all this changed after the war when he decided one night to go to the Hammersmith Palais to watch and listen to the sound and the antics of the "Original Dixieland Jazz Band". This group of five energetic young Americans, who caused a sensation when they came to London in 1919 with their jumpy new sound, included Larry Shields on clarinet. After hearing what Larry could make the instrument do, young Harry was hooked. The clarinet suited him down to the ground because, being on the small side — Harry was only 5ft. 6in. and weighed a mere 9½ stone — he could easily carry it around while acting daft in front of the band, or slip it under his arm when singing a

△ *Harry Roy fronts the band for a recording session in 1934. Note the two pianos — played by Ivor Moreton (foreground) and Dave Kaye. Also in the picture are Maurice Sterndale (violin), Joe Daniels and Bill Currie (drums), Tommy Venn (guitar), and Nat Temple (alto saxophone) who later led his own orchestra at the Club Royal.*

vocal. Indeed, as he became a co-leader of his brother's band — known as "The Darnswells" — it was Harry's showmanship and peppy singing style that became the band's main attraction to the public and earned it an enviable reputation.

By the middle Twenties, the band had become the "Lyricals" and their growing success meant them receiving a modest recording contract as well as undertaking a few overseas tours. In 1930, by which time he had formed his own band, Harry Roy achieved a huge success at the Bat Club in London, and was invited to open at the new Leicester Square Theatre which was then a major British showcase for RKO films. In those days it was common practice to have a live performance in between feature films. Later in the Thirties, mainly for reasons of economy, this part of the show was taken over by cinema organists who were to be seen and heard at the end of the film rising up in front of the screen in a blaze of sound and coloured lights.

Harry Roy and his RKOleans, as they came to be called, flitted across Leicester Square to the Café Anglais in 1933, and then in the following year came the little man's big chance when he was invited to take over as the resident dance-band leader at the plush Mayfair Hotel following the departure of the famed Ambrose and his Orchestra. Harry quickly established his outfit as one of the top bands in Britain, broad-

casting regularly on the BBC and becoming a prolific recording star as well as popular vocalist and songwriter.

During the mid-Thirties, by which time Syd had given up on his own career to take over the management and business affairs of his younger brother's booming music empire, Harry Roy and his band were topping the bill at Variety theatres all over Britain. But the public who flocked in their thousands to see and hear them mainly wanted to watch the energetic little man in front of the orchestra, for you never quite knew what tricks he would get up to next. Almost all of his numbers contained some ad-lib elements, which turned every performance into something of a surprise. Harry's many fans called him "Little Hotcha Ma-Cha-Cha" because of his diminutive size and his liking for bright and jazzy numbers — epitomised by his signature tune *Bugle Call Rag*. A sizeable section of the public also enjoyed his semi-clowning, larger-than-life singing style, often considered to be similar to that of Al Jolson, but in a British sort of way.

In August 1935, Harry caused a different kind of sensation when he married Miss Elizabeth Brooke at Caxton Hall Registry Office. His bride was known to popular newspapers at the time as "Princess Pearl", for she was the headline-catching daughter of Sir Charles and Lady Vyner Brooke, the white Rajah (and Ranee)

PRINCESS PEARL on "MY HOME WITH HARRY ROY"

RADIO PICTORIAL

LUXEMBOURG and NORMANDY PROGRAMMES

3D

HARRY ROY AND PRINCESS PEARL
to be married next Tuesday, August 6

△ Harry Roy and his bride-to-be, "Princess Pearl", appeared on the front cover of "Radio Pictorial" in August 1935.

of Sarawak, in north-west Borneo. Elizabeth's great-grandfather, Sir James Brooke (1803-1868) the first Rajah, was one of the most famous and romantic figures in the old British Empire. Educated at Norwich, he ran away from school and forged an illustrious career in the army in the Far East, before sailing by private yacht to Borneo in 1838. Three years later he helped the island's ruler to suppress a rebellion in Sarawak, a territory the size of England, and was promptly invited to rule over the country's half-million people.

Harry Roy met Elizabeth at a Mayfair party in 1932, but he waited more than two years before proposing to her, at Christmas 1934 — by letter sent to her jungle home in Sarawak! The letter took a month to arrive out there, but Elizabeth's answer was delivered in person within eight days — that's how long it took her to fly back to Britain by Imperial Airways flying boat! No wonder the newspapers splashed the story, for it was a fairy-tale romance.

Thousands of people turned out to see and cheer the happy couple as they set off for their honeymoon, spent in America. They later appeared together in a film entitled "Everything is Rhythm" in 1936 and the marriage lasted for a creditable 12 years which, for show business,

was quite something even in those days. They had two children — Roberta, and David who bore a striking resemblance to his famous father. Following a divorce in 1947, Harry married his second wife, the Windmill dancer Sonia Stacpoole, in July 1948 and remained happy ever after.

Harry Roy continued his upward climb in popular esteem throughout the Thirties, helped by some remarkable musicians in his band — notably the brilliant piano duettists Ivor Moreton and Dave Kaye, who featured in many of his top-selling records, plus drummer Joe Daniels, Arthur Calkin (string bass) — and, later, pianist Stanley Black — all of whom teamed up with the boss to form a small group known as "Harry Roy and his Tiger Ragamuffins".

During the war, Harry Roy led the resident band at such legendary night clubs as the Embassy, one of the bright spots in blacked-out London, and in answer to an appeal from ENSA he took his band out to military stations overseas to entertain the troops, which meant forsaking his £4,000-a-week earnings in Britain.

After the war, despite the decline in decent dance band music, Harry continued leading orchestras at many of his old London haunts — including the Café Anglais and the swish Mayfair Hotel — but the writing was on the wall for the big bands and he retired from the scene as the Beatles era got under way in the Sixties. Then, for four months in the summer of 1969 he came back from retirement to lead a Dixieland band at Sherry's renovated dance hall in Brighton, even though he was on the verge of 70.

His widow, Sonia, recalled: "He was a demon for work and he couldn't bear being idle." He also had a wonderful sense of humour, as many musicians readily recall, which lasted throughout his life. Laughter and happiness were evident to all who saw him on stage throughout his long career.

Harry Roy often boasted that he'd never had a day's illness in his life, but his luck changed a couple of weeks after his 71st birthday when he suffered a fatal heart attack at his London home and died on February 1st, 1971. But that was not the end of the Harry Roy story, for on the first anniversary of his death, a group of friends met at the band leader's home and, together with his widow, formed the Harry Roy Appreciation Society dedicated to preserving his memory and keeping alive the music he made popular. The society now has members in many parts of Britain and overseas, has its own newsletter, club badge and tie. □

Jack Jackson

(1907-1978)

Many of the band leaders featured in this book faded from the scene after the war or continued with smaller musical combinations in a different manner. Some of them went on to broadcast exclusively over the radio, whilst others went to sea on cruise ships and passenger liners. One exception, however, was Jack Jackson who built an entirely new career for himself as a record spinner and in the process became a household name.

Not many dance band leaders ever went on safari, but in 1926 both Jack Jackson and pianist Billy Mayerl took part in an ill-fated visit to South Africa. As a member of the trumpet section of Bert Ralton's Havana Band, Jackson — still in his teens — had already had experience in military bands before travelling the world playing with pick-up dance bands on various ocean liners. The South African tour was several months old when, on 16th January 1927, Ralton — a popular American saxophonist — was accidentally shot and killed during a big-game hunting expedition. The tour came to an abrupt end and the band was forced to return home.

Far from hindering Jackson's promising career, however, the unfortunate incident provided an opportunity to join Jack Hylton's orchestra, the undisputed top band in the country at that time. He soon made a name for himself by playing "hot" trumpet, and for the next few years was prominent on many of Hylton's finest recordings. Although Jackson had already made earlier records, as a teenager, with Ronnie

△ Jack Jackson was an early exponent of "hot" trumpet.

Munro's orchestra, it was the Hylton discs which brought him to wider public attention.

Jack Jackson was born at Belvedere in Kent in 1907 and was taught the cornet from the age of six. After a brief spell in Barnsley, where he played with a local brass band, he returned to London and turned professional after a spell studying trumpet at the Royal Academy of Music, and eventually found fame both as a dance band leader and, after the Second World War, as one of the earliest "disc jockeys" (DJs as they are now called), working firstly for the BBC and then Radio Luxembourg.

None of this would have been possible had he not survived a remarkable incident when only 17 years old. During a world cruise on the *ss Samaria*, he and his fellow musicians slipped over the side for a swim. Unfortunately someone unwittingly pulled up the ladder and despite their frantic cries for help, they were on the verge of drowning, or being eaten by two circling sharks, when an Arab dhow rescued them in the nick of time!

In 1929, after growing tired of touring Britain and the Continent, Jackson moved from Jack Hylton to play firstly with Howard Jacobs at the Berkeley Hotel, then to Percival Mackey and Arthur Lally, both at the Savoy. In March 1931 he joined Jack Payne and the BBC Dance Orchestra, where he remained for the next two years. Payne and Jackson had highly contrasting personalities, however, and a clash was almost inevitable. Payne was methodical, precise

△ *Always in a hurry, Jack Jackson, pictured here posing with his band during filming for a 1930s movie, wrote his signature tune "We're Gonna Make Those People Sway" whilst sitting at a table in the Dorchester Hotel.*

and business-like, whilst Jackson was a totally independent, carefree extrovert with a mischievous disposition. Opinions differed and finally came to a head, with Jackson speaking his mind and walking out to form his own band in February, 1933.

Within six months he had acquired the coveted Dorchester Hotel spot, and opened on 1st August the same year, his earliest HMV recordings being under the title of *John* Jackson and his Orchestra. John was also the name of the first son born to Jackson and his South African wife in Spring 1934. His successful tenancy at the Dorchester, a new and lavish building in Park Lane, lasted for five years until a problem with the management over salaries caused him to leave and take his band on tour.

Among the girl vocalists who joined the band in 1934 were the American blues singer Alberta Hunter, and Peggy Cochrane, who later married Jack Payne. Originally trained as a classical pianist and violinist, Peggy broke her arm and had to turn her musical ambitions elsewhere, deciding instead to become a dance band vocalist. Fred Latham was the regular male singer, and although able to mimic Bing Crosby, usually sang with a soft voice which matched the

warmth of the sound emanating from the instruments behind him. Perhaps the band's most famous singer, however, was Sam Costa, who later became a successful disc jockey in his own right, but first found fame with Kenneth Horne and Richard Murdoch in the highly popular radio show "Much Binding in the Marsh". Based on a fictitious wartime RAF base, this programme continued well into the 1950s.

In 1933, Jackson wrote the band's signature tune, *Make Those People Sway*, after simply slipping away to a quiet table during the first rehearsal at the Dorchester. It took him little more than a few minutes to complete the song, entirely characteristic of a man who knew exactly what he wanted, and achieved it as quickly as possible. He was also one of the few band leaders who used a closing theme tune, *Dancing in the Dark*, which epitomised his matter-of-fact approach to his paying clientele. His music was tuneful but never brash, sometimes sentimental yet never slushy, but above all, was acceptable to a wide ranging public.

Jack Jackson regularly took part in BBC radio programmes such as "Band Call", "Salute to Rhythm" and "Band Parade", the latter as its compere, and whilst on tour in early 1939, increased the size of his band and added the popular young singer Mary Lee. In October 1940 he took up his final London residency, this time at the Mayfair Hotel. Wartime, of course, slowed everything down. The pre-war dance band bubble was beginning to deflate, and at an increasingly rapid rate. Most people stood still and waited to see what would happen next, but Jackson was always in a hurry which, allied to his breezy, happy-go-lucky attitude, fitted him well for a fresh challenge.

While most of his fellow dance band leaders bowed to the inevitable, after changing post-war fashions, and economic austerity forced many of them out of business, Jackson easily slotted into a new mould. With a warm, friendly personality and no time for pomposity, he was the ideal choice to host a new post-war radio show, finally laying down his trumpet and conductor's baton in 1947. Thus began the second phase of an active career in show business.

Jack Jackson's "Record Round Up" began on 10th January 1948, initially as an afternoon show, but within six months, its popularity saw it transferred to peak listening time at 11pm, starting on 26th June the same year. It was the first late-night record programme to run for a whole hour, popular radio shows of the period rarely lasting more than 30 minutes. It usually began with Harry James' version of *Carnival*, and ended with *Dancing in the Dark*, played not by himself, but by the great American band leader, Artie Shaw.

The programme was full of fast-moving chat, and unusual revolutionary sound effects, made even more light hearted and entertaining by the use of Jack's fictitious cat, "Tiddles". It was later followed by "Record Roundabout" and "Jackson's Jukebox", the latter on Radio Luxembourg, eventually becoming simply "The Jack Jackson Show". Much of the material for these programmes was recorded in the state-of-the-art studio he set up at Puerto de la Cruz, in Tenerife, one of the Canary Islands. The tapes were later flown straight to the BBC in London, or to Radio Luxembourg.

Like so many other active brass players, Jack Jackson eventually contracted a lung disease and returned to the British Isles. He died at his Jersey home on 14th January, 1978, aged 71. He is remembered now perhaps more for his record programmes than for his dance band days, because he made an indelible mark as a unique pioneer in early popular music broadcasting. His radio programmes also reached a much younger and wider audience than his dance band ever did. Nevertheless, both equally important parts of his career were strongly connected by a common theme, which he would have been happy to acknowledge from an early age. For Jack Jackson was, above all else, an "entertainer". □

Joe Loss
(1909-1990)

It is perhaps forgotten these days that a band's popularity over half a century ago depended very largely on its ability to provide strict tempo music for dancing. Apart from the leader, who occasionally raised a baton to show who was in charge, the men in the band remained fairly static. As for the clientele, whether formally dressed or not, the big question for young fellows and their fancied ladies was whether they could do the latest dance craze, be it the palais-glide, tango, or fox-trot. In the 1930s and 40s there were many top-flight dance bands who broadcast regularly from posh London hotels, but the vast majority of ballroom enthusiasts were to be found tripping the light fantastic at the local *Palais-de-Danse*. One band leader who became well-known at dance halls throughout Britain, began his career playing the violin in cinemas to accompany silent films. He eventually reached the top of his profession and confirmed his talent by

▽ *Hugely popular, Joe Loss became a dance band legend in his own lifetime.*

△ *Joe Loss was one of the few bands to continue broadcasting successfully after the Second World War, both on radio and television*

staying there for over half a century. He made over a thousand records, and many wartime romances blossomed as the boys and girls of blacked-out Britain waltzed and jived to the lively music of Joe Loss.

Joe had the longest career as a band leader in British dance music history. He started as a violinist accompanying silent films, formed his first band while still in his teens, became the youngest bandleader in the West End of London at 21, and was still in the forefront of the music business when he died 60 years later. An impressive record by any standards, particularly as the Joe Loss orchestra was mainly regarded as a "palais band" churning out hits of the day. But it was a remarkably efficient and successful palais band which always managed to fill ballrooms and sold thousands of records from pre-war 78s to latter-day LPs and CDs.

That, however, was all in the future when Joshua Alexander Loss was born in Liverpool Street, London, on 22nd June, 1909, where his father worked as a cabinet-maker. Before the First World War had finished, the nine-year-old Joe was already playing the violin, going on to study at the London School of Music and eventually winning a scholarship to Trinity College of Music, giving recitals, and becoming a music teacher himself.

Though professing to dislike dance music and jazz, at 17 he formed an outfit called the "Magnetic Dance Band", which included a young baritone saxophone player and future band leader called Harry Gold. It wasn't very successful, however, so Joe went back to playing the violin for 30 shillings a week at the Coliseum Cinema, Ilford, accompanying silent films, then moving to the Rialto Cinema in London's Coventry Street doing the same job. He later worked at the Chinese Café in Blackpool, returning to London to join the band playing at the Wimbledon Palais de Danse as deputy leader. It was there that he began to take an interest in dancing, though from the musicians' point of view rather than the dancers'. He learned all there was to know about strict tempo, and when he felt the time was ripe, at the advanced age of 21 he took his courage and his fate into his hands and formed a small band to play in the style of Oscar Rabin's Romany Band at the Astoria Ballroom, Charing Cross Road. Joe's growing reputation earned him the job of relief leader at the very exclusive Kit-Cat Club, where he was quickly promoted to musical director.

It was with this early eight-piece band that he made the first of many BBC outside broadcasts from the Kit-Cat in 1933, producing his first records for the Edison Bell Winner label the same year. It says much for Joe as an employer that the only personnel changes during the rest of the 1930s were when the band grew to an eleven-piece over the years.

In 1934, Joe's regular vocalist (Jimmy

Messini) left and was eventually replaced by two gentlemen who were to become immensely popular in their own right, although their real names may not sound familiar nowadays ... Henderson Rowntree from Hartlepool, and James Montgomery Fyfe, a stalwart tenor from Scotland. Very soon, however, the listening public got to know them by their professional names — Chick Henderson and Monte Rey.

In August 1935, a budding 18-year-old croonette made her first broadcast with the Joe Loss band, singing the top hit of the day *Red Sails in the Sunset*. Her name? — Vera Lynn, later a celebrated Dame of the British Empire.

In 1937, Joe recorded a little known number called *Let's Dance at the Make-Believe Ballroom*, which became his band's original signature tune, but his biggest hit in the Thirties was *Begin the Beguine* with a Chick Henderson vocal that was recorded on 5th July, 1939, barely two months before the outbreak of war. Chick, who joined the band in 1934, recorded *My Prayer* on the reverse side of the record, and also *That Sly Old Gentleman from Featherbed Lane*. For all three of these he received the standard session fee of £4 and no royalties!

Imagine Chick Henderson earning only £1 6s 8d for making each one of the three best records in dance band history and one which kept his name alive years after his death. It could have been as a result of this that Chick left the Loss band shortly afterwards to join Harry Roy at the Café Anglais. Monte Rey, clad in colourful Latin costumes, sang in a near-operatic and non-rhythmical voice, but the fiery "Latin" was actually an amicable, mild-mannered, middle-aged Scotsman — but that's show business for you!

Early in the war, Monte sang in his appropriately robust style on a rare record of *There'll Always Be an England* and *Lords of the Air* labelled as by Joe Loss and his "Concert Orchestra", which was quite a contrast to the series of strict tempo dance records he did about the same time with a small combination in the style of Victor Silvester. They were in addition to the big band's normal output, so we can see that Joe Loss was also a businessman with his finger firmly on the public pulse.

The war gave Joe the opportunity to leave the Astoria and take his band show to the forces overseas, following which he embarked on a tour of the music halls and ballrooms on the home front. Joe Loss may have begun as a society bandleader, but his real *forté* was playing for the mass public. He never disappointed them, nor did his public ever let him down, ever enthusiastic and always there to support him.

From the moment he started making a name for himself as a leader, Joe Loss never again touched his fiddle in public (unlike Ambrose) neither did he compose music for his band nor do any of his own arranging. In fact, the Joe Loss band of the Thirties tended to reflect the latest American styles. This happened with his tremendously successful records of Glenn Miller's *In the Mood*, and Woody Herman's *At the Woodchoppers' Ball*, carbon copies that outsold the originals in Britain. Joe even claimed *In the Mood* for his later signature tune.

In the post-war years he added singers like Rose Brennan, Howard Jones, and Elizabeth Batey, a South Shields girl known in her home town as "Little Betty Batey" when she sang in a seaside concert party in 1935.

The Joe Loss band continued with one night stands, which by now included a fair quota of society and even royal engagements, as well as residencies at holiday camps, voyages on the Cunard liner *QE2*, playing for the World Ballroom Championships and, of course, still more records. In the 1970s, he even went out on the road with a smaller band playing pop music, however regrettable his old fans may have found it. But that was typical of Joe Loss all through his life and career ... identifying a public need, and then supplying it.

During the 1980s Joe was the subject of a "This Is Your Life" television programme, not before time some people thought. He died on 6th June, 1990, aged 80, one of the last survivors of a profession which had brought so much pleasure to so many people. Some of those who danced and fell in love to his music later brought up their children and grandchildren to hear and appreciate it. ☐

▷ Monte Rey — a fiery 'Latin' singer was actually a Scotsman called James Montgomery Fyfe.

Roy Fox
(1901-1982)

Earlier this century there was fierce competition between major shipping lines who vied with each other to win the famous "Blue Riband" for the fastest trans-Atlantic sea crossing. The mighty and luxurious ships of Britain's celebrated Cunard Line had a firm grip on the title, and their prowess instilled as much pride in the average British schoolboy as it caused envy in the boardrooms of foreign shipbuilders. Nowhere was that feeling felt more keenly than in Germany, where the 56,550-ton *Bismark* — planned as the world's biggest passenger liner — was being constructed at Hamburg. But the year was 1914 and all work stopped on it until after the First World War when, as part of German reparations to the Allies, she was handed over to Britain and acquired by the White Star Line, who then renamed her the *Majestic*. She was put on the prestigious Southampton to New York run, making her maiden voyage in May 1922,

△ *Softly-spoken Roy Fox originally hailed from America.*

and brought over many famous American people — film actors, politicians, businessmen — and also dance band leaders who were the "pop stars" of that era.

But when the *Majestic* docked at Southampton on 25th September, 1930, there were no cheering crowds to greet one of America's up-and-coming band leaders, Roy Fox, who had arrived with six fellow musicians from the States to begin a two-month appearance at London's newly-opened Café de Paris. For Roy was little known in this country at the time, but the unobtrusive yet polished manner of this balding young American, and his cultured "whispering cornet" style of playing, soon

endeared him to the British public and his eight-week engagement in London stretched through the years to become a lifetime's attachment to our dance band era. Despite health problems, he went on to lead orchestras in most of the West End's top night spots and eventually became a British citizen.

It is a paradox that three of the most important figures of the Dance Band Days in Britain during the Thirties were Americans — Roy Fox, Charlie Kunz, and Carroll Gibbons. All liked life in this country so much that they settled down, married, and eventually died here.

Roy Fox was born at Denver, Colorado, on 25th October, 1901, and taken to Los Angeles when only a few months old. He grew up in the then little-known suburb of Hollywood, 10 years before it became the film capital of the world. Roy's parents were ardent members of the Salvation Army and when only three years old he was already singing with them in street choirs, and by the age of 13 he was playing the cornet in a local band. Roy went on to gain useful experience with a succession of well-known bands on the American night club scene, including the Gus Arnheim Orchestra at the Coconut Grove in Hollywood. One evening in 1927, as he finished playing a short trumpet solo with the band, a dancing couple approached and the man complimented him, adding: "You play the trumpet so softly, just like a whisper. It sounds more like a violin than a horn". Roy thanked him for his tribute, and only learned of the man's identity later — it was world-famous violin virtuoso Jascha Heifitz! This one remark made all the difference to Roy's future career, for he perfected his softly-softly style and became known as America's "Whispering Cornetist", confirming it by adopting the 1920 hit song *Whispering* as his signature tune from then on.

While in Hollywood he met many famous stars, once falling in love with blonde bomb-shell Jean Harlow, but before their love could blossom into anything concrete Roy was offered that eight-week stint at London's Café de Paris, beginning on 29th September, 1930. He hast-ily assembled a group of six other Californian musicians and embarked on the *Majestic* from New York, planning to rehearse with his new band on the way over. But he reckoned without the *Majestic's* reputation as a bad sea ship. She was top heavy and rolled like a drunken sailor in the Atlantic swell. Rehearsing was impossible and it was a party of green-looking bands-men who stepped giddily, but thankfully, off the ship at Southampton ... just four days before their opening night. As a result, all but one of the sophisticated dancers at the Café that evening were not greatly impressed with the new band. But the one exception made up for all the rest. He asked Roy Fox to play his favourite number, the new hit then sweeping through Britain after its earlier success in the USA — *Without a Song*. The requester was none other than the debonair Prince of Wales, and from then on whenever the future King arrived in the ballroom they would strike up the music for that song.

When the band's two-month contract at the Café de Paris was over, the sidesmen went back to the USA but Roy decided to stay on in England to build up a new career over here. His talent as a trumpet soloist, as well as his ex-perience as a band leader, attracted the new Decca recording company and they offered him £50 a week to organize a studio band. Roy had already made a few records for Decca within a month of his arrival in London, but it was not until the New Year that he began recording in earnest, eventually making over 400 titles for Decca during the next five years. One of his first successes was giving a job to a young guitarist who had been heard busking on the streets of London around Christmas time in 1930. The young fellow was called Al Bowlly, who went on to become a crooning legend.

By being able to pick and choose musicians for Decca's recording bands, Roy Fox gradually formed the nucleus of what was to be his reg-ular band in 1931, including pianist/arranger Lew Stone, Jack Jackson and Max Goldberg on

▷ "Little Mary Lee", originally a Glasgow school-girl called May McDevitt, was only 13 when talent spotted by Roy Fox in March 1935. She joined the band the following year and was recording hit songs with them by the age of 15!

trumpet, trombonist Lew Davis, Billy Amstell on tenor sax, violinist and future film music composer Ben Frankel, Spike Hughes on string bass (before he became a renowned music critic) and Bill Harty on drums.

In May 1931 a successful businessman named Jack Upson, who had made a fortune with his Dolcis Shoe shops throughout Britain, decided to invest his excess profits in a new night club called the Monseigneur Restaurant in Piccadilly, and he invited Roy Fox to become its first musical director. For light music during lunch-time, the Monseigneur booked a small, mainly string ensemble under the direction of a young Italian-born violinist called Anunzio Mantovani, soon to become immensely popular with his "Tipica Orchestra".

Every Wednesday evening from 10.30 till midnight, Roy Fox and his band broadcast from the dance floor at the Monseigneur and it was through this exposure on the wireless rather than via the wealthy patrons dancing to his band in Piccadilly that his reputation for good music grew. The BBC even put the programme out on short wave so that people overseas could tune in ... and during the winter of 1931/2 one of those eagerly listening to the broadcasts from a mountain village high up in the Swiss Alps was Roy Fox himself! For after only four months at the Monseigneur he had been taken ill with pleurisy, caused by overwork. In addition to playing at the restaurant, Roy and the band also appeared nightly at a nearby cinema in what was then called "Cine-Variety" — providing a live stage show before the main feature film came on.

What with this engagement, the broadcast rehearsals, and late-night dancing at the Monseigneur, it is no wonder that Roy collapsed with exhaustion in October 1931. His doctor ordered him to take a complete rest and so he went to Switzerland for six months, during which time his band continued at the Monseigneur under the able direction of Lew Stone. His musical arrangements, plus the incomparable singing of Al Bowlly and the talented antics of an up-and-coming young trumpeter called Nat Gonella, contributed enormously to the growing reputation of the Roy Fox band. Every Wednesday night after listening to the broadcast in his Alpine refuge, Roy would telephone the Monseigneur and speak to Lew about the programme, otherwise he might have lost touch. On his return to London, restored to health, in April 1932, Roy picked up where he'd left off and it was not long before he was adding further engagements to his already hectic programme, including a prestige

△ Roy Fox with singer (and pianist) Peggy Dell at the Kit-Cat club in 1933.

booking twice nightly at the London Palladium, where he became a major attraction.

However, the Monseigneur management objected to this doubling of stage work with his duties at the restaurant, so Roy felt that the only course was to part company. The management offered the job to Lew Stone in view of his success at moulding the band's style, and in the event nearly all the musicians elected to remain under Stone's leadership, only trumpeter Sid Buckman, who was also a singer and deputy leader of the band, went with Fox when he opened at the Café Anglais on 24th October, 1932. Roy's new band was built around Buckman and a quartet from the Spider's Web roadhouse on the London outskirts. This consisted of drummer Maurice Burman, trumpeter Les Lambert, tenor saxist Harry Gold and guitarist Ivor Mairants (the latter three forming the Fox vocal group aptly called "The Cubs") and, perhaps most important of all, pianist Jack Nathan, whose arrangements formed the style of the new Fox band for the next six years. They went to Brussels that December for a Royal Command Performance before the Belgian King and Queen, and were also honoured by being asked to appear at the 1933 British Royal Command Performance. On 16th January, 1933, Roy Fox moved yet again — this time to the Kit-Cat Club, returning a year later to the scene of his first British residency, the Café de Paris. August 1934 found his band playing at the Deauville Casino in Normandy where he proved as great an attraction to French audiences as he did in London.

Unlike trumpet-playing band leaders of the calibre of Louis Armstrong, Nat Gonella and, in later years, Harry James and Charlie Spivak, Roy Fox never made his own instrument the focal point of his band's performances. He did, indeed, have a whispering sound through the use of a mute, which he stuffed tightly up the horn of the trumpet, but in time he used his instrument less and less, being content to introduce his broadcasts with a shy, almost whispered "Hello, Ladies and Gentlemen, this is Roy Fox speaking" in a gentle American accent. That was the extent of Fox's showmanship, his self-effacing demeanour making the point that it was the music, not the leader, that was important. And it was really top class dance music that his band played.

After a year and a half during which his radio admirers had got used to hearing the Roy Fox band without the distinctive tones of Al Bowlly (who had stayed on with Lew Stone) it found a new voice in Denny Dennis, known as "The English Bing Crosby". He wasn't of course, but there was enough tonal resemblance to almost warrant the description. He was joined in the vocal team by his brother Barry Gray, whose voice was a light, almost falsetto tenor, as opposed to Denny's mellow baritone. Then there was trumpeter Sid Buckman, a 14-year-old Glaswegian schoolgirl called Mary Lee, and a robust contralto and pianist from Ireland called Peggy Dell.

Roy Fox and his band went from success to success, gaining a new record contract with HMV and appearing in films like *A Night Like This*, *On The Air*, and *Radio Pirates*, but the leader of the band was clearly not a well man. For the second time since coming to London Roy's career was interrupted through illness, and he did his last recordings for HMV in August 1938. After that the band broke up. To give him more time for recuperation, and some much-needed sunshine, Roy went to Australia and wound up directing Jay Whidden's band at the St. Kilda Palais in Melbourne. Whidden was an American who had worked in Britain during the 1920s and 1930s, had returned to the Biltmore Hotel in Los Angeles, and ended up in Australia. When war was declared in 1939, Roy Fox was unable to return to this country, spending the time in America to no great acclaim, though he did play at the Rainbow Room in New York, where Ray Noble had made his name.

After the war, he returned again to Britain leading a band of excellent quality, a richly-toned ensemble which made four records for Decca in 1946 but he never got the prestige dates its fine sound and style warranted. The band did mostly summer seasons and one-night stands at venues like Seaburn Hall, Sunderland, Green's Playhouse in Glasgow, and the Palace Ballroom, Douglas (Isle of Man). Sid Buckman was happy to return to his old boss, as was Bobby Joy, a child vocalist who had joined the pre-war band in 1935 to sing lachrymose songs like *It's My Mother's Birthday Today*, but the era of big dance bands was passing. Roy Fox was announced as going to open his own club, to be known as the Circus Room, but it never materialised. One provincial concert was cancelled through lack of support from a post-war public which didn't want to know about "The Whispering Cornetist", and his lack of good fortune was confirmed when the Inland Revenue made him bankrupt in 1951 with tax debts of nearly £10,000. He won his discharge in 1964.

Roy Fox became a theatre agent in 1952, again without conspicuous success, and in later years he and Mrs. Fox (the former Irish beauty queen Eileen O'Donnell) moved to Brinsworth House in Twickenham, the Benevolent Home for retired entertainers, where he passed away on 20th March, 1982, at the age of 80. His life ended some 6,000 miles from where it started, but in a country where he was loved and fondly remembered by so many of the British public who accepted the whispering American as one of their own. □

△ *Singer Denny Dennis, formerly an electrician in Derby, became known as "The English Bing Crosby".*

Geraldo

(1904-1974)

Born into a humble East End family, Geraldo was to top Britain's orchestral tree for over 30 years. First he found fame with his Gaucho Tango Band; then he created his own special sound, featuring the finest musicians and arrangers. Soon, millions were dancing to his distinctive style. To many, he was "Britain's Glenn Miller" ... entertaining the troops in wartime, boosting public morale and even earning the snide compliments of "Lord Haw-Haw"! He played for films and starred in revue ... and his broadcasts were legendary. His was the first band to be seen on television in peacetime, and his long career saw many changes — yet he remained faithful to good music, pleasantly played. Style and sophistication, charm and charisma ... this was Geraldo's legacy.

△ *Geraldo (real name Gerald Bright) had a twin brother, called Sidney. Both went to the Royal Academy of Music.*

'Hello again! We're on the radio again;
We know we're modest when we say
That when we play that it's gonna get cher,
In such a way that it can upset cher, betcher;
You'll agree, we've lots of personality,
And as you recognize the style
We need not tell you the name's Geraldo,
Let's just call it the band you prefer, Yes, Sir!'

This happy-shouting signature tune was one of the best-known during the Second World War. It inevitably heralded a feast of lively music — broadcast each week to millions throughout Britain —- and the band was one of the most successful in the land, led by a man who always seemed to know exactly what the public wanted.

Geraldo's real name was Gerald Walcen Bright, born on August 10th, 1904, in London's East End. For almost 40 years he was at the top of the British entertainment scene, as pianist, bandleader and showman, while his bands played everything from the tango to the classics. His music was sometimes compared to Glenn Miller's and, like the American, he braved many dangers by touring Britain during the war. When peace came, his was one of the first showbands to be seen on television.

Geraldo came from a working-class Jewish immigrant family engaged in the rag trade, but despite such humble beginnings he himself was always suave, polished and with a meticulous approach to his role as a band leader. He hired only the best musicians and demanded the same high standards from them that he set himself. "Musical ability and hard work, that's what you need for success," he would say proudly in his gravelly Cockney accent.

Gerry and his twin brother Sidney (later to lead the orchestra) were piano prodigies. Both were accepted for the Royal Academy of Music, and won their diplomas there, even though the family wanted the lads to carry on in the clothes business.

Gerry first played piano at a cinema in London's Old Kent Road, then got a job playing the organ at a fashionable restaurant in the Strand, though he had never played an organ in his life! Amazingly, he lasted a whole week before being asked by the management to leave. Having then spent all his spare time studying the organ, he cheekily returned to the same restaurant a few months later as "a fully-experienced organist".

Gerry was always a go-getter. He was also a great traveller and when he was only 18 decided to go abroad to pick up a few ideas. Exactly where he went still remains a mystery — it might have been central Europe or even South America, which would tie in with his later "gaucho" image; but Gerry was just as likely to have been in Paris, watching "Apache" bands in smoky cafes.

After playing piano in Liverpool, and at Blackpool's Metropole, and Tower Ballrooms, he started his own band just down the coast at the Hotel Majestic, St. Annes-on-Sea, with a group of five musicians, which he called "Gerald Bright and his Celebrity Orchestra". Blackpool-born Cyril Grantham, who became a star vocalist with Geraldo retained happy memories of those early days: "The five musicians would go on stage, then there would be a long wait before Geraldo would make his dramatic entrance ... wearing a cloak! It was quite a sight — he looked like Dracula!"

The band's broadcasts on the BBC's North Regional programme helped spread the word, and soon Gerry was moving back to London, launching himself as "Geraldo's Gaucho Tango Orchestra" at the Savoy Hotel in August 1930. The band had greasy moustaches, slicked-down hair, extravagant outfits and played fiddles and accordions. After a successful season at the Savoy, alternating with Carroll Gibbons, they made their first record, *Masks and Faces* ("La Cumparsita") on 22nd November, 1930. They were also booked by Charlie Chaplin for his film "Modern Times". They later recorded as "Geraldo and his Rumba Band" and in 1933 were chosen for a Royal Command Performance. The band was so convincingly Latin American that when they were presented to the Prince of Wales (later King Edward VIII) after the Royal Command Performance he spoke to them in Spanish!

"I couldn't understand a word," said Gerry later. "When HRH had finished speaking I had to explain 'Your Highness, I am English'." "The devil you are!", exclaimed the astonished prince. As one observer wryly put it: "They were more like Aston Villa than Pancho Villa."

However, the popularity of his tango style soon began to fade and Geraldo began working on a smoother sound. By 1934 he relaunched himself as "Geraldo and His Sweet Music" featuring vocals by Monte Rey (real name James

Montgomery Fyfe) and Cyril Grantham, who also played clarinet and alto, with the Top Hatters and the Geraldettes. The new signature tune was *I Bring To You Sweet Music*. Gerry's twin brother Sidney, who had been playing piano with Jack Hylton's Kit-Cat Band, Van Phillips and Al Starita, then joined as deputy leader.

Geraldo became a big name on the radio with his programmes "Music Shop", "Milestones of Melody", "Dancing Through", "Band Box" and, possibly the best-known of all, "Romance In Rhythm", a fortnightly series conceived with top song-writer Eric Maschwitz and introducing, among others, Anne Ziegler and Webster Booth. Gerry was also musical director for Herbert Wilcox Productions at Elstree studios, and he and his band appeared in many Wilcox films, including "Limelight" with Anna Neagle and Arthur Tracy, "Brewster's Millions" with Jack Buchanan, "The Gang Show" with Ralph Reader, and "Sunset in Vienna" with Lilli Palmer.

Gerry had always been a hard worker but this was a purple patch! He also played for C.B. Cochran revues ("Lights Up" starred Evelyn Laye and Doris Hare) and radio shows such as "Up With The Curtain" with Tommy Trinder. Gerry was also a good friend to jazz and swing fans (when it suited him) and held special "Jazz Jamboree" and "Sunday Night Swing Club"

▽ *Cyril Grantham was with Geraldo until the outbreak of war when he joined the Royal Navy, later taking part in the raid on Dieppe and receiving the DSC from King George VI. After the war, he directed his own band at the Dorchester Hotel for 10 years.*

△ *Geraldo pictured in 1933 with his Gaucho Tango Orchestra, mainly consisting of piano accordionists. Edward, then Prince of Wales, liked the music and thought Geraldo was Spanish. But he was born in London's East End!*

sessions at the Gaumont Suite, London and St. Martin's Theatre.

At one time he had 200 musicians on his payroll and worked 18 hours a day on arrangements and rehearsing. His daily broadcasts featured the arrangements of George Evans, who eventually created an individual style for the band with emphasis on woodwind. Spirits were high — made even higher when four of the boys won the prestigious Henry Hall swimming cup for broadcasting bands. Gerry held a slap-up dinner at the Savoy to celebrate — and almost dropped the handsome trophy at the presentation!

The band recorded pre-war at the Abbey Road studio in London, and Cyril Grantham vividly remembered vocalists and band all crammed around one microphone. He also recalled Gerry buying a huge Humber car on the proceeds and nearly having a heart attack when he noticed a long scratch on its paint-work. Some joker had stuck on a piece of tape with a "scratch" attached!

Al Bowlly did some of his best work with Geraldo around this time. Later vocalists were Dorothy Carless and her sister Carole Carr, Doreen Villiers, Beryl Davis, Sally Douglas, Eve Boswell, Len Camber, Johnny Green, Archie Lewis, Dick James (later a famous music publisher) and comedians Derek Roy and Jackie ("Umbrage") Hunter. Dorothy Carless was a particular favourite of Gerry's because she could sing both soprano and contralto.

The band travelled extensively during wartime, often by night to the accompaniment of bursting bombs. There were several narrow escapes. Once their train was machine-gunned just before reaching London and several musicians lost their sheet music in the uproar; but the band still managed to be on the air, as scheduled, at 8.15am, after 24 hours travel. No wonder the treacherous William Joyce, broadcasting over German radio as "Lord Haw-Haw" paid them the ultimate compliment: "*Britain may be blitzed, but its premier dance band is carrying on regardless.*"

Gerry was now the BBC's Director of Dance Music and supervisor of the Bands Division of ENSA — dubbed "Every Night Something Awful" by some Servicemen, but officially the

▽ *Dorothy Carless was a pianist before joining Geraldo as a torch singer.*

△ *Vocalist Eve Becke was always beautifully dressed — her brother was a famous London fashion designer.*

Entertainments National Service Association. A typical day saw him make a studio broadcast at 10am, rush to a factory for an ENSA show at lunchtime, record in the afternoon, then leave to play for the first house at Golders Green Hippodrome or Chiswick Empire.

On ENSA's behalf he took his orchestra to the Middle East, North Africa, Belgium, and Italy. Once the band was involved in a plane crash near Palermo, Sicily, from which they all miraculously escaped. They also went to France, Holland and even to Berlin itself, where a photograph taken in 1945 shows the band members, smart in their uniforms, outside the Chancellery — Hitler having vacated!

Geraldo was the first bandleader to appear on TV after the war. Later, he became musical supervisor for the Cunard/White Star Line, and what became known as "Geraldo's Navy" gave many British jazzmen the opportunity to make expenses-paid trips to New York's night clubs to hear the latest musical developments. Gerry often left the band in the more than capable hands of Robert Farnon, recently demobbed from the Canadian Army, whose AEF Band he had been leading during the war. One of Bob's first actions was to engage Eric Delaney as his new drummer.

Gerry's ambition was to have his own symphony orchestra, and he once staged a concert at the Royal Albert Hall, London, with a 70-piece orchestra, playing everything from jazz to Shostakovich. He also issued a famous challenge to Sir Malcolm Sargent, who, on a "Brains Trust" radio programme, had criticised dance band music and leaders who "could not read music." Said Gerry: "I am prepared to conduct Sir Malcolm's orchestra through any classical piece he cares to name, if he will conduct my orchestra through any swing composition that I care to name." Jack Hylton had made a similar challenge to Sir Dan Godfrey in the 1930s. Like that particular gauntlet-throwing exercise, this challenge was never accepted.

The band broke up in the early Sixties and Geraldo became a theatrical agent booking bands and producing records, working from a suite of offices in Bond Street, London. His room was often to be seen piled high with paper, dominated by a vast desk with two telephones and pet budgerigars in a cage to keep him company. Geraldo had a little white house in St John's Wood, with an all-white sitting room containing a large white piano, but no pictures or photographs. He also had a small flat in Harley Street, London, and a lovely country home at Worth in Sussex, which was cylindrically built with a huge aluminium flue for a chimney. In his more leisurely moments he enjoyed the occasional glass of champagne and driving fast cars.

His last public appearance was in February 1974 at the Congress Theatre, Eastbourne, featuring his concert and dance orchestras in a programme that ranged from Ravel's *Bolero* to a Judy Garland medley (vocals by Rosemary Squires). Three months later — on May 4th, 1974 — he died.

He had been scheduled to do a broadcast for Capitol Radio on his life and music. He taped the first part, then went to Switzerland for a holiday with his wife Manja, but suffered a heart attack and died in hospital at Vevey, on the shores of Lake Geneva. Perhaps the best epitaph is to recall his sign-off line from his radio show, delivered in that ripe East End accent: "On behalf of me and the boys, cheerio and thanks for listening." □

△ *Comedian Derek Roy first found fame as a wartime vocalist with Geraldo at the BBC.*

59

Nat Gonella
(1908-1998)

There wasn't a great deal of home-grown jazz to be heard in Britain in the late Twenties and early Thirties. This was hardly suprising because the public had never been brought up to jazz, didn't like it, and as a whole didn't want to know! Even visits by such American jazz greats as Louis Armstrong, Fats Waller and Duke Ellington, who appeared on the music hall circuits, were appreciated only by musicians and a handful of fans who made up the Rhythm Clubs which existed in those days.

True, there were occasional jazzy records by such as Joe Daniels and his Hot Shots, and George Scott-Wood and his Six Swingers, but though these featured top musicians from the ranks of the popular dance bands they were never very high on inspiration and the essential free-wheeling spirit of jazz. But there

△ Nat Gonella invariably wore a striped jacket or suit.

was one man who more than any other, helped to educate the British public to it. He was a young Cockney of Italian descent named Nathaniel Charles Gonella, born in Islington, North London, on 7th March, 1908, the middle one of seven children.

When his cab-driver father died at the early age of 44, his mother couldn't cope with all seven kids, his younger sister Jessie, and 4-year-old Adolphus James (soon nicknamed Bruts, for brother, by Nat who knew that a boy called Adolphus would have little chance of surviving in a rough and tough area like Islington) were taken into care at St. Mary's Guardians School just off the Seven Sisters Road. It turned out to be a good move for the youngsters and in later years Nat paid tribute to the school and its principal, one George Johnson, who were far

removed from the Dickensian image of Mr. Wackford Squeers and "Dotheboys Hall".

The school had its own brass band and it would be nice to report that young Nathaniel was attracted to it for musical reasons. Not so! He only wanted to wear the band uniform. When it was gently pointed out that wearing the uniform entailed actually *playing* something, Nat chose the big drum. In time though, under the tutelage of the music teacher, a former Army bandmaster named William Clarke, he took up the cornet and soon made enough progress to realise that he wanted nothing more than to spend his life making music.

But when he was 14 it seemed as though that ambition was to be denied him, an attack of rheumatic fever apparently leaving him with a weakened heart. He took up the violin and tenor horn instead, but it wasn't the same somehow. On leaving the Guardians School young Nat became an errand boy, until one fateful day he was passing a music shop when he was arrested by the sight of a gleaming second-hand cornet in the window.

The only trouble was that it cost £3 10s. an astronomical sum for one earning only 18 shillings a week. However, negotiations with the shop keeper proceeded apace, and on promising to pay 5 shillings down and instalments of half a crown per week, the happy youngster took his prize home. Despite the warnings of the heart specialists the previous year, Nat found to his great joy that he was playing with even more verve than before. And he continued to do so for the next 50 years! Gonella found another uniform to wear when he joined the St. Pancras British Legion Brass Band, then got his first

△ *Nat Gonella and his Georgians in a scene from the 1937 film "Variety Parade".*

professional engagement touring the halls with impresario Archie Pitt's "Busby Boys", a stage band led by Bert Gutsell, later known as famous Blackpool band leader, Bertini. At that time (1924) Archie Pitt's 26-year-old wife took Nat under her wing and introduced him to jazz when she gave him a few Bix Beiderbecke records with a wind-up gramophone to play them on. Mrs. Arche Pitt was, of course, the fabulous Gracie Fields, though little known in those days.

Archie Pitt was responsible for another milestone in Nat's life, when he changed the instrumentation of the "Busby Boys" to include five trumpets rather than cornets. If Nat had liked the sound of the cornet, he loved the trumpet even more, becoming still more enthusiastic about his new career when he was joined in the Boys by another ambitious trumpeter ... his young brother Bruts! Altogether, the Gonellas were on the road for four years in two long-running Pitt shows, "A Week's Pleasure" and "Safety First". When the latter show ended its run in Margate, all the "Busby Boys" were sacked, however, and so Nat decided to try his luck at dance band playing with Bob Dryden's band, staying for three years and playing in both Manchester and Belfast, before returning to Margate.

Nat was becoming a restless soul, however, and his next stop was at Brighton's Regent Ballroom with Archie Alexander's band ... only to find that Bruts was playing virtually across the road at Sherry's. From there Gonella went right into the big-time with Billy Cotton and his band, earning an unheard of £8-10s. a week, and playing alongside Sydney Lipton, trum-

peter/vocalist Sid Buckman, trombonist Joe Ferrie, and saxophonist Mick Burberry.

Nat Gonella had by this time come under the influence of Louis Armstrong, who later became a personal friend, but it is well to dispose of the generally held conception of Gonella as no more than an Armstrong copyist, both as instrumentalist and singer. True, "Satchmo" — as Armstrong was called — may have been an initial influence and inspiration but that would be true of almost any trumpet player in the 20th century. As for singing, that was 100% Gonella, stemming more from London Music Hall than from New Orleans. Incidentally, the first time Nat's tortured tones were heard on record was with Billy Cotton's band (at that time a surprisingly "hot" outfit offering plenty of scope for his trumpet solos and scat singing) as part of a vocal trio in *That Rhythm Man* in August 1930, his first solo vocal being on *Bessie Couldn't Help It* a couple of months later.

The next year the entire Cotton brass section consisting of Gonella, Buckman and Ferrie, moved *en masse* to join the band Roy Fox was forming to open the Monseigneur Restaurant in Piccadilly Circus. It was here that Nat became a great favourite with radio listeners, particularly with his versions of *Oh Mo'nah, How'm I Doin'?* and, of course, the song with which he is always associated, and which he adopted as his signature tune, *Georgia On My Mind*.

When the Monseigneur management asked Fox's deputy Lew Stone to take over as musical director, Nat stayed on for three years. As well as playing with Stone, Nat did recording sessions with Stanley Black's Modernists, Edgar Jackson's Dance Band, American pianist Garland Wilson, and the great Ray Noble and his New Mayfair Dance Orchestra.

Nat played on the only live engagement Noble ever fulfilled on this side of the Atlantic, when he took his orchestra, otherwise purely a studio recording group, to the Kurhaus at Schveningen in Holland for a month's residency. Nat also fronted a group of Lew Stone sidesmen, including his brother Bruts, Eddie Carroll and Al Bowlly, for six titles under his own name for Decca records. Later, he joined forces with Brian Lawrance and his Quaglino's Quartette, with whom he had been topping the bill at the old Holborn Empire, for another six recordings. But it was only a matter of time before Nat was on the move again as a leader in his own right.

His "Georgians" started as a "band-within-a-band" to relieve the full Lew Stone orchestra at the Monseigneur, but eventually became an autonomous unit when Nat finally left and signed contracts for music hall tours and to record for Parlophone. The Georgians were a completely new band with Nat on trumpet leading Pat Smuts (tenor sax), Harold Hood (piano), Jimmy Messini (guitar and vocals), Charlie Winter (bass) and Nat's first boss, Bob Dryden (drums).

The popularity of Nat Gonella and his Georgians was such that in the first year of their existence they toured the country and made dozens of records, with many more to come in later years. They are all typical of the hybrid mixture of dance music, jazz, novelty jive numbers and outright corn that was the Gonella stock-in-trade in the pre-war years, earning him the great reputation that we still recall today.

These mid to late Thirties were the heyday years of Nat Gonella. After touring Sweden and Holland at the outbreak of war, Nat and his vocalist wife Stella Moya fled from Holland to Cannes, where they managed to catch a boat filled with refugees headed for Gibraltar. Here they were lucky enough to board a collier bound for Liverpool, eventually winding up on Merseyside with only the clothes they stood up in — and Nat's beloved trumpet!

Although the time was hardly propitious for such a move, Nat decided to go all out with a big band called "The New Georgians", touring the halls, ballrooms and Service camps until the day came when, like so many men of his age, Nat was called up, initially posted to the Pioneer Corps. Nat, who had never known any other life but music, was like a fish out of water at first, but with his record in entertainment he was soon asked to join the first "Stars in Battle-dress" group of entertainers. Only for a while,

△ Stella Moya was Nat Gonella's wife in wartime and together they escaped Hitler's invasion of Holland by fleeing to England via Southern France.

though, for he was posted to North Africa. Here again luck was on his side for he was invited to join the Royal Tank Regiment Band.

Just before D-Day he was invalided out with a duodenal ulcer, and had to face the problem of resuming his former status in the dance band business. To be honest, he didn't find it very easy, although it started well enough, when under Jack Hylton's fatherly eye, Nat took a big band over to Holland where he had always been regarded as some sort of musical god. The band included Bruts Gonella and singer Helen Mack, who did Nat the best turn of his life when she introduced him to his third and last wife, Dorothy.

There was a predicably disastrous venture when Nat, the sternest of traditionalists, led a band attempting to play the new "be-bop" style, then it was back to the music halls for a tour with his old friend Max Miller, just when variety was dying on its feet. He welcomed the boom in traditional jazz with the formation of his "Georgia Jazz Band", went into partnership with Acker Bilk, did summer seasons in Jersey, and tours of Sweden and Germany, all climaxed by the star spot in "This Is Your Life" in 1960.

But from then on the Nat Gonella story runs out of steam. The occasional date in what was left of variety led to a tour in "Those Were The Days", which must have seemed a fate worse than death to a man who still considered himself a vital performer and a timeless musician. But worse was to come ... engagements as a solo performer in whatever venue would have him, all the way down to seedy pubs and working men's clubs. Nat and Dorothy moved from Blackpool to live in Gosport when he had to give up the trumpet because the strain on his heart and lungs became too much. He died, aged 90, in August 1998. ☐

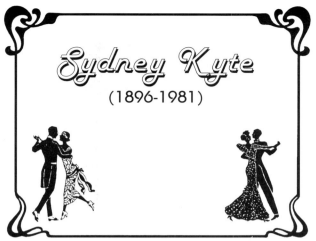

Sydney Kyte
(1896-1981)

△ *Sydney Kyte was immaculate, even at the mike.*

Sydney Kyte, a genial, immaculate and dignified man, was born at Stamford Hill, London, in 1896, one of eight children of a tailor. At 15 he won a scholarship to the Royal Academy of Music, successfully studying violin, viola, piano, clarinet and saxophone. When he left four years later, the First World War had begun, and he volunteered for the Life Guards, combining regular army duties with playing in the regimental band.

He then served in France as a dispatch rider, although the motor-cycle he rode took second place in his affections to the horses he had become accustomed to in the Life Guards. It was therefore no surprise that after the war he joined the Household Cavalry and began using his musical training by leading the unit's string orchestra at Buckingham Palace and Windsor Castle. Leaving the army and wanting to get back to his first love of music, Sydney decided to form a small band of his own for society functions.

He then went to the Savoy Hotel as deputy conductor of the Orpheans under Debroy Somers, took part in some of their recording sessions and worked with the Savoy Havana Band at Claridges and the Berkeley. In 1929 he took his band, which included such future leaders as Maurice Winnick and Billy Thorburn, to Ciro's Club where they began broadcasting one night a week. After two years he moved to his best-known residency, the Piccadilly Hotel, from where he was on the air every Monday night.

Sydney was too old for active service in the Second World War, but the band entertained the forces in this country and he himself did his bit as an air raid warden near his home in Temple Fortune beside Hampstead Heath, where he and his wife, Amy, lived for almost 50 years. After the war he returned to broadcasting in "Music While You Work" and other BBC assignments.

During more than 30 years as a bandleader Sydney Kyte earned a highly respected name for himself. Listeners may recall his theme song *Tune In, Keep Listening*, written specially by two other well-known BBC artistes, Harry S. Pepper and John Watt, although he never recorded it.

Sydney was well into his retirement when he died at his home in Great Leighs, near Chelmsford, Essex, on 29th July, 1981, at the age of 85. □

Victor Silvester

(1900-1978)

Slow, Slow, Quick-Quick, Slow . . .

"Ladies and gentlemen, take your partners for a waltz in the ballroom of memories" . . . such an introduction can only bring to mind one man — the tall, handsome and debonair Victor Silvester, whose orchestra brought the elegant melodies of the dance floor to a vast listening public via radio, television and records.

His cheery greeting was "Hello there, everyone". His signature tune was *You're Dancing on My Heart*, and each week millions of people throughout the world tuned in to his BBC radio programme and watched his "Television Dancing Club", which ran for 17 years. His "Record Request" programme on the BBC World Service ran for a staggering 28 years.

From basic steps to the latest sensation, Victor taught Britain (and most of the British Empire) to dance. He also launched the finest strict tempo band in the land, which sold more records of its type than any other dance orchestra in the world. His music was specially arranged for dancing tempo, and he never tried to tinker with that winning formula.

Victor Silvester was a master showman who created a unique sound — a solo violin soaring over a small intimate orchestra. Dance fads may change but the exquisite Silvester style lives on, shimmering in a land of dreams. Listeners are transported to a bygone age in which soft lights cast their glow on a lavish

△ *Victor Silvester played the sweetest music ever written for ballroom dancing . . . and always in strict tempo. For more than 40 years his silken arrangements kept feet tapping, from the green lanes of Oxford to the Australian outback.*

ballroom . . . elegant dancers glide effortlessly across the floor . . . and, in the background, a sweet orchestra plays. Oscar Grasso's violin, rich in tone, fashions an ethereal melody while the conductor, impeccably dressed, admits you happily to a world of wonder.

Throughout his life, Victor Marlborough Silvester blended considerable charm with a fierce determination to succeed. Dancing's somewhat "sissy" image was the ideal cover for a man who loved a scrap and could sniff out new opportunities. Victor never claimed to be an instrumentalist — and that got him into trouble with more established band leaders — but he did possess an impeccable sense of rhythm. And he ran a loyal band.

Born on 25th February, 1900, he was the second son of the Vicar of Wembley, Middlesex. His elder brother had been called Temple after the then Archbishop of Canterbury (Frederick Temple) and the youngest Silvester was due to be dubbed Marlborough after the Bishop of that diocese. However, he was spared this heavy epithet (as a first name at least) by the news of a famous British victory in the Boer War, which came through on the day he was born. Hence the first Christian name, though Marlborough was retained as the second. After the two Silvester boys, four sisters were born — Gwen, Joyce, Mary and Joan.

Because the Bishop of London held an annual ball at Lambeth Palace for the sons of the clergy, Victor was soon taught to dance. He learned quickly. He also learned to play the piano, his tutor being an aristocratic Prussian lady "who rapped my knuckles smartly with her cane whenever I slouched or played a wrong note." Home life was never comfortable. His mother — a strict, but fair, lady of Lancashire/Scottish descent — also kept a cane for use at meal times and Victor was in awe of his father. Boarding school was even worse. After running away several times he lied about his age and volunteered for the Army soon after the outbreak of the Great War. He was only 14, but claimed to be 18, and his strongest memory was of waiting three hours with 19,000 other soldiers in snowstorms on Epsom Downs for the commander-in-chief, Lord Kitchener, to inspect his London Scottish regiment. "We wore kilts and it's a miracle we didn't freeze to death," he later recalled in his autobiography. "At least an officer had the presence of mind to march us the 10 miles back to barracks to warm us up. If we had gone back in the cattle truck we would have stiffened up!"

Later, Victor saw the horrors of the Western Front and was wounded in the leg as a stretcher bearer in northern Italy in 1917 while serving with the British Ambulance Unit. He was awarded the Italian Bronze Medal for Valour for his part in evacuating the wounded after the battle of San

Gabriele and returned home for commissioning at Sandhurst as an officer in the Blues (the Royal Horse Guards) just before war ended. Yet his career was destined for the palais glide not the military two-step, his first forays being with Belle Harding's dance escorts in the Twenties. His father (with whom he had never really seen eye to eye) is said to have observed this period of Victor's career with some degree of shocked disbelief, and declared that he never thought the day would come when his son would turn gigolo and throw aside the chances of becoming a Field Marshal! But Victor was tall and athletic and popular with the ladies he was required to partner. He soon fell out with the grumpy Miss Harding but greater things lay ahead.

In 1922 he won the World Ballroom Championship foxtrot and waltz titles with Phyllis Clarke. Five days earlier he had married another dancer called Dorothy Newton, a forthright lass who he met at a tea dance in London's Empress Rooms. Together they demonstrated the latest dance crazes — the Charleston, the Black Bottom (called after the mud at the bottom of the Mississippi), the Heebie Jeebies, the Yale Blues, the Stomp, the Rhythm Step and the Baltimore — and started a high class dance school at 20 New Bond Street. One of their pupils was a wide-eyed girl called Estelle

▽ *Victor leads the band which helped to create the unique Silvester sound. The musicians included Oscar Grasso (violin), Ben Edwards (drums), Rico de Stefano (accordion), George Senior (string bass), Charlie Spinelli (alto sax), and pianists Eddie McAuley and Cecil Norman.*

Thompson, later to become the film star Merle Oberon. The Silvesters appeared on an instructive series of cigarette cards and enjoyed years of success, demonstrating their art throughout Europe. They also acquired an elegant flat in Dover Street, London.

In 1928 Victor and Dorothy collaborated on the highly successful book *Modern Ballroom Dancing*, incorporating controls issued by the newly formed Imperial Society of Dance Teachers which restricted ballroom dancing to four basic steps — waltz, foxtrot, quick-step and tango. The first edition of 5,000 copies soon sold out; another 20,000 were printed and sold out within six weeks. By the end of the year more than 100,000 copies had been sold. Thirty years later more than 50 editions had been printed and sales had soared to one million.

In September 1930 Victor first came to nationwide notice while promoting the Charleston Blues — "The very latest hit straight from Manhattan" — with Carroll Gibbons and Christopher Stone on the wireless from London's Savoy Hotel.

One of the dubious benefits of fame was the need to go on tour. Before dancing a demonstration at Rochdale, Lancashire, Victor demanded his fee of £21 in advance from a dodgy promoter. It came in the shape of 168 half-crowns. Victor stuffed some in the pockets of his dress suit — clanking as he danced! — and hid the rest of the coins in the dance hall cistern to collect later. That was a night to remember; so was the night he danced a fox-trot (a step originated by the American vaudeville star Harry Fox around the turn of the century) with the great Russian ballet dancer Anna Pavlova, who was fascinated by ballroom dancing.

The famous ballroom orchestra was formed in 1935 for a precise reason. For years Victor and Dorothy had found difficulty in obtaining strict tempo records exactly suitable for dancing — mainly because most of the recording bands tended to play their orchestrations in the tempo they thought most suitable for a particular tune. But the new guidelines on competition dancing required musical accompaniment to be played with metronomic exactitude to match the discipline of the steps; any deviation could lead to a dancer's banishment from competition. It was too good an opportunity to miss.

First, Victor made strict tempo recordings, using society pianist and top jazzman Gerry Moore. The records were snapped up by dancing teachers, and commended by dancing journals, so Victor then launched his first band, which comprised two pianos (one to provide the "lemonade", the trickling notes between the chords in the top octaves); an alto-sax doubling on clarinet (Charlie Spinelli); bass (George Senior) and drums (Ben Edwards). Pianists included Gerry Moore, Felix King (later a bandleader in his own right) Eddie Macauley and Ernest Wilson, who also arranged.

"A good solid beat with the melody predominating all through" was the message. Victor made it clear what he wanted and stuck to it through 43 years of recording. The first of four titles rehearsed by the band, *You're Dancing on My Heart*, was recorded in August 1935 and became the signature tune. The orchestra's closing tune was called *Don't Say Goodbye*, a famous Robert Stolz melody.

"I agreed to record four titles every month for a fee of £5 a session, the musicians receiving their usual rate of £3 a session," said Victor. "Actually, I would have done it for nothing. The important thing was to have my name appearing regularly on gramophone labels and for my type of dance music to become popular."

At the end of 12 months his contract with Parlophone was renewed. Instead of a fee he received a small royalty on the retail price of the records, then costing 1s 6d. By then he had also added an accordion (for tangos etc.) and a violin (played by the inimitable Oscar Grasso) to add the soft, melodious tone which was thereafter a main feature of his music.

Victor was one of the first dancers to direct a band and his fame had spread. He was friendly with such leaders as Jack Hylton, Jack Jackson, Geraldo, Jack Payne, Sydney Lipton, Billy Ternent and Eric Robinson, but he upset certain members of the profession who objected to a non-player fronting a band.

Eventually he was able to form two distinct groups, the "Ballroom Orchestra" for quick-step, foxtrot and waltz, and the "Silver Strings", which was the ballroom orchestra augmented by 15 strings and woodwind, for tango, rumba, samba and Viennese waltz.

Victor's first composition (with Ernest Wilson) was *Spurs of the Gaucho*, a natty tango. Together the duo produced some 200 tunes in 12 years, all recorded by Columbia. Other hotshots included the famous *Golden Tango* (originally called *Gold of the Incas*). Fans included concert pianist Eileen Joyce, Latin American rumba king Edmundo Ros, and Glenn Miller, who in December 1944 offered Victor a tour of the

United States "as soon as the war is over." Within days, Miller was lost on a plane trip over the Channel and the tour never materialised.

Victor enjoyed a friendly rivalry with Joe Loss, as both featured strict tempo music; he was also an admirer of Palm Court virtuoso Albert Sandler and moved in high society circles. In February 1937 the band auditioned for the BBC and were taken on by the then Director of BBC Variety, Eric Maschwitz. They were booked for six broadcasts, then a further six, and so on, each broadcast promoting a corresponding rise in record sales. In 1941 Victor launched the BBC "Dancing Club" from the Paris Cinema in Lower Regent Street, London, a series which was interrupted only when "Lord Haw Haw" cheekily used the programme to bridge the gaps between broadcast dance sequences with German propaganda! Instead of leaving a pause for listeners to write down the latest steps, Victor began repeating them so "Haw Haw" couldn't insert his messages!

The versatile "Poggy" Pogson replaced Charlie Spinelli (who died young in May 1941) on alto/clarinet, and classical violinist Alfredo Campoli (using the soubriquet Alf Campbell) replaced Oscar Grasso, who had been called up. The melodies continued to flow after the war when Grasso returned and television made more fans (including the Queen and Queen Mother, who called him "Victor one, two, three") aware of his easy elegance and the unique sound of his orchestra. The Carlton Rooms, Maida Vale were adapted for "Television Dancing Club", a weekly series which harnessed the post-war boom in ballroom dancing and included his son, Victor Silvester junior, who ran the band when Victor was injured in a car crash in the snow in 1956. Young Victor (who battled back after a grenade blinded him in one eye in a wartime incident) gradually took over more of the conducting duties.

In the 1940s Victor had formed a Jive Band, featuring ex-Squadronaires sidesmen Tommy McQuater (trumpet) and George Chisholm (trombone), to fill a new and exciting void in the market. It was shrewd thinking. Not only was dancing's staid old image shattered; the Silvester sound now encompassed the complete dance hall range, from modern waltz to jitter-

△ The swirling gaiety of the ballroom is captured in this picture from the BBC's "Television Dancing Club" with Victor conducting the orchestra.

bug, and record buyers came in all ages. Victor's famous "Ballroom Orchestra" sold more pure dancing records than any other band in the world, including 23 tangos, recorded on Parlophone in which extra violins were added to create the true "Argentine" flavour. The arrangements earned great praise in many of the countries that specialised in authentic Latin American music.

Victor Silvester had brought dance music back to basics, and it proved a blueprint for success. Perfectly groomed and as upright as ever, he continued to demonstrate the latest dances with an almost military grace while his dance studios thrived. Friends and colleagues, including the faithful Grasso (who died, aged 68, in 1982) and drummer Ben Edwards, paid heartfelt tribute in a special "This Is Your Life" programme in 1958. Victor was awarded the OBE in 1961 for his services to dancing.

The Silvester activities continued right up to Victor's death, in August 1978 in a swimming tragedy while on holiday in France — by which time his everlasting fame was assured. The impact of his unique style found its evidence every weekend when thousands of couples went dancing at their local Palais. They dressed up to the nines and danced on crowded floors. It may have been a crush, but for a few hours stardust was being sprinkled on a humdrum world.

They owed much of that to the genius of Victor Silvester.	□

Mantovani

(1905-1980)

In the mid-1920s a small sized "Radio" record of *Persian Rosebud* — a new song by Horatio Nicholls — featured organist Charles D. Smart and an anonymous violinist, known to his friends as "Monty". His brief solo added to the listeners' pleasure; but who could have foretold that this talented young Italian was destined for world fame?

He was born Annunzio Paolo Mantovani, in Venice on 15th November, 1905. Four years later, his father (Bismark) and mother (Iparia) came to England, bringing with them little Annunzio and his two-year-old sister Remila, but leaving behind a baby sister, Elsa, in the care of an aunt. She rejoined her family in England when she was 12. The Mantovanis settled down in Britain, Iparia being particularly happy here.

Bismark Mantovani, who had been a professor at two Italian

△ *Venetian-born Mantovani's orchestra was a firmly established British favourite for half a century.*

conservatories, was a distinguished violinist. He had toured North America under the baton of Pietro Mascagni, composer of the opera *Cavalleria Rusticana* and also played under Saint-Saens, Richter and Toscanini. He had come to London as leader of an orchestra supporting an Italian opera company appearing at Covent Garden.

Under his father's watchful eye Monty studied piano, counterpoint and harmony; and at the age of 14 he took up the violin under other tutors. Even while very young he was devoted to music and determined to succeed. At 17 he was a professional violinist, playing at hotel restaurants in various parts of the country. In 1923 he formed a Quintet for the Midland

Hotel, Birmingham, his players including a Londoner of Greek parentage named George Melachrino who went on to earn a name for himself in light music. Monty's first gramophone records were probably made in 1927 for Imperial, a label for which he recorded until the early 1930s, disguised as "Leonelli Gandino" for violin solos, and as "Gandino and his Orchestra" for light orchestral items, selections from stage musicals, and the like.

However, from 1927 to 1932, Mantovani often joined the dance bands assembled, for recording purposes only, by Harry Hudson. Heard on the Winner or Radio labels, they had names like the Plaza Band, Deauville Dance Orchestra and Radio Rhythm Boys.

In 1927, Monty assembled a small orchestra to play dance music at one of London's most prestigious hotels, the Metropole, recording for Regal from January to May 1928. Among the orchestra's violinists was Monty's father, who remained with him until 1935 when, suffering from asthma, he retired.

Monty's expertise on the violin was effectively demonstrated on two occasions — in 1930 when he gave a recital in London's Aeolian Hall, and in 1931 at Queen's Hall, where he played Saint-Saens' *Violin Concerto in B Minor* to rapturous acclaim, even earning a "Bravo!" from Sir Thomas Beecham, and excellent press notices the following day. In July, 1931, Mantovani left the Metropole for the newly-opened Monseigneur Restaurant (later a cinema) where he stayed until August 1934, not only entertaining customers in that select

△ *The young Annunzio Mantovani (second from right) with his Quintet at the Midland Hotel, Birmingham in 1923. George Melachrino is second from left.*

establishment but reaching out to a much wider audience through his lunchtime broadcasts. While at the Monseigneur, his recently-formed little Tipica Orchestra, playing British, American and European tunes, with a particular fondness for tangos, competed for popularity with the superb bands of first Roy Fox and then Lew Stone, acquitting itself very well.

From August 1932 to February 1935 Mantovani recorded for various labels, appearing (often heavily disguised) on Sterno, 4-in-1, Cinecord, Plaza and Silvertone. The last of these labels bore the inscription "Chosen for Selfridge's by Christopher Stone." Did those buying records supposedly featuring Charles Baxter, Jean Jacques, Paul Monty, Patna, Lew Roberts or Dick Rose, know that all had been made by Mantovani? It seems highly improbable.

During his sojourn at the Monseigneur, Mantovani courted Winifred Kathleen Moss, the beautiful daughter of a City company director. They were married on 4th August, 1934, settling first at 55 Grove Park Road, south-east London, where their son Kenneth was born the following year, moving further up the street to No.76 after the war; and then, in the late Forties, to St. John's Wood. Later in life, they purchased a ranch-style house in Branksome Park, Bournemouth, which they called

"Greensleeves", and when retired in 1976 they moved to Canford Cliffs at Poole, Dorset.

The Mantovanis enjoyed a deeply-caring marriage. With her charming smile and friendly personality, Winifred gave him her unwavering encouragement, and in every way enriched his life. A daughter, Paula, was born in 1939. Although a disciplinarian (as he had to be) when directing his orchestra, Mantovani was an affectionate father and, in the fullness of time, became an indulgent grandfather.

He left the Monseigneur for the Café de Paris, but then secured a Gaumont-British Pictures contract to tour cinemas with a "stage" orchestra. This was followed by a short stay at the Hollywood Club. However, in 1935 he went to the San Marco Restaurant. For much of that year he recorded for Regal-Zonophone, featuring the well-known George Barclay as his male vocalist, and Stella Nelson (later called Stella Roberta) as his "croonette", the name by which girl singers were then dubbed by *Radio Pictorial* magazine.

George Barclay, who sang for such famous bandleaders as Charlie Kunz, Billy Thorburn and Felix Mendelssohn, left Mantovani in 1937, but Stella Roberta continued to sing, broadcast and record with Monty's various orchestras for several years ... and not every one knew she was the bandleader's sister!

△ *Mantovani's sister, the singer Stella Roberta, was the cover girl for this issue of "Radio Pictorial" magazine in September 1937.*

Her real name was Remila Brunelda Mantovani, and like her brother (and sister Elsa) a Venetian, born in 1907. Photographs from the Thirties show her to have been a very pretty girl, while gramophone records reveal that she had a distinctive voice.

By the summer of 1935, piano-accordionist Ronald Binge had joined the Tipica Orchestra and much later he composed the beautiful *Elizabethan Serenade*. Binge, born at Derby in 1910, left Mantovani in the autumn of 1941 to join the R.A.F. He died at Ringwood (Hants) in September 1979.

At the end of October 1935, Mantovani began recording for Columbia, but his style of music remained virtually unchanged. Early in 1937 the word "Tipica" was dropped from his title and the size of the orchestra was subsequently increased. At the start of 1940, he transferred to Decca, for whom he was to record for the next 35 years until his retirement. Throughout the war years, Mantovani continued to play dance tunes, but light orchestral music was beginning to take over. In the early post-war period he directed theatre orchestras for a succession of important productions, including Noel Coward's "Sigh No More" (1945), "Pacific 1860" (1946) and "Ace of Clubs" (1950); Leslie Henson's "Bob's Your Uncle" (1948); and Vivian Ellis's "And So to Bed" (1951).

Although now firmly established in public affection in this country, Mantovani knew his style had so far created little attraction in America. Decca, too, were aware of this and it was felt that something should be done to increase record sales there. But how could this be achieved without lowering the high standard which Mantovani never dropped, although often subjected to great pressure?

He took a bold step, by commissioning Ronald Binge to provide a distinctive new sound — and supremely inspired, Binge came up with the "cascading strings" effect, creating a virtual waterfall of silvery melody on violins, unlike anything heard before. Tasteful, arresting, and very moving, his wonderful arrangements were to make Mantovani internationally famous.

The first composition arranged in this manner was *Charmaine*, an old tune first heard in 1926. The second composition was *Diane* which had appeared the following year. Both were waltzes by Erno Rapee, a Hungarian conductor and song composer who had settled in America. They had been played and sung for a quarter of a century by various bands, but when recorded by Mantovani and his Orchestra in February 1951, and paired together on Decca F.9696, they created a sensation. The record sold a million copies, an amazing number for the time.

Later hits in this style included *The Song from the Moulin Rouge* and *The Melba Waltz*, both recorded in 1953, by which time Mantovani's name had become indelibly associated with soaring, singing strings, and an almost sensuous treatment of song melodies and light classical compositions, performed by a concert orchestra of symphonic proportions.

Mantovani's "champagne music" proved irresistible to North Americans. After making an initial tour over there in 1954, he returned to Canada and the USA every year from 1955 to 1969, playing to packed houses. Among the music he played were some pleasing compositions of his own.

Immensely popular in Britain too (he had become a naturalised British subject in July 1935) he had his own television series. In September 1955 he received a golden disc in recognition of the incredible sales of *Charmaine* and in 1956 won the Ivor Novello Award as the year's most outstanding personality in popular music. He became the first artist to sell a million LPs in stereo, and the total sales of his albums eventually mounted to a staggering 35 million!

These albums, with their beautiful covers, had titles like *Songs to Remember*, *Operetta Memories* and *Latin Rendezvous*. They kept Decca profitable where otherwise it might have failed. The last album appeared in 1975, the year when ill-health compelled Mantovani to retire. In 1977 he entered a nursing home in Bournemouth, and in October that year his beloved Winifred died. Afterwards, the family moved him to another nursing home in Tunbridge Wells, Kent, where he died on 30th March, 1980. With his passing, an era also came to its close.

Other musicians directed concert orchestras of very high standard — including George Melachrino, Peter Yorke, Ron Goodwin, Ray Martin and Frank Chacksfield — but there was only one Mantovani. With his outstanding gifts he might well have become one of the great violinists, or a famous symphonic conductor. Instead, like Eric Coates, he remained faithful to light orchestral music, eschewing the classical heights.

Let us be grateful he chose the path that he did. Maestro Mantovani gave even the simplest tune a lustre that transformed it into something magical. Furthermore, to his very great credit, although he took the world by storm, he never neglected home and family. Modest and rather shy, he will long be remembered. Meanwhile, his music lives on. □

△ *Mantovani with his happy family in the mid 1960s — wife Winifred, daughter Paula, and son Kenneth.*

Edmundo Ros
(born 1910)

As the bulky American musician sat down at the piano and weaved his giant hands effortlessly over the keys, only a drummer remained on stage to provide the soft percussion accompaniment. But the result was electric and the audience at that London night club in August 1938, was spellbound. The pianist was "Fats" Waller, and his rhythmic backing was provided by a young, unknown drummer called Edmundo Ros, newly arrived in England from South America. Sadly, Waller died young whilst still in his prime, but Edmundo Ros went on to create an entirely new style of British music ... eventually retiring to his sunshine home in the Mediterranean.

Born at Port of Spain, the capital of Trinidad, on 7th December 1910, Edmundo Ros was initially marked out to enter the legal profession, but reduced family circumstances caused him to volunteer for the Army instead. Once in uniform he quickly joined a military band and after his training, secured the post of timpanist with the Venezuelan State Symphony Orchestra. He then opted to take up a state scholarship which he had won and, in 1937, made his way to England to study at the Royal Academy of Music.

71

◁*Edmundo Ros and his Orchestra were seen regularly on TV's "Come Dancing" programme.*

Grove, the latter eventually being renamed the "Edmundo Ros Club", whose genial host was held in great respect for many years.

The band's original name followed a reference to "the three R's", made by Winston Churchill in the House of Commons. Not realising that it meant "reading, 'riting and 'rithmetic", Edmundo responded by naming his new band "Ros's Rumba Romeos." This was short-lived, however, and quickly dropped after the Cosmo Club manager described it as both stupid and too long! For a signature tune, Ros cleverly adopted *The Cuban Love Song* and in 1949 he had a top hit in both the UK and America with *Wedding Samba*.

In common with most students, he found it difficult to make ends meet at first, but after joining the pioneer Latin American group of Don Marino Barreto, he eventually formed his own band in 1940. He took early advice from Victor Silvester, who explained that the British public needed something a little less rigid than true Latin American rhythms. Edmundo took the point and adapted his music to such an extent that for the next 35 years he became an extremely well-known and popular figure. His infectious enthusiasm endeared him to all radio listeners, and, coupled with live performances both on television and at West End night clubs, secured for himself a place in musical folklore.

Edmundo's new band made its first appearance on 8th August 1940, at the Cosmo Club in Wardour Street, which was also doubling as an air raid shelter! The word quickly got around, however, and it was not long before people were arriving in large numbers, not just to escape the German bombers but mainly to listen to the music. Edmundo then became a victim of his own success and was soon forced to move out when his clientele outgrew the premises. His next appointment, at the St. Regis Club in Cork Street, was even shorter, lasting only two weeks before a German bomb demolished it. Happily, there then followed long and successful associations with other night clubs like the Astor, the Bagatelle, and the Coconut

It was a colourful and rhythmical combination which, together with his bubbling personality, made Edmundo Ros so well-liked, for he was Latin American in style yet distinctly British in character. Almost single handedly he introduced the public to a new type of dance music which several bands later successfully copied, until it became an integral part of the British ballroom scene. It was epitomised by the long running TV show "Come Dancing", a much-loved programme which was never complete without a separate Latin American section encompassing the rumba, cha-cha-cha, samba and *paso doble*, all dances popularised in the early days by Edmundo Ros and his band.

In 1966, at the height of his fame, his career was severely disrupted by a serious road accident in which he suffered a fractured pelvis. This eventually led to arthritis and after a painful few years he was forced to retire through ill-health in 1976. He then led an active life in Spain, living with his wife Susan in a villa overlooking the port of Javea, in Alicante province. Well known among the growing British expatriate community in the area, despite his years he is often to be seen singing — and dancing! — at local get-togethers on the Costa.

Edmundo Ros introduced Britain to a brand new style of Latin American carnival music — and the public took him to its heart. □

Oscar Rabin
(1899-1958)

The Hammersmith Palais had been a well-known dance hall since November 1919 when it opened with the Original Dixieland Jazz Band from America making the music. During the Twenties and Thirties most British bands appeared there. In 1935 Oscar Rabin successfully took over the stand for five years, his residency being terminated only by the outbreak of war.

The band was actually known as "Oscar Rabin and his Romany Band with Harry Davis", the explanation being that Oscar was a short, fat, bald and very shy man who preferred to hide behind the big bass instrument in his own saxophone section, while his long-time partner Harry Davis — tall, elegant and handsome — conducted the band with emphasis on showmanship rather than direction.

Both men were born in 1899, Davis in London and Oscar Rabinowitz in Latvia, being brought to England as a four-year old refugee with his parents. Mr. Rabinowitz worked at his own trade as a cobbler in the East End of London, while young Oscar took violin lessons sponsored by Maidstone Violins who provided free tuition for deprived youngsters.

On his way to school he used to listen to the sound of someone playing a violin, coming from an upstairs window overlooking the street. Young Oscar was fascinated, particularly when he discovered that the violinist was blind. When asked if he would guide the sightless musician in exchange for lessons *and* his own violin, he quickly agreed. All this expert tuition gave him enough grounding for a scholarship to the Guildhall School of Music at the age of 13.

After his studies he jobbed around the London music scene, playing in a pit orchestra when 14, and at various locations including Lyons' Corner House in Coventry Street, and the Trocadero Restaurant. At 22 he was leading his first band at the Derby Palais, then in 1924 formed his long-lasting partnership with guitarist-singer Harry Davis. It was at this point that Oscar realised his true function was as a backroom boy rather than standing out in front playing the violin, so he took up the saxophone and buried himself in the background while allowing Harry to conduct the band.

▽ *Oscar Rabin (with violin) and his Romany Band at the Hammersmith Palais in 1938. Harry Davis is seated (left) with his daughter Beryl (centre).*

▷ *Pretty little Beryl Davis, see here at 15, left school to become a singer with the Oscar Rabin band in 1938. But her father, Harry Davis, was able to keep a protective eye on her for he was the orchestra's leader.*

After long stints at Southend and Hull, the late 1920s saw them at the Wimbledon Palais, by which time the Romany Band, as it was known in the early days, had grown to a nine-piece and earned a spot at the Royal Palace Hotel in Kensington, later transferring to the Astoria Ballroom in Charing Cross Road.

Oscar and Harry made 65 recordings for the Sterno label, during the 1932-34 period and gave five years sterling service at the Astoria as the dancers' favourite band, with its appropriate signature tune, Jerome Kern's sparkling *Dancing Time*.

In August 1935 came the move to Hammersmith Palais, where Rabin consolidated his popularity, also with his records for the Rex label, including one with Al Bowlly, others with regulars Eve Becke, Garry Gowan and a very young Beryl Davis, Harry's daughter. On leaving the Palais in 1940, the band dropped the "Romany" from its name, and started a nationwide variety tour. It was now a 16-piece big band, as modern as any, and often broadcast as BBC "Band Of The Week".

In 1951 Harry Davis and his family emigrated to America and he was replaced as leader of the Rabin band by clarinet player David Ede. The band was so successful at the Lyceum, just off the Strand, that Oscar was made a director of the owning company,

▷ *A quiet, shy man, Oscar Rabin preferred to hide behind his bass saxophone, leaving the running of his band to Harry Davis.*

Mecca. But in June 1958 he had a heart attack and died while receiving treatment for diabetes which had plagued him for years.

Meanwhile, Harry Davis lived on for a further 38 years, dying at Christmas 1996 in Los Angeles, aged 97. His daughter Beryl continued her career into her 70s, singing cabaret on American cruise liners. □

◁ *A national institution and treasure, Dame Vera Lynn, perhaps more than any other British singer, epitomised our wartime fighting spirit. A firm favourite with all the Services (as indicated here), she came to symbolise everything patriotic about our "green and pleasant land". During a long and successful career, she sang with many different bands, although Billy Cotton parted company with her after only three days because he thought she would never make the grade! In later years she regularly turned out for the British Legion Festival of Remembrance at the Royal Albert Hall, invariably bringing a tear to the eye with old favourites such as "There'll Always Be an England", and "There'll Be Bluebirds Over, the White Cliffs of Dover".*

Billy Merrin
(1900-1980)

Anyone who remembers shopping at Woolworth's before the war will readily recall those small shellac records which were on sale for sixpence. Played on a wind-up gramophone, they brought a touch of dance band magic into the lives of ordinary people in small town England who never had a chance to visit a posh London hotel, and hear in person the big names of the period.

Those first 78 rpm records in the early Thirties, made by the Crystalate company, were known as "8-inch Eclipse" and featured such bands as Bertini, Jay Wilbur, and Syd Roy (Harry's brother). Competition between rival record producers was fierce, and in August 1935 Crystalate launched a 9-inch series for sale at Woolworth's under the new Crown label. The first record featured Mrs. Jack Hylton and her band, with the lady herself doing the vocal of *In a Little Gypsy Tea Room*. Her husband at this time was still a leading name on the up-market HMV (His Master's Voice) label.

The second "sixpenny" record band employed by Crown, in September 1935, was a provincial outfit that rose swiftly to national prominence — Billy Merrin and his Commanders. Although they had already made several earlier recordings for such labels as Sterno, Plaza and Rex, the Commanders turned out no fewer than 66 Crown titles in 18 months, and soon soared to popularity throughout the country.

Born at Nottingham in February, 1900, Billy Merrin started work at a local lace factory but, at the age of 17, joined the Royal Naval Air Service as a wireless operator. It was a further ten years before he became a professional musician, however, playing the banjo for Conri Tait's band in the Sheffield area. In 1930 he joined Alan Green at the Nottingham Palais, playing piano, alto sax and also singing, before opening there a year later with his own band, making his first broadcast soon afterwards.

In 1933 he successfully transferred to the rival Victoria Ballroom, soon progressing to

▽ *Billy Merrin turned down several opportunities to move to bring his band to London, preferring instead to remain a big name in the provinces.*

Birmingham where he boasted his own recording studio at the Futurist cinema. Now dubbed "King of the Midlands", Billy rivalled the Blackpool-based Bertini band as the most famous in the provinces, regularly turning down offers of permanent work in London because, in his own words, "I would rather be a big fish in a small pond than a small fish in a big one". He nevertheless accepted occasional guest appearances in the metropolis which, together with regular radio broadcasts, kept him well in the public eye.

With his colourful Commanders, he toured extensively and appeared in Sandy Powell's famous film "Can You Hear Me Mother?" For several summers he also became a popular fixture at the St. Lawrence Hall, Ramsgate, but the war unfortunately brought this to an abrupt end. He remained active during hostilities, however, continuing to broadcast and playing briefly at the Plaza Ballroom in Derby. As a successful song-writer, he also owned a music publishing business in London and later toured as a one-man variety act.

After the war, the teetotal, non-smoking musician, who enjoyed playing tennis to keep fit, reformed the band and enjoyed three summer seasons at Herne Bay, juxtaposed with winter work in Nottingham. He gave up full-time band leading in 1951 and became a musical entrepreneur, also managing and accompanying his singing *protegé* Penny Nicholls, with whom he successfully toured the music hall circuit for almost a decade.

In 1960 he was musical director for a successful revival of the show "No, No Nanette" and in 1962 led a revamped Black and White Minstrel Show on a prolonged tour of Australia and New Zealand, eventually returning home three years later for a final summer season at Scarborough, in the company of northern comedian Harry Worth. He retired to Brighton later the same year, where he lived until his death on 24th July, 1980.

Unusually, Billy Merrin used two equally well-known signature tunes, opening with *Troubles Are Like Bubbles* and closing with *Cheerio*, both of which he composed himself. Despite being largely a provincial band, he always attracted top quality vocalists, including Helen Raymond, Pat Hyde, Ken Crossley, Rita Williams, Harry Bentley, and the ever-popular Sam Browne.

Provincial and disarmingly modest he may have been, but second-rate he most certainly was not. □

Sydney Lipton
(1906-1995)

S ydney Lipton, another London East Ender, was born on 4th January, 1906, and like so many other dance band leaders was a juvenile prodigy. He started on the violin at the age of seven, but his hopes of becoming a great soloist were dashed when he folded a deck-chair clumsily and severed the tip of his left index finger. Coming from a poor though musical family, Sydney soon realized he had to make some contribution to the Lipton coffers so, as a concert career was out of the question, he found employment after school hours in cinema and theatre orchestras.

△ *Sydney Lipton with his daughter Celia, who went on singing to the end of the century.*

At 17 he turned professional with the Murray Hedges quintet at Edinburgh's Palais de Danse ... a long way from home, but it gained him valuable experience. When they came south to the Regent Ballroom at Brighton, where they were booked to play opposite Billy Cotton and his band, as well as Syd Lipton on

violin the group included
Joe Ferrie on trombone
and Clem Bernard on
piano. When Cotton went
to Southport for a season
he asked the three young
men to join him.

Although Billy Cotton
still had some years to go
before being really established as a big name, as far
as the three young fellows
were concerned it was a step up the ladder.
Cotton later moved down the coast to the
Liverpool Rialto, but Syd refused to go, having
been offered the leadership of the local Southport
band, which included the pianist Dave Kaye who
later became one of Harry Roy's "Tiger
Ragamuffins". When the job at Southport eventually ended Syd returned to London to join
Ambrose for broadcasts and recordings when a
larger string section was called for.

Billy Cotton then offered him his old job back
with no hard feelings in regard to the Southport disagreement, and Sydney Lipton started
his recording career proper with Cotton's London Savannah Band at the Astoria Ballroom,
Charing Cross Road, in 1928. He stayed with
Cotton when the band went into Ciro's Club,
but to his mind there was too much touring
involved, especially for a married man with a
young daughter. He didn't know then that, just
a decade later, she would be singing with her
father's own band, as well as those of Lew
Stone and Jack Hylton. In addition, Celia Lipton
starred in many London and Broadway
musicals.

Instead of touring with Cotton, Lipton formed
a band at the Royal Palace Hotel, Kensington.
His combination included alto-sax player Harry
Hayes, accordionist-songwriter Billy Reid, and
singer-pianist Ronnie O'Dell. The supporting
band was led by pianist Leslie A. Hutchinson,
later famously known as "Hutch". When Syd's
contract expired he moved to the Grosvenor
House in Park Lane, from where the BBC began
regular broadcasts of late-night dance music.

Little did Sydney Lipton realize that his
tenure at the Grosvenor would last for 36 years,
apart from his wartime service. He had what by
latter-day standards would be called an all-star
line-up, including future bandleader Ted Heath.

It was quite strong in the vocal department too,
Celia Lipton being joined by Jack Plant, Harry
Bentley and Chips Chippendall, with Cyril
Grantham and George Evans adding their con-
siderable singing talents to those of such occas-
ional guests as Al Bowlly, Nat Gonella and Sam
Browne. But the war came and Sydney Lipton
enlisted first in the Royal Artillery, and later the
Royal Corps of Signals. Like Sydney Kyte, he
was also a motor-cyclist and was "Mentioned In
Dispatches" for his service, later being de-
mobbed with the rank of Captain.

The last thing he felt like doing after the war
was to take up the reins again at Grosvenor
House, but the hotel management made him an
offer he couldn't refuse, so back he went to
Park Lane with a completely new instrumentation of strings, harp and rhythm. Eventually,
however, he returned to a more conventional
dance band format, employing a new generation of musicians like Peter Knight, Syd
Lawrence, Bill McGuffie and Harry Hayes, who
brought along his wife Primrose (née Orrock)
as vocalist.

Sydney Lipton made many records before the
war for Regal Zonophone, Sterno, Decca and
Columbia, but like Sydney Kyte he had merely
ticked over without scoring any famous hits.
From his office at Steinway Hall, near Hanover
Square, he had started an entertainment
agency long before the war, and this became his
principal interest when he retired in 1967.

Although born a real Cockney, Sydney Lipton was always well-spoken with a rich, mellow
voice, tall and elegant in appearance ... a fine
figure to front a band and impress musicians
and listeners alike with his personality. It was in
his 90th year, while on holiday at his daughter's home in Florida, USA, that he died in July
1995.

□

Billy Ternent
(1899-1977)

Billy Ternent was born in North Shields on 10th October 1899, learning the violin at eight years of age, turning professional at twelve, and conducting in George Black's Tyneside theatres at 16, being too young for call-up in the Great War. His next job was in the band at the Terrace Tea Rooms in Fenwick's department store in Newcastle. Then he went to London for service in Jack Hylton's Kit-Cat band alongside Ted Heath, Al Starita, Sidney Bright and Len Fillis, among others. Being a multi-instrumentalist, capable of playing everything in the band, it wasn't long before this general utility man was promoted to the main Hylton orchestra.

Ternent's achievements as a musician, and his superb orchestral arrangements for the band, of which he was Hylton's deputy conductor, are detailed in the chapter on his boss.

Owing to complex music union regulations, when Jack Hylton went to the USA in the mid-Thirties he was only allowed to take his vocalists and arrangers with him, leaving the rest of the orchestra behind in England. Although Billy also went to the States, in January 1936 he returned to conduct the band when it backed a 12-year-old girl called Pat Sibley. *Moanin Minnie* and *Why Did She Fall for the Leader of the Band?* were the first records of a young lady who then went on to sing as a 16-year-old with Ambrose and become a firm wartime favourite with the troops. Her stage name was Anne Shelton.

On the outbreak of war in 1939, the Hylton organisation split into two, one band under

△ *Billy Ternent was deputy leader of Jack Hylton's band before forming his own orchestra.*

Freddy Bretherton's leadership for stage work, the other given into Billy Ternent's hands and summarily dispatched to BBC studios in Bristol and Bangor to escape the Blitz. Here the Hylton band became the BBC Dance Orchestra, featuring Billy Ternent's Sweet Rhythm, a wonderfully nostalgic style of scoring which he was to use with only slight variations until his death 37 years later. Augmented, the band played for many of the BBC's variety programmes and such featured comedy shows as "Danger — Men At Work", "The Old Town Hall", "Old Mother Riley" and, of course, "ITMA" for which Billy Ternent wrote the ever-familiar signature tune.

Unfortunately, he was dogged by ill-health for much of his life, undergoing many operations, and it was this which necessitated his giving up the job as leader of the BBC Dance Orchestra in favour of Stanley Black. In due course he toured with his band in the George Black show "If It's Laughter You're After", playing for the troops overseas, then returning to broadcasting after the war when he put in three years' service as musical director of "Variety Bandbox". He accompanied Frank Sinatra on a tour of Britain in 1953, with the first half of the programme as a showcase for the band ... with some regrettably unfunny comedy. Also as a conductor he took over the reins at the London Palladium during the 1960s and directed "Those Were The Days" from the City Varieties Theatre, Leeds.

Unlike some other band leaders Billy Ternent was quite happy merely having a dance band with a rich, mellow ensemble sound which was

△ Billy Ternent (front row, fourth from left) pictured with Jack Hylton (centre, in the trilby hat) and band at the Paris Opera House in 1931.

highly individual. He took the "Ternent sound" to ballrooms, society dances, everywhere from the Royal Albert Hall to Butlin's. His public was everywhere, and they always welcomed the strains of his famous signature tune *She's My Lovely*, the Vivian Ellis melody which Billy Ternent made so much his own for nearly 40 years.

The much-admired "Ternent sound" dated back to 1936 when he toured the USA with Jack Hylton. Billy was enraptured by the American sound of such bands as Hal Kemp and his Orchestra, and later adopted this style on his return to Britain when he began the formation of his own orchestra. His was not a swing band, but he played up-tempo pieces in a crisp and well-controlled style which contrasted well with the sheer romanticism of the ballads popular at that time.

Billy Ternent was a typical no-nonsense Geordie who never lost his Tyneside accent — blunt and outspoken, sometimes difficult to get on with, but highly respected despite all that. One musician said of him: "He had a fierce bark, but no bite, and beneath his prickly exterior he was really a nice fellow. He was a perfectionist and a strict disciplinarian, an outstanding musician and a real pro of the old school who just couldn't tolerate inefficiency".

Bill Ternent's long bouts of ill-health finally took their toll, and he died on 23rd March, 1977, half way through his 78th year. □

▽ Billy Ternent, as deputy leader of Jack Hylton's orchestra, invited a 12-year-old schoolgirl called Pat Sibley to sing with the band in 1936. The records she made led to stardom ... after she changed her name to Anne Shelton.

79

Lou Preager
(1906-1978)

In 1942, two years after Oscar Rabin had left, the Hammersmith Palais saw the entry of the longest-serving maestro at the venue, Lou Preager and his Band. Like many other band leaders, Lou was an East Ender, born literally within the sound of Bow Bells on 12th January, 1906. He was somewhat of a prodigy, playing piano at the age of four, giving classical recitals and tuition at 10, accompanying silent films at 11, and playing in Joe Young's dance band while still at school.

Music was still only a sideline for him while he worked first for a solicitor, then a chartered accountant and later an advertising agency, but the young man would never have been happy keeping it as a mere hobby. While still a teenager, he had a spell in revue as pianist, actor and comedian, then had the chance to turn professional with Maurice Harford's band at the Piccadilly Hotel.

In search of as much and as varied experience as he could get, Lou played Russian music in a department store restaurant during the afternoons, and in the evenings played the accordion in a continental trio at a Park Lane restaurant. He became deputy leader of Bert Firman's band, then when the band went to Paris he improved his knowledge of the Argentinian tango by guesting with a Latin orchestra and then spent three winter seasons, from 1929-1931, at the world-famous Shepherd's Hotel in Cairo.

Returning to London, he learned that there was a vacancy at the Monseigneur Restaurant for a tango band to play opposite Roy Fox. Lou hastened to form a group, including Eugene Pini playing violin beside Sydney Lipton, which got the job and eventually made its radio debut from 2LO at Savoy Hill. Later, Syd Lipton had his own band at the Grosvenor House Hotel,

including the pianist/accordionist Billy Reid, later known as the writer of such world hits as *The Gypsy*. After working at the Monseigneur, Lou formed an 11-piece band which he took into Ciro's Club, where he was personally asked for by the then Prince Of Wales (later King Edward VIII) who considered him to be the finest exponent of the Argentinian tango in this country. Then followed the five-year engagement that really established the name of Lou Preager, at Romano's Restaurant in the Strand, with the appropriate signature tune *Let's All Go Down The Strand*.

Lou built up quite a following with his broadcasts from Romano's, so it was only logical that in 1938 he should take the band on a year-long music-hall tour, followed by another residency at the Haymarket Brasserie and a summer season at the Spa, Scarborough. More touring ended at Caproni's in Bangor, as in fact did Lou's civilian activities, for it was now wartime. Lou went to France to play for the forces during what was known as "the phoney war", but there was nothing phoney about the retreat from Dunkirk with the Preager band under fire.

Back in England, Lou joined the Ambulance Service and then volunteered for the Intelligence Service as an interpreter, but while working for his commission he was badly injured when a lorry in which he was travelling was involved in a horrific crash. After spending

▽ *Lou Preager led his band at London's famous Hammersmith Palais for 17 years.*

the best part of a year in hospital, Lou received his discharge from a war he had never really had a chance to take part in. His elbow having been shattered, he could no longer play piano or accordion so he settled for a return to band-leading, taking up the reins again at Green's Playhouse in Glasgow and then at the Streatham Locarno.

When Lou Preager took over the stand at Hammersmith Palais De Danse in 1942 he had no idea that he would spend almost the rest of his professional life presiding over the dancers and their music at that venue, with *On The Sunny Side Of The Street* as his band's signature tune. Probably the highspot of Lou's tenure there was his Hammersmith Palais Song Contest under the title "Write A Song For £1,000". This got off to a fine start in 1945 with nationwide publicity when two middle-aged ladies, a former music-hall singer named Emily Beadell, and café pianist Nell Tollerton, submitted an old-fashioned waltz which was derided by swing fans and the music business alike.

Remember *Cruising Down The River?* Lou had faith in the song, which was catchy enough in its own way, and offered to underwrite its publication himself. Fortunately, a publisher quickly accepted it, and the ladies not only won the £1,000 prize but made over £50,000 in royalties from best-selling records both here and in America!

Although he made over 80 records in the first five post-war years, Lou Preager was quite content to stay at the Palais in Hammersmith, which had now become his spiritual home. When he finally left there after 17 years he led his band to the Lyceum Ballroom, taking over from the late Oscar Rabin, until he had to retire from active leadership through ill-health. He remained in the business, however, buying the Carlton Ballroom in Slough and running it successfully until stopped by a heart attack, which forced him to sell out in 1967. Nine years later, he moved to Palma, Majorca, but his retirement in the Mediterranean sunshine lasted for only two years before his death out there in November 1978.

Lou Preager, though perhaps not one of the biggest names in British dance music, had the kind of band that was the backbone of the musical profession. He had his own special niche and his own special public, which must have comprised millions of ballroom dancers over the years. Many men of music would like to have earned such an epitaph. ☐

Billy Thorburn

(1900-1971)

Billy Thorburn, who later built up a reputation for himself and his band under the unusual title of "The Organ, the Dance Band and Me", was born at North Kensington, London, on 12th May, 1900, the son of the verger at the parish church of Holy Trinity. Due to his father's position, he became a regular attender at the various church services and, after a spell as a boy soprano in the choir, his burgeoning musical talent was so irrepressible that he was appointed organist and choir-master at the incredibly early age of nine! And he held that job for eleven years, apart from a short spell as a volunteer in the Royal Flying Corps during the last year of the Great War.

As Britain shook off the awful trauma of that conflict, Billy felt he needed a change too, so he got a job as pianist in a small jazz band at the Regent Palace Hotel before joining Jack Hylton in 1922, who was then leading a dance orchestra playing in the rooftop ballroom at the

△ A laughing Billy Thorburn pictured with his band at rehearsal in 1938.

Queen's Hall. Shortly after his marriage in 1923 Billy joined Carroll Gibbons as a second pianist under Debroy Somers at the Savoy Hotel, playing in the Orpheans and the Sylvians, also broadcasting as a pianist called "Uncle Jazz" for a children's hour programme from the BBC's new wireless station 2LO, then based at Savoy Hill.

When the well-known American composer George Gershwin came over to England in the summer of 1925, Billy Thorburn was chosen to partner him in a piano duet of his famous new number *Rhapsody in Blue*, which sought to combine a classical theme in a modern musical setting. From the Savoy, Billy moved to the Piccadilly Hotel band led by Sydney Kyte before joining Jack Payne in 1932 where he remained for four years after which he formed his own 12-piece orchestra known as "Billy Thorburn and his Music", playing at Bournemouth's Royal Bath Hotel in the summer of 1936.

It was a stroke of bad luck that gave Billy his biggest push up the ladder of success. In December 1936, Jack Hylton and his band had to call off an intended broadcast at short notice and the BBC's staff organist, Reginald Foort, had the unenviable task of mustering a replacement group of musicians within a few hours. Billy and a few of his pals responded immediately, and despite there being no time for rehearsal they somehow cobbled together a half-hour show called "A Programme of Rhythm Music", combining Billy's pleasant dance band sound with organ music played by Reginald Foort. The listening public loved it and begged for more. In April 1938, records began appearing under the title "The Organ, the Dance Band, and Me", but no name of pianist or organist was given on the label. It was not until the following November that the pianist was revealed as Billy Thorburn and his organist being H. Robinson Cleaver. The latter played a three-manual, 8-unit Compton organ which had been specially installed at the studios in Abbey Road, London, where all the records were made.

For 15 years — from 1938 until 1953— Billy Thorburn's "The Organ, the Dance Band and Me" combination recorded almost 300 songs for Parlophone, including many wartime hits like *I've Got Sixpence* and *Don't Sweetheart Me*. Most of them had Robinson Cleaver on the Compton, although several other organists "ghosted" with the band but declined to be named, probably because of their contracts as cinema organists. In fact, Robinson Cleaver was renowned for his broadcasts from the organ at the Regal Cinema in Bexleyheath, Kent. Born at Eckington, Derbyshire, in 1906, he enjoyed one of the longest careers in music history, for he was still playing the organ and promoting concerts in Llandudno, North Wales, well into his 80s.

When "The Organ, the Dance Band, and Me" was finally disbanded, Billy Thorburn continued to make records for several years with his Strict Tempo Music before he finally retired from show business. He spent the last 10 years of his life, with his lovely wife Ivy, as the landlord (and lady) of the "Green Dragon", a pub in Barnet, Hertfordshire. Even then, he would often delight his regulars by playing a few rippling tunes on the piano in the bar.

Billy Thorburn, renowned for his mild-mannered, easy-going personality, as well as his superlative musical talent, died in April 1971 within a year of completing his allotted span of "three score years and ten". □

▽ The well-known radio organist H. Robinson Cleaver, for many years a vital part of Billy Thorburn's band.

The Accordion Bands

Don Porto — Rossini — Primo Scala
(Harry Bidgood) — Eric Winstone
Billy Reid — George Scott-Wood

The early-1930s saw the introduction of the cinema organ into dozens of newly-built auditoriums all over the country. It quickly became a firm favourite with a public which "went to the flicks" at least once a week, and when a relatively new instrument suddenly gave them an opportunity to experience similar sounds in the dance hall, a new style of music emerged. It soon took over in popularity from the ukulele and its versatility was instantly recognised by one man in particular. Fronting several different groups, including his own conventional dance band, Harry Bidgood, alias Don Porto, Rossini and above all, Primo Scala, became the biggest name among the Accordion Bands ...

House lights dimmed, the audience hushed, and a growing air of expectancy spread all around. Suddenly, a crescendo of sound filtered into the auditorium and a spotlight settled on the orchestra pit. Then, as if by magic, a beaming organist rose majestically and effortlessly into view, thrilling everyone with the all-conquering and powerful sound of the mighty Wurlitzer. Invariably there was a round of applause as the soloist launched forth into his signature tune.

The time was anything between 40 and 65 years ago, and the organist could have been Reginald Dixon, Sandy MacPherson, Sidney Torch, Reginald Foort, Robin Richmond, or a whole host of other famous names. Everyone loved the sound of the cinema organ but only a privileged few ever got to play one. The next best thing, however, was a musical instrument which caught on in the 1930s, and quickly

△ Primo Scala (alias Harry Bidgood) made more accordion band records than anyone else.

took over in popularity from the ukulele. It was the piano-accordion and it came in many sizes, allowing everyone with a musical touch to enjoy a personal taste of an organ in miniature. It soon became all the rage and many towns in England vied with each other to produce the best local accordion bands.

By 1933, the "squeeze-box", as it was affectionately known, was making an indelible mark on the dance band scene. With three accordions (sometimes many more), replacing the front-line melody-making instruments, and backed by the usual rhythm section, the overall sound was often as good, if not better, than many conventional bands. The new genre was not without its critics, however, and as one wag remarked: "A gentleman is someone who knows how to play the accordion — but doesn't!"

A number of different names, began to surface on major record labels — but were not always what they seemed. The first was "Don Porto and His Novelty Accordions" who appeared on the 8" Eclipse records sold at Woolworths for sixpence. When these were phased out in favour of the 9" Crown label, a new name emerged — "Rossini's Accordions" — but clearly not formed by the famous classical composer who died in 1868.

Even more up-market was the 10" Rex label which retailed at the princely sum of one shilling, on which the Latin-sounding "Primo Scala and His Accordion Band" were the star turn. With such famous vocalists as Vera Lynn, Cavan O'Connor, Dan Donovan, Pat O'Malley, Sam Costa and Donald Peers, the accordion had arrived.

△ *Multi-talented George Scott-Wood, managed to play in several different bands all at the same time. He was equally at home with an accordion, dance band, or playing hot-tempo jazz.*

However, most of the public never realised that all three bands were one and the same! All were directed by Harry Bidgood, a Londoner born in 1898. After starting his musical career as a pianist with the famous De Groot orchestra at the Piccadilly Hotel, he became the recording manager for Vocalion before transferring allegiance in 1932 to a rival firm, Crystalate. Between 1925 and 1937 Harry Bidgood made hundreds of records with his conventional dance band — also using a variety of different names — and made several hundred more with his accordion bands between 1933 and 1944 — a truly prolific output in a relatively short space of time.

When Don Porto and Rossini disappeared from the recording studio, Bidgood's best-known pseudonym took over and lasted into the early 1950s. "Primo Scala" was a cleverly constructed hybrid, contrived from the forename of Italy's heavyweight boxing champion, Primo Carnera, together with the surname of a man who won the famous Irish Sweepstake, Signor Emilio Scala. It was an exotic-sounding title which perfectly complemented the atmosphere of an accordion band, and to which the public took a shine. Everyone agreed that the bread-and-butter name Harry Bidgood somehow did not have the same ring about it. Indeed, when he died in 1957, Harry was better remembered for his Italian *nom-de-plume* than his true English name!

There were many other accordion groups playing at the same time, but the only one which seriously rivalled Primo Scala, was the London Piano-Accordion Band, led at different times by Billy Reid (1902-1974), George Scott-Wood, and Eric Winstone. Billy Reid's band invariably teamed up with youthful vocalist Dorothy Squires, who went on to become an international star in her own right. Billy, meanwhile, left to concentrate his attentions more on music publishing and composing.

Multi-talented George Scott-Wood, born in Glasgow in 1903, recorded for the Regal Zonophone label and made several tracks between 1934 and 1940, many with Sam Browne as vocalist, during which time he also busied himself with his own jazz group called the Six Swingers. He also found time to perform with several other groups. Despite his heavy work load, and just like Harry Bidgood, he managed to maintain a high standard of music which the public thoroughly enjoyed — bouncy, catchy, melodic and tuneful — everything which the modern successor to the old concertina was capable of achieving via its bellows and keyboard. George Scott-Wood died in 1978.

During the war, Eric Winstone (1915-74), was extremely popular as a solo accordionist and also with his swing quartet, where his virtuoso playing was well supported by a string bass, guitar and vibraphone. He later recorded for Regal with the bigger London Piano-Accordion Band, before finally switching to his larger-than-life dance orchestra which enjoyed several post-war hits. He retained his smaller accordion ensemble for radio broadcasts, however, especially the ever-popular favourite programme, "Music While You Work". His main vocalists were Alan Kane and Julie Dawn.

▽ *The first recognised leader of the London Piano-Accordion Band was Billy Reid, who later became a successful music publisher.*

△ *Primo Scala (real name Harry Bidgood) was the most popular and prolific of all the British accordion bands. Between 1933 and the end of the Second World War he made hundreds of recordings, in addition to many more under his own name with a conventional dance orchestra. The female singer in this picture is Nina Delmonte.*

Although the piano-accordion was actually invented in the 19th century (no less a composer than Tchaikovsky used it in his *Suite No. 2*), its rise to popularity in the 20th century was caused almost entirely by its sudden availability to a mass market. Most 1930s music magazines contained dozens of adverts for the instrument, usually encouraging payment by instalment, or the "never never" as it was cynically termed in those days. There was even a magazine called *The Accordion Times* which enjoyed a healthy life span before succumbing to new musical trends and fashions.

The most famous brand name was Hohner, which advertised widely and sold thousands of instruments. The company also organised an annual accordion rally at the Central Hall, Westminster, where on one notable occasion no fewer than 40,000 devotees crammed themselves into a space which would today horrify anyone involved with health and safety. There were no reports of mass riots, however, and everyone clearly enjoyed themselves.

Versatility and volume of sound made the accordion an ideal instrument for both indoor and outdoor concerts, and many famous singers, both sacred and secular, used it to accompany themselves. When placed in a group, however, the options were vast, and accordion bands were extremely popular for all types of dancing

▷ *Post-war band leader Eric Winstone's early career included a spell as a successful piano-accordionist. He often appeared on the BBC programme "Music While You Work".*

Although the instrument is still widely used, its heyday has long gone, replaced firstly by the electric guitar, and more recently by synthesisers and electronic and computer gadgetry. Its bigger brother, the cinema organ, has fared much worse and was in grave danger of extinction until a number of enthusiasts dismantled, removed and have since restored, several examples of this magnificent "King of Instruments" from a bygone era.

Novelties they may have seemed, but the best accordion groups were genuine dance bands, capturing the spirit of an age when tastes were simple, pleasures uncomplicated, and enjoyment easily fulfilled. They provided extra dimensions of sound in a single and highly mobile instrument, sounds perhaps equalled by the piano, but surpassed only by the enormous but very static cinema organ. Small wonder that piano-accordions were so popular. □

The Service Bands

Squadronaires — Skyrockets
Blue Rockets — Blue Mariners

For a decade before the Second World War, Britain's finest dance band musicians mingled with the cream of society. They wore evening suits and played in plush salons for society parties. Yet when the call came they quickly donned khaki, Air Force or Navy blue, and carried on playing, their brilliance undimmed by the black-out or German bombers. Every branch of the armed forces had its own music makers, known collectively as the Service Bands

The Squadronaires (officially called the RAF No.1 Dance Orchestra) was formed in 1940 with members drawn largely from the Ambrose Orchestra. Led by Jimmy Miller and later by Ronnie Aldrich, the unit disbanded in the early Sixties. Signature tune: *"There's Something in the Air"*. Star Players: George Chisholm, Froggy Ffrench and Tommy McQuater.

The Skyrockets (The No.1 Balloon Centre Dance Orchestra) rivalled the Squadronaires for popularity. Air Ministry used it for propaganda broadcasts to the Luftwaffe; later it gave public concerts and made scores of recordings. First leader was George Beaumont, soon to be succeeded by trombonist Paul Fenoulhet. Signature tune: *"A Stairway to the Stars"*. Star players: Pat Dodd and Chick Smith. Later the band became resident at the London Palladium.

The Blue Rockets (Royal Army Ordnance Corps) was the Army's answer to the two RAF bands. Formed by Eric Robinson, later a noted conductor of classical music, it first specialised in swing arrangements of the classics. Signed a year's recording contract with HMV in 1942 but was briefly disbanded after a Press outcry over bandsmen being "toy soldiers." Re-formed, it played on until the early Fifties, led by Eric Tann and Benny Daniels.

The Blue Mariners Band (Royal Navy) was led by pianist George Crow and featured clarinet and ace saxophone player Freddy Gardner.

When war clouds gathered over Europe it looked like the end for Britain's dance bands. Their fans were joining up and the best venues were closing down, but the Army, Navy and RAF wanted big band music to boost morale so the musicians were conscripted, donned uniform, stayed as a unit, and kept faith with the beat. From the Blitz to VE-Day (and beyond) the bands played on.

At airbases, ballrooms and barracks all over Britain the sweet sounds of good music were kept alive by the best instrumentalists in the land, bearing rank and blowing a storm. In the darkest days, when the Nazi threat was just a Channel away, they kept the feet tapping. Some of the more cynical Press called them draft-dodgers; others called them heroes.

It all started in 1940 when Wing Commander Rudy O'Donnell, Director of the RAF's Central Band Wing, began recruiting dance band musicians. He was convinced they would be as big a morale booster as military bands and string orchestras, so recruits were formed into five-piece bands before dispersing to RAF Stations throughout Britain.

▷ *Eric Robinson who conducted the Blue Rockets.*

Their rank was "aircraftsman second class/general duties" — the lowest of the low. The pay was low, too — 3s 6d a day (17½p) with bed and board, and at the RAF School of Music headquarters at Uxbridge the beds were indeed boards. The welcome was also uncertain. As Sid Colin, one of the intake, recalled in his book *And The Bands Played On*: "The regulars greeted the musicians' arrival with wry amusement. 'Wo ho, the snake charmers,' they called. They stood around the parade grounds in their stiff new uniforms and asked themselves what nice boys like them were doing in a place like that." Fourteen men were selected to become the RAF Number One Dance Orchestra — known collectively, though unofficially, as the Squadronaires. Some of them had been with Ambrose at the Mayfair; all had played with big-time West End bands. They included trombonist George Chisholm, pianist Ronnie Aldrich, trumpet aces Tommy McQuater and Kenny Baker (who also played for the RAF Fighter Command band) saxes Andy McDevitt and Jimmy Durrant, drummer Jock Cummings and the aforementioned Sid Colin on guitar. Under Jimmy Miller, another ex-Ambrose man, they turned into one of the finest swing bands to be heard outside America.

In January 1941 a radio concert by the Squadronaires was described by an enthusiastic columnist in *Melody Maker* magazine as: "The greatest dance band performance ever broadcast this side of the Atlantic." Nine months

△ *The Squadronaires at a wartime dance. Trombonist George Chisholm is second from the left, and trumpeter Kenny Baker on the far right.*

later he enthused about another Squadronaires session: "This is the greatest jazz this country has ever produced." Even allowing for wartime patriotism it was quite a compliment. The standard was no surprise, and after the war many sidesmen continued in the manner to which they'd grown accustomed, with such bands as Ted Heath.

Playing everything from Dixieland to Jive, the Squadronaires was the first British service band to make its mark. Later came the Skyrockets (the No.1 Balloon Centre Dance Orchestra), the Blue Rockets (Royal Army Ordnance Corps) and the Blue Mariners (the Royal Navy), all forerunners of the post-war big band boom. Other outfits represented the Ack Ack Corps, Bomber Command and even a London Fire Force Band which was described by *Melody Maker* in October 1942 as "easily our second best National Service band."

Freed from the petty regimes of assorted pre-war bandleaders (and promoters) players were allowed to experiment, extemporise and expand their repertoire. The Squadronaires in particular created adventurous swing which, thanks to quality recordings, can still be savoured and admired more than 50 years later.

Most of the bands' gigs were held in hangars, Naafis or works canteens packed to

⊲ *The Royal Army Ordnance Corps band, known simply as the Blue Rockets, being conducted by Eric Robinson.*

the rafters with airmen, soldiers or factory workers — though the Squadronaires reached an even wider audience by being featured in the 1943 Powell-Pressburger film "The Life and Death of Colonel Blimp", starring Roger Livesey, while the Blue Rockets starred in "Swinging Into the Attack", a flag-waver made by the Ministry of Information and including numbers by Spike Hughes.

Strange things happen in war. One mixed-up journalist filed a story that dear old Charlie Kunz had been jailed in the Tower of London for passing on coded messages to the Germans via his piano broadcasts, while a French bandleader was said to have been wounded fighting for the Finnish army in Russia. Stranger still was the situation in which sidesmen ineligible for military service found themselves earning better money than ever before in civilian life because the call-up had taken most of the best players — who, in comparison, were earning less.

There was also the ticklish problem of how such free spirits as the Squadronaires (who included a high proportion of Scottish-born session men) would take orders from the English top brass. Sid Colin tells the story of a furious commanding officer who demanded to know why half the band had left midway through a mess dance. "Taking a break, sir", explained sergeant (acting) Jimmy Miller. "I want the full band back at the double," ordered the enraged CO. When the order came to revert to full strength the band did just that — removing their mutes and playing with such power in the tiny hall that much glassware was reportedly smashed and

officers were half-deafened by the din.

The Blitz made heavy demands on travel and performance. Once the band was playing at Bristol when a bomb literally blasted them out of the hall and they finished the night dragging victims from bombed houses. At other times the blackout and second-rate equipment took its toll of quality. Some public address systems were so bad as to howl piteously when approached. The band called it "The Grapes of Wrath, With Music."

Some of the Squadronaires had played pre-war as a group called "Heralds of Swing" and George Chisholm always insisted that the Squads were a collective organisation, catering for intimate jazz and full-blown big band alike. Certainly it was ripe for ideas, with Chisholm, Aldrich, Durrant and Jimmy Watson doing most of the arranging. Its style was compared with the Jimmy Lunceford band, one of America's most vibrant outfits, and its propaganda value was immense — being beamed to Germany on the same wavelength as that used by the Luftwaffe broadcasting network!

The band played on into the post-war era under Ronnie Aldrich, disbanding as a civilian group in the early Sixties. It made scores of records. Their signature tune was "There's Something in the Air", usually sung by Jimmy Miller.

The Skyrockets were the Squadronaires' greatest rivals, founded in 1940 by a group of musicians who were on, of all things, a training

▷ *The British Band of the AEF (Allied Expeditionary Force) seen in 1944, conducted by George Melachrino.*

course at Blackpool to become balloon rigger fabric workers. Trombonist Paul Fenoulhet, a former arranger for Carroll Gibbons at the Savoy, took over as leader from George Beaumont when the latter was posted to another station and the band really took off when it was posted to Fighter Command and received official recognition as a Service dance orchestra.

It recorded for Rex and Parlophone and continued into the post-war years, owned by 13 of its members who employed the remaining musicians. Fenoulhet was seeking the more lavish André Kostelanetz sound and there were disputes about the band's direction before it became resident at the London Palladium, where it accompanied Danny Kaye among others. Woolf Phillips replaced Fenoulhet, who became conductor of the BBC Variety Orchestra, and the group finally disbanded in the mid-Fifties. Star soloists were Pat Dodd (piano), Chick Smith (trumpet) and Pat Smuts (sax) with Glaswegian Benny Lee (later a comedy regular on "The Braden Beat" and other radio programmes) on vocals. Such illustrious post-war musicians as pianist and conductor Stanley Black, later director of the BBC Dance Orchestra, and George Melachrino, director of the British band of the AEF, also made their names with RAF bands.

Considering the conditions (wartime and post-war) under which they played, many of the service bands attained a marvellous proficiency. The Navy's Blue Mariners, led by pianist George Crow, provided an ideal showcase for the brilliance of Freddy Gardner, described as Ray Noble's favourite alto player and a clarinettist of liquid delight. The RAOC Blue Rockets were formed by Eric Robinson, formerly a guitarist with Eric Wild's Tea-Timers (as seen on early TV) and later a conductor of orchestral light classics whose programme "Music For You" ran as a regular television series in the Fifties. The Rockets also featured trombonist Eric Tann (later leader) and top saxophonists

Benny Daniels and Bertie King. In various forms they survived until the early Fifties but without ever rivalling the RAF dance bands in popular appeal.

It says something for the quality of all the British service bands that not only did they withstand the war — and the awesome competition of Major Glenn Miller's 40-piece Army-Air Force Band and Sam Donohue's powerful US Navy Band — but that they emerged, refreshed and resilient at the peace, after a playing renaissance born out of conflict. The Squadronaires, Skyrockets, Blue Rockets and the rest bequeathed a proud legacy of fine musicianship. As death and destruction rained down, they continued to swing. □

▽ *Paul Fenoulhet leader of the Skyrockets — after the war he conducted the BBC Variety Orchestra.*

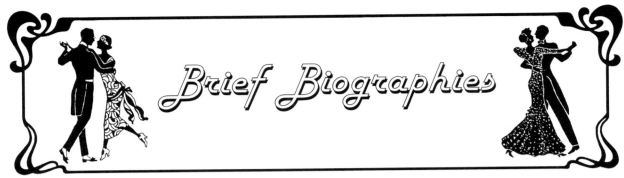

Brief Biographies

2LO Dance Band — Led by pianist Stanley Holt (died 1978), it was the BBC's first resident dance band on the wireless, lasting for 18 months, following which it was superseded by the Savoy Orpheans and Savoy Havana Bands, from the end of 1924.

'Wag' Abbey — Real name Charles Abbey, but acquired his nickname through a non-stop talking habit. He first recorded under his own name in 1922, but also later as Victor Sterling when he played xylophone solos.

Lou Abelardo — An American singer who came to England in 1929 and made a lasting impression singing with Ambrose. He made a handful of recordings with a band under his own name before returning to the United States two years later.

Paul Adam (1914-1978) — Born Carl Tauber, of Austro-Polish descent, Londoner Paul Adam changed his name in 1942 and led his Mayfair Music at several well-known Metropolitan night clubs. He was also a regular broadcaster, including a long run as a presenter of "Housewives' Choice". A real extrovert, he spent almost as much time socialising with his customers as he did playing music.

Edgar Adeler (1896-1985) — A South African band leader who toured Europe and Asia, with Al Bowlly as his singer, eventually arriving in England and performing briefly in concert with Bowlly, Al Starita and Len Fillis.

Alyn Ainsworth (1924-1990) — (see also Northern Dance Orchestra) — After making an early appearance as a boy soprano with Herman Darewski, he worked as an arranger for both Geraldo and Oscar Rabin, before beginning a long association with the Northern Dance Orchestra. A true northerner born in Bolton, he backed many famous shows, including Jimmy Clitheroe, Ken Dodd, and "The Good Old Days" from the Leeds Variety theatre. After moving from the BBC to Granada Television, he worked as a musical director in London, and also took part in several Royal Variety Performances.

Ronnie Aldrich (1916-1993) — (see Chapter on Service Bands) — A founder member of the wartime RAF Dance Band No. 1, better known as the Squadronaires, he traded his piano for the leader's baton in 1951, and stayed in charge until the band's demise in 1964. Thereafter he concentrated on composing, arranging, and conducting his own orchestra.

Alfredo (1891-1966) — His real name was Alfred Gill, but adding a letter 'o' to his Christian name produced the right type of image for the leader of a genuine gypsy band of musicians recruited from several countries. Resplendent in traditional silk costumes, they cut a dashing image and were extremely popular throughout the 1930s. Prior to this he led a more conventional 1920s band which was the first to wear white waistcoats with black ties and dinner jackets.

Nat Allen (1909-1964) — After learning his trade with several bands in the 1930s, Nat formed his own band which appeared regularly on radio and television for several years after the war, especially on "Kaleidoscope". At one point he even had his own show. He was also the first band to appear live from a Scottish ballroom during "Come Dancing" from the Glasgow Locarno. A popular raconteur he once succeeded a young, unknown manager at the Ilford Palais called Jimmy Saville.

Les Allen (1902-1996) — London-born but taken to Canada by his parents at an early age, Les returned in 1924 as saxophonist and co-leader (with Hal Swain) of the New Princes' Toronto Band. When Hal left two years later Les took the band to Berlin, before hitting the big time as the star vocalist with Henry Hall's BBC Dance Orchestra from 1932-4. He then formed his own instrumental group called the Melody Four, and a vocal group called the Canadian Bachelors, before moving back to Toronto in 1948.

Billy Amstell (born 1911) — Playing saxophone with several top bands, including Roy Fox, Ambrose, and Geraldo, he rubbed shoulders with all the famous names in London and went on to become a veteran band leader with his Dixie All Stars Jazz Band. In 1987 he played for Princess Anne at the Mayfair Hotel Diamond Jubilee, the same year that his autobiography *Don't Fuss, Mr. Ambrose* was published.

Micky Ashman (born 1927) — After playing the double bass with Mike Daniels, Humphrey Lyttelton, Chris Barber, and Lonnie Donegan, Micky formed his own traditional jazz band in 1958, performing until the mid-Sixties.

Stan Atkins (1902-1973) — In 1935 he was chosen to front a band which deputised for Oscar Rabin at the Hammersmith Palais, following which, in 1940, he became resident at the new and ultra-modern Embassy Ballroom in Welling, Kent. Packed to its 1,500 capacity throughout most of the war, the regulars danced on a beautiful Canadian maple-wood floor, usually ignoring the bombs raining down outside. The band was often supplemented for wartime broadcasts, especially "Music While You Work" and "Saturday Night at the Palais", by members of the nearby RAF-based band, later to become famous as the Skyrockets. Stan retired in 1952 after more than 20 years as a band leader.

Jos Q. Atkinson — Determined not to go down the Tyneside pits as a coal miner, Jos conducted choirs and theatre orchestras from his earliest teenage years, before enlisting under age in the First World War. An enthusiastic ornithologist and angler, between 1925 and 1939 he made more than 700 broadcasts with his own dance orchestra, as well as running other bands in several north-eastern hotels, music halls, and cinemas. Jos was not an abbreviation, but the Q stood for Quarrie.

Howard Baker (1902-1985) — After forming his first band at the age of only 22, he became something of a dance band entrepreneur and, at one point in the mid-1930s, was broadcasting with the Howard Baker Radio Band, in addition to running six other London bands, and a further 15 in the provinces! His nickname, unsurprisingly, was "The Gig King". One of his recordings featured 17-year-old Vera Lynn, whom he personally presented with the original disc of *It's Home*, when she became the subject of the television programme "This Is Your Life". He played his trumpet until 1960 and only gave up band leading in 1967, after an unprecedented 21-year run at the Kursaal, Southend. In between times he played all over the country and, via his highly successful agency, discovered and promoted many famous names, including the Dagenham Girl Pipers. In later years he regularly came out of retirement

▽ *This RAF band, pictured in 1942, was formed by two musical brothers — Alfie Khan (left) on clarinet, and brother Dave (far right) on trumpet. The saxophonist in the centre is Charlie Barlow, who enjoyed a 50-year musical relationship with Blackpool.*

to lead his band at the annual RAF Battle of Britain Ball at London's Grosvenor Hotel.

Kenny Baker (born 1921) — After finding fame as a trumpet soloist with both Ambrose and Ted Heath, Kenny formed his famous Baker's Dozen which seemed to pop up everywhere in the 1950s. He later moved away from variety to pure jazz.

Kenny Ball (born 1930) — After serving an apprenticeship with Sid Phillips and Eric Delaney, he formed his own traditional jazz band in 1958, when dancing became a standard feature of television programmes such as "Six Five Special", "Oh Boy" and "Easy Beat".

Claude Bampton (1908-1969) — Most famous for leading a blind band in 1937 (which included George Shearing on piano), he was disappointed although not surprised that the public did not support it on tour – mainly because the organisers misguidedly insisted on highlighting the musicians' physical defects via the spotlights. His other more conventional band was called the Bandits.

Chris Barber (born 1930) — Forming his first band in 1949, Chris Barber burst on to the popular music scene in the mid-50s, when he did more to popularise traditional jazz then any other British musician. Appearing alongside pop stars on television shows, his bouncy early style had the crowds flocking to theatres throughout the country.

Charlie Barlow (1913-1993) — Initially a saxophone player in Bertini's band at the Blackpool Tower Ballroom, he played in wartime RAF service bands before returning to England's premier seaside resort in 1945, firstly leading a band at the Winter Gardens, then reverting to the Tower where he was nicknamed "The King of Swing". When fire gutted much of the Tower complex in 1956, his band's instruments suffered considerable smoke and water damage, but Charlie managed to rescue his music library by throwing it out of a window! In all he spent no fewer than 46 years with the Blackpool Tower Company, a remarkable record but, in 1976, at the age of 63, he left to take his band on tour and, trooper to the end, continued playing one-night-stands until shortly before his death.

Stanley Barnett — After a residency at Madame Tussaud's Ballroom in the early-30s, he performed at Glasgow and Margate, before returning to London where, like many other bands, he disappeared from view during the war years.

Don Marino Barreto (1908-1995) — A Cuban-born pianist who, after recording *Rhapsody in Blue* as a double-sided solo, was at the forefront of 1930s British Latin-American music with his Cuban Orchestra and Rumba Band, a member of which was the young Edmundo Ros. His son (who sported the same name as his father) continued the tradition after the war.

Carl Barriteau (1914-1998) — Born in Trinidad, he came to England in 1937 at the invitation of Ken "Snakehips" Johnson, and reformed the latter's band after the ill-fated wartime performance at the Café de Paris. A virtuoso clarinet player, Carl continued to lead various jazz-influenced dance groups until the 1950s pop music scene drove him abroad, eventually settling in Australia where he continued to perform up until his death.

Billy Bartholomew — Although British he led a successful international dance and jazz band in Germany between 1926 and 1939, returning home at the outbreak of war. Al Bowlly was the vocalist on several records made in the late Twenties.

Reginald Batten — Succeeded Bert Ralton as leader of the Savoy Havana Band in 1923, and also played with, and occasionally directed, the Savoy Orpheans.

Sydney Baynes (1879-1938) — Most famous for his compositional waltz *Destiny*, Sydney Baynes led a large and popular orchestra which played just about every type of music. Unfortunately, at the height of his fame he died following an appendix operation.

BBC Bands — It was only natural that the fledgling BBC should have its own resident dance orchestra and, in 1926, the London Radio Dance Band was formed at Savoy Hill. Led by violinist Sidney Firman (older brother of John and Bert) the baton was passed on to Jack Payne's BBC Dance Orchestra in 1928 — which was in turn succeeded in 1932 by a youthful Henry Hall. At the outbreak of war, Jack Hylton was asked to form a new Dance Orchestra fronted by his right hand man, Billy Ternent, who, in 1944, handed over to Stanley Black. In 1952 it was succeeded by the BBC Show Band led by Cyril Stapleton who, when it was officially disbanded five years later, turned it into his own orchestra. Meanwhile, various provincial bands had emerged, the most famous of which was the Northern Dance Orchestra led by Alyn Ainsworth, and later popularly known as the NDO under Bernard Hermann. In London there were two parallel bands, the Variety Orchestra led firstly by Rae Jenkins, and

△ *Claude Bampton's All-Blind Band with pianist George Shearing (left).*

later Paul Fenoulhet, and the latter by Frank Cantell, Bob Busby and Harry Rabinowitz. After being merged into the Radio Orchestra in 1964, the band was then jointly-led by Malcolm Lockyer and Paul Fenoulhet, before finally receiving the economic chop in 1990.

George Beaumont — (see Service Bands).

Ivy Benson (1913-1993) — A remarkable personality, Ivy, formerly a saxophonist in Teddy Joyce's all-female band, shot to prominence during the Second World War when her All-Girls' Band was officially appointed to the BBC — an event which caused considerable ill-feeling among many of her male rivals (the exception being Joe Loss), who believed the girls' talent to be inferior. It had to be admitted, however, that her personnel was always changing because it regularly fell prey to male admirers, particularly American servicemen — with marriage the inevitability of the time. Nevertheless, indomitable Ivy, born in Leeds, not only survived the opposition and staffing difficulties, but went on to greater things, tour-

ing with her band well into, what for other people, would have been their retirement years.

Always resplendent in a long evening gown, Ivy managed to keep the band on the road until the 1980s. Her signature tune, *Lady Be Good*, was highly appropriate, because she finished her career as a popular organist in the seaside resort of Clacton in Essex, regularly entertaining until the day she died.

Bertini (1889-1952) — Arguably the biggest band name in the English provinces, rivalled only by Billy Merrin and his Commanders from the Midlands, Bertini (real name Bert Gutsell) was based at Blackpool's Tower Ballroom where he provided high-quality professional entertainment, both for locals and the many thousands of provincial holiday-makers who regularly flocked to Lancashire's most famous seaside resort.

Harry Bidgood (1897-1957) — As a director and arranger of studio bands, he was responsible for hundreds of records between 1925-1936, firstly for Vocalion and then for Crystallate. On stage he went under the colourful name of "Primo Scala". See the chapter on Accordion Bands.

△ *This official BBC postcard shows Sidney Firman conducting the London Radio Dance Band, the predecessor to Jack Payne who took over in 1928.*

Big Ben Banjo Band — Initially a novelty creation by Norrie Paramor, it included such outstanding musicians as Eric Jupp (piano), George Chisholm (trombone), Tommy McQuater (trumpet) and Bert Weedon (guitar) — so it was hardly surprising that it was an instant success. The band made many recordings between 1954 and 1966.

Acker Bilk (born 1929) — Somerset-born Bernard Stanley started out with Ken Colyer in the early-50s traditional jazz boom, before fronting a highly popular band of his own. Trading on his new stage name and West Country accent, Acker Bilk quickly became a star attraction.

George Birch — (see The Stardusters).

John Birmingham (1889-1928) — His band played at the Hotel Cecil and made a few recordings in the mid-Twenties. Sadly he died

tragically by falling from the balcony of his Earls Court flat in London when looking out for some friends he was expecting.

Wally Bishop (1895-1966) — Cardiff-born, he first played for the local Lionel Falkman orchestra before forming his own group called Waldini's Gypsy Band. Touring all over the British Isles on successful one night stands, they also became summer season celebrities in several different seaside resorts, including a seven-year stay at Llandudno, and a four-year stint at Ilfracombe. He never retired and was on tour in Germany when he became terminally ill.

Billy Bissett (born 1906) — Although he only played in England for three years before the Second World War, experienced Canadian band leader Billy Bissett was extremely popular. After visiting America in 1939 the war prevented him from returning to fulfil an engagement at the Café de Paris (later bombed in 1941), and so he stayed put and changed his name to Billy Bishop and his Music from Mayfair. He then became a stockbroker before eventually retiring to California. Married to Jack Hylton's former American singer, Alice Mann.

Black Diamonds Band — The Zonophone studio recording band from 1907-1931, directed in the 1920s by George Byng.

Stanley Black (born 1913) — During his early career he led bands called the Black Hand Gang, and the Modernists, but shot to fame as a prolific composer and arranger who, after several stints as a pianist with bands such as Ambrose, Ray Noble, Lew Stone, Maurice Winnick, and Harry Roy, took over the BBC Dance Orchestra from 1943-1952. During this time he successfully led a rigorous weekly schedule of performances, including backing many famous shows, such as "Ray's a Laugh" and "Much-Binding-in-the-Marsh". He was also an arranger for the Decca record company and wrote more than 100 film scores.

Blue Jays — Harry Hudson's house band on Edison Bell records.

Blue Lyres — An Ambrose band directed mainly by Arthur Lally, which played initially at the Café de Paris and later at both L'Hermitage (formerly the New Princes' Restaurant), and Dorchester Hotel. Its outstanding recordings, however, were actually "ghosted" by the Ambrose orchestra. When Lally became ill at the Dorchester, his place was taken by Peter Rush (died 1972).

▽ *Ivy Benson was a saxophone player who became a band-leading phenomenon, easily outlasting her contemporaries by touring with her all-girls band (right) into the 1980s. She then continued as a solo artiste until the day she died in 1993, aged 79, playing the organ at functions in Essex, where she was a popular attraction, especially among those of older years who remembered her from her prime.*

Blue Mariners — (see chapter on Service Bands).

Blue Mountaineers — A recording band of the early-Thirties led by Joe Brannelly (born 1900), featuring such famous names as Ted Heath, Nat Gonella, Sam Browne, Cavan O'Connor and Phyllis Robins.

Blue Rockets — (see chapter on Service Bands).

Josephine Bradley (1893-1985) — Sometimes described as the female equivalent of Victor Silvester, her largely studio-based orchestra played strict-tempo dance music, specifically to meet public demand. The musicians involved were often loaned from other famous bands, especially Geraldo's, but Josephine's name on the record was all that was needed to sell copies in vast numbers, even when a jazz group was assembled under someone else's direction.

Joe Brannelly — (see Blue Mountaineers).

Larry Brennan (died 1949) — Born in a Yorkshire vicarage and intended for the ministry, he ran away from home at the age of 14 and joined the band of the Seaforth Highlanders! At the end of the Great War he formed his own band and played at several leading London hotels, before plying his wares at the Moulin Rouge in Paris. He then made his way to Sweden via a nine month residency in Berlin. When asked to play for the Swedish Royal Family he was accidentally mistaken for an ambassador and feted with a limousine, royal salute and musical fanfare — until he explained the misunderstanding! Returning to England he became a familiar figure in Blackpool during the 1930s and alternated with Bertini and Norman Newman at the Tower Ballroom.

△ The gigantic shadow of Blackpool Tower was a familiar sight to everyone who flocked to the undisputed Mecca of northern seaside resorts, especially dancers at the Tower and Empress ballrooms. Larry Brennan (above) was a big-pre-war favourite at both venues, as was Bertini (top right), whose main provincial rival was Billy Merrin (bottom right), who hailed from the Midlands.

Freddy Bretherton (1908-1954) — A Lancastrian piano player from Ramsbottom who played and arranged for Sydney Lipton and also fronted bands for both Jack Hylton and Edgar Jackson, eventually ending up as musical director to the Crazy Gang at London's Victoria Palace.

Philip Brown (1895-1955) — Originally in charge of the Midlands-based Dominoes Dance Band, he then worked for the BBC as Controller of Dance Music from 1936 until the end of the Second World War, after which he left to form an agency.

Sandy Brown (1929-1985) — Scottish born Sandy led another of the 1950s traditional jazz bands which had London hopping to its rhythms.

Teddy Brown (1900-46) — Nobody could miss Teddy Brown, all 5ft. 2ins. and 26 stone of him! Born in America as Abraham Himmelbrand, he first appeared in London in 1925 at the Café de Paris, where his band made several recordings. Subsequent records were mainly of his virtuoso xylophone playing. He died after a heart attack while performing on-stage at the Wolverhampton Hippodrome.

Mick Burberry (1899-1998) — A saxophone playing Londoner who, as a young man, used to watch the Original Dixieland Jazz Band at the Hammersmith Palais. He formed his first band on Merseyside, returned to London, and then accepted a job at St. Moritz in Switzerland. Back in London he was offered

△ Bertini's Band, seen here at Blackpool's Tower ballroom, was once virtually a permanent fixture at Lancashire's premier holiday restort.

work by Billy Cotton and stayed for the next 14 years, during which time he claimed he learnt all about cabaret but forgot how to play his musical instrument! He then moved to Edinburgh and finished up as band leader at the prestigious Gleneagles Hotel but — where Henry Hall started it, Mick finished it — because in the 1960s it quickly became obvious that the younger generation no longer welcomed traditional dance band music, and it was time to retire.

Tito Burns (born 1921) — Leader of the Tito Burns Sextet, he was popular after the war with his breezy accordion playing. He worked with both Jimmy Edwards and Frankie Howerd

▷ Teddy Brown and his xylophone

and also toured extensively, eventually moving into theatrical management, at one point looking after Cliff Richard.

George Byng (see Black Diamonds Band).

Café Colette Orchestra — An early-1930s BBC radio band led by Walford Hyden, and purporting to broadcast from a fictitious café in Paris. Suitably continental in style, and often dressed in silk, it played many foreign dances such as the tango, and paso doble.

Eddie Calvert (1922-1978) — "The Man with the Golden Trumpet" first played in northern brass bands before joining Billy Ternent and Geraldo. He then became a celebrity recording artist in the 1950s, with his hit records *O Mein Papa* and *Cherry Pink and Apple Blossom White* turning him into an overnight star. He died young, however, ten years after emigrating to South Africa.

Phil Cardew (1903-1960) — Arranger, clarinet and saxophone player with several bands in the 20s and 30s, including Fred Elizalde, Jack Payne, and Jack Hylton, he became famous as leader of the Band Waggoners, the group which backed Arthur Askey and Richard Murdoch's wartime classic comedy show, "Band Waggon".

Don Carlos — (see Abe Walters).

△ *A highly popular musician, Sydney Baynes died prematurely, at the height of his fame.*

Eddie Carroll (1907-1969) — Pianist and arranger who played with Al Starita, Spike Hughes, Henry Hall, and Lew Stone, he formed his own band in 1935 and played at various London clubs. In 1936 he ran a band for Henry Hall on the maiden voyage of the *Queen Mary* when he unwittingly composed his popular signature tune *Harlem*. — unfortunately without realising he had unconsciously borrowed the melody from American band leader Benny Moten. The case was subsequently settled out of court. Eddie's successful career was almost totally extinguished by the war and, although he later made various attempts to re-form his band, never really got going again, dying alone and penniless, but a gentleman to the end.

Benny Carter (born 1907) — An outstanding and versatile American musician who specialised in the alto-saxophone, but also played trumpet, clarinet and piano. Early on he established himself as an arranger with Fletcher Henderson, Duke Ellington and Benny Goodman, before arriving in England in 1936 where, in addition to being staff arranger for the BBC Dance Orchestra led by Henry Hall, he made several fine recordings with British musicians.

Frank Chacksfield (1914-1995) — After forming his own band in 1936, he became an accomplished Army wartime arranger. When hostilities ceased he was signed up by Decca, and in 1953 earned a gold disc for his theme-tune *Limelight*, which catapulted him to fame and kept him in the public eye for the rest of his prolific recording and performing career.

John Chilton — Author and trumpet player, he led an appropriately named traditional jazz band called the Feetwarmers, who were a popular part of the late 20th century music scene, often backing the singer George Melly.

George Chisholm (1915-1997) — An irrepressible Glasgow-born trombonist who successfully integrated dance band music and true jazz. Among others, he played with Fats Waller, Louis Armstrong, Lew Stone and Ambrose. After becoming a member of the RAF-based Squadronaires band from 1939-1950, he joined the BBC Show Band, where he quickly gained a reputation as a clown, specialising in interrupting dialogue with well-timed musical raspberries. Particularly prominent in the "Black and White Minstrel Show", he continued with his own group, the Gentlemen of Jazz, right up until his demise.

Johnny Claes (1916-1956) — British-born but educated in Europe while accompanying his travel-loving mother. A pupil of Nat Gonella he shone brightly as a young instrumentalist, and set London ablaze during the war years with his hot-tempo band called the Clae Pigeons. After returning home to Belgium he enjoyed a brief career as a racing car driver before dying prematurely from cancer.

Al Collins (1900-1964) — A violinist, Al was born in London, but was taken to America by his piano teacher at the age of only 14. When war broke out he enlisted in the American Navy, and later teamed up with the then unknown solo pianist Billy Mayerl in

▽ *Canadian Billy Bissett made a big impact during his three-year stay in Britain before the war.*

△ *Talented pianist Eddie Carroll never really enjoyed the success he deserved, and died in obscurity.*

Richmond, Virginia. Returning to the UK in 1919 he worked almost exclusively for the Savoy hotel group right through to the end of the last war, on account of which, although still relatively young, he was dubbed "The Oldest Inhabitant", or "The Hermit". After appearing for an afternoon tea dance at either Claridges or the Berkeley, he thought nothing of then turning up for late night dancing at the Savoy itself, priding himself on being able to cater for every type of dance, ancient and modern. A lover of all music, he also played in several different symphony orchestras.

Ken Colyer (1928-1988) — An unashamedly New Orleans post-war jazz band leader who remained firmly loyal to his beliefs in the traditional style. Chris Barber and Acker Bilk both played with him in the early-Fifties.

Frank Cordell (1914-1980) — Later to become a household name as musical director of HMV records, where his studio orchestra backed many top singers, he was an outstanding young jazz pianist. Wartime service in the RAF saw him as leader of the Middle East Command Orchestra in Egypt, and when hostilities ceased he became a top orchestral arranger.

Coventry Hippodrome Orchestra — Renowned for its weekly lunch hour broadcasts throughout the Thirties, firstly under the baton of Charles Shadwell (*q.v.*) and, from 1936 under William (Bill) Pethers. The star performer was invariably pianist Jack Wilson (*q.v.*) and his Versatile Five.

Dr. Crock — (see Harry Hines).

George Crow — (see Service Bands).

Tommy Dallimore — He and his band featured in a live post-war Radio Luxembourg programme hosted by Geoffrey Everitt, in which they were challenged to play a nominated dance tune without music or rehearsal. If they failed, then the challenger won one guinea!

Chappie d'Amato (1897-1976) — A prominent saxophonist, clarinettist, pianist, guitarist and singer with several bands before the war, including Jack Hylton and Jack Jackson. He then became a popular band leader in his own right, often performing at Hatchett's Restaurant in London.

Benny Daniels — (see Service Bands).

▽ *Tito Burns, on accordion (left) leading his Sextet in 1949. The singer is Cab Kaye and the two eventual band leading saxophonists are Ronnie Scott (left) and Johnny Dankworth.*

Joe Daniels (1908-1993) — A childhood prodigy on the drums, he eventually became a showman percussionist with Harry Roy. During a recording rehearsal in the mid-1930s, while waiting for other musicians who were late, he experimented with what became his famous Hot-Shots (including Ted Andrews, father of famous daughter Julie), playing mainly up-tempo music bordering on jazz. One of the few bands to survive after the war, he changed to pure Dixieland when the early-50s trad jazz revival occurred, playing regularly at Butlin's holiday camps between 1957-1974.

Mike Daniels — With his Delta Jazzmen, he faithfully recreated New Orleans jazz from the early part of the 20th century, making good use of a brass bass in his rhythm section. Extremely popular in the Fifties and Sixties.

Johnny Dankworth (born 1927) — A rare jazz talent who began working on Atlantic ocean liners, and played with Tito Burns before forming his own septet in 1950. He soon became a household name and, together with his singer-wife Cleo Laine, remained extremely popular for many years.

Herman Darewski (1883-1947) — Russian-born but British by upbringing, he led his own band from 1927 and for many years was a regular at the Winter Gardens in Blackpool. In 1930 he broke new ground by playing at Bentall's department store in Kingston, attracting 35,000 people in 10 days! He is perhaps better remembered now, however, for his music publishing company which he formed in 1916 after a brief spell with Francis, Day and Hunter. He also left a legacy of many songs and light orchestral pieces, particularly marches.

△ Top — Joe Daniels (drums) and his Hot Shots.
△ Above — Herman Darewski, who was rarely pictured without his hat!
▽ Below — Phil Cardew.

Max Darewski (1894-1929) — A pianist and composer who made several records in the mid-Twenties, before dying prematurely.

Harry Davidson (1892-1967) — Pre-war leader of the Commodore Cinema Orchestra, Hammersmith, he was later synonymous with the radio programme "Those Were the Days", which ran from 1943 to 1966, fronting a large orchestra mainly for old-time dancing. Harry, born at Croydon, Surrey, was a well-trained and versatile professional musician, equally at home on piano or strings. His first broadcast, from Leeds in 1924, began a tradition which lasted for more than 40 years, a time scale rarely matched by others. Every week, couples all around the country tuned in their wireless sets, some of them donning evening dress, as Harry Davidson invited them to "Honour your part-ners" because, in those time-honoured words, "It's time for old time". Whether it was a Viennese waltz, Dinky one-step, Military two-step, Eva three-step, the Veleta, or the Lancers, Harry Davidson will forever be remembered as the foremost proponent of old-time dancing.

Harry Davis (1901-1996) — Long-time conductor of the band belonging to shy Oscar Rabin (*q.v.*), who preferred to stay at the back, hidden by his bass saxophone, leaving Harry, much more of an extrovert, to wield the baton up front. One of the band's singer was Harry's daughter, Beryl.

Syd Dean (1907-1993) — A band leader for more than 50 years, Syd played all over the UK, including the Channel Islands. Although he later adapted his sound to appeal to a younger audience, he decided to retire in the 1960s when the new generation of popular music

△ *Harry Davidson, the doyen of old-time dancing.*

lovers moved rapidly away from melody-based tunes. Nevertheless, he often dusted off the ageing cobwebs to perform at functions in the Brighton area, a part of the country with which he was associated for more than 40 years.

David de Groot (1880-1933) — A popular Dutch violinist and naturalised Briton who led a string orchestra at the Piccadilly Hotel, London, from the early stages of the First World war until 1930. Much of his repertoire was light classical but some was genuine dance band music.

Eric Delaney (born 1924) — After playing briefly with Ambrose during the war, he then worked for both Nat Temple and Geraldo before forming his own band in 1954, not a good time to branch out on one's own. Confounding everyone, however, he centred the band around his own extrovert timpani playing and, using tuned drums, had an immediate hit-record with *Oranges and Lemons*, used for many years by the BBC as the call sign for their Overseas Programme. He subsequently toured with great success, all over the country.

Albert Delroy — An accordionist who first broadcast with Troise and played at several London clubs before joining the wartime RAF. Thereafter he formed his own trio and broad-cast with several orchestras, specialising in Continental music.

William (W.F.) de Mornys (1891-1979) — Although not strictly a professional musician, Belgian-born William de Mornys deserves recognition as the most important dance band

▽ *Geoffrey Everitt (right) challenges Tommy Dallimore and his Band during a Radio Luxembourg show.*

△ Multi instrumentalist and band leader, Chappie d'Amato.
◁ Accordionist Albert Delroy began his career with Troise.

impresario of the 1920s, effectively shaping and ensuring the music's future. Settling in England after the First World War he was responsible for opening several important dance halls, starting with Rectors in Tottenham Court Road, followed by the Birmingham Palais which he converted from an old ice rink, and London's famous Hammersmith Palais, a former roller skating rink and redundant aircraft factory! He then offered to change the prestigious Savoy Hotel ballroom into a public venue, an immensely successful business venture which resulted in the formation of the resident Savoy Havana and Savoy Orpheans bands, both of which he effectively owned — and personally organised. He was responsible for importing several famous names from America, including Rudy Vallee and Carroll Gibbons (*q.v.*), and also "discovered" Ramon Newton, Debroy Somers, and Billy Mayerl. Always with a penchant for the unusual, in 1925 he organised the Orpheans in a live, but very risky radio broadcast from an aeroplane flying over London, when another of his discoveries, Billy Thorburn, almost fell out of the aircraft, together with his piano! De Mornys could best be described as "a leader of band leaders" — a very important influence in the early days of the genre.

Dick Denny — Following nine years leading a band in India, he returned to England in 1936 when he toured the music halls. After the war he played several summer seasons at Butlins.

▽ Shy violinist Al Collins was for many years a highly-respected leader of the dance band at London's Berkeley Hotel (seen right).

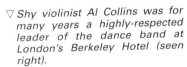

Reginald Dixon (1904-1985) — For more than 50 years "Mr. Blackpool" thrilled dancers and listeners at the Tower Ballroom, dispensing every conceivable type of music and rhythm on the mighty Wurlitzer, often introduced by his inimitable version of *Oh, I Do Like to be Beside the Seaside*. Although an adopted Lancastrian, Reginald hailed from Yorkshire and at the time he compered the radio programme "Housewives Choice" his accent contrasted sharply with other announcers on the BBC. At the height of his fame he was a national institution, and the dance floor was always packed when he was performing. Unsurprisingly, he was awarded the MBE for services to music.

Dan Donovan (1901-1986) — More famous as a singer with various bands, including Debroy Somers and Henry Hall, he actually began by leading a small group in Cardiff, and later formed another band 12 months prior to the war, succeeding Brian Lawrance at the Lansdowne House Restaurant. He reverted to solo singing after hostilities ceased, and took part in several radio broadcasts.

Leslie Douglas (born 1914) — A singer with Henry Hall in the mid-30s, he served in the wartime RAF where he led the Bomber Command Dance Orchestra. When the fighting was over he toured widely abroad, with Pearl Carr as his singer, before returning home to several residencies and radio broadcasts.

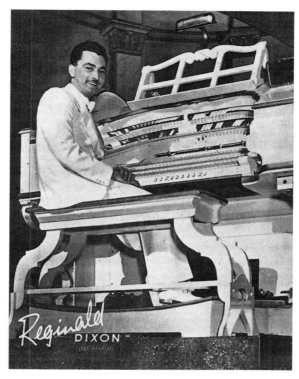

△ *"Mr Blackpool". Reginald Dixon's organ playing at the Blackpool Tower ballroom was a standard feature for dancers over a period of almost 50 years.*

▽ *Eric Delaney confounded all his critics by starting a successful band in the 1950s, a time when other band leaders were handing in their batons.*

△ George Elrick, the "Housewives' Choice".

Rudolph Dunbar (1907-1988) — A native of British Guiana, he appeared in several Broadway revues before coming to England with Lew Leslie's famous musical "Blackbirds". Competent on both saxophone and clarinet, he led his own band called the African Polyphony at Princes' Restaurant, before trying his hand at composing.

Durium Dance Band — Durium was a recording company which produced single-sided cardboard records in the early-Thirties. Among its house-bands were Arthur Lally, Lew Stone, Phil Cardew, Peter Rush, and Sydney Kyte.

David Ede (1926-1965) — In 1951, on the departure to America of Oscar Rabin's front man Harry Davis, young clarinettist David Ede was promoted from within the ranks to succeed him. It proved to be an inspired choice because the band starred at the Lyceum Ballroom in London's Strand until Oscar's death in 1958. A transfer to the Wimbledon Palais lasted until 1965, when impresario Bernard Rabin (Oscar's eldest son) realised the quickly-changing public pop scene required something new. With Bernard's blessing, and as a reward for all his hard work, the Oscar Rabin Band became David Ede and his Band — but not for long, because David was drowned in a boating accident at Blackpool during his first engagement. Trumpet-player Terry Reaney took over for the remainder of the season, following which the band broke up, a sad ending to the final chapter of Oscar Rabin's dance band legacy.

Ray Ellington (1916-1985) — London-born with an American father and Russian mother, he had a vibrant personality, and both sang and played drums for Harry Roy's band. After the war he formed his famous Quartet which played in theatres and clubs all over Britain and Europe. He also made many radio and television broadcasts, notably in the "Goon Show", where his musical and spoken contributions were always memorable.

George Elrick (born 1903) — An early singer and drummer with Henry Hall's BBC Dance Band, George — a native of Aberdeen — briefly borrowed Lew Stone's band before branching out on his own in 1937. After making several recordings he officially retired as a band leader after the war, but his popularity resulted in a number of later studio recordings in the 1950s. His geniality and versatility saw him quickly established as a favourite presenter of "Housewives' Choice", but when he mischievously hummed and sang along to the famous signature tune, *In Party Mood*, without realising the microphone was still switched on, he feared the sack. However, he was surprised to discover that his huge radio audience loved it, and henceforth his jaunty parting refrain "I'll see you all again tomorrow morning", became an integral part of his daily routine.

Alan Elsdon — Another popular post-war traditional jazz band leader who continued playing through towards the end of the millennium.

George Evans (1915-1993) — Much sought-after for recording sessions as a tenor-saxophone player and vocalist, he worked with Lou Preager, Nat Gonella, Sydney Lipton, Benny Carter, and Geraldo, the latter also as a successful arranger. In 1945 he formed a unique but relatively short-lived big band with ten saxophones and five trumpets. A lengthy spell of ill-health and immobility interrupted events but in 1949 he took to the road once more, enjoying considerable success until his first retirement in 1959. When his wife died in 1982 he again returned to music making and to celebrate his 70th birthday formed a huge band with no fewer than 11 saxes, 10 brass, four rhythm and three vocalists, which performed several concerts during the next 18 months.

Tolchard Evans (1901-1978) — A famous songwriter who, early in life, also led his own bands, notably in Southend where the rhythm of the train along the mile-long pier inspired him to write *Lady of Spain*. Among his many other successes was Maurice Winnick's first signature tune *Lend Me Your Ears*.

Digby Fairweather — An active post-war trad. jazz trumpeter, band leader and broadcaster who did much to keep the dance band genre alive on the media.

Lionel Falkman (1903-1963) — With musical talent inherited from his Russian ancestry, young Lionel won several Eisteddfod prizes as a violinist and by the age of 12 was leading a musical hall orchestra in Abertillery. Moving to London in 1919 he played in top symphony orchestras before retracing his steps to the Welsh border two years later when he founded the Newport College of Music. In 1921 he became the first cinema orchestra leader to broadcast anywhere in the country, appropriately from the Capitol in Cardiff. After a spell in Manchester, in 1937 he moved to the Lyons Corner House in London's Oxford Street, where he formed his famous Apache Band, making more than 140 appearances on "Music While You Work". His violin was a 200-year-old Italian instrument, donated anonymously by a lady in a Rolls Royce who appeared one day at the theatre, handed it to a stage doorman and promptly departed!

Harry Farmer — Led a wartime group in the Royal Armoured Corps featuring his electric organ which had to be transported around on a heavy truck! Post-war, his catchy dance rhythms were extremely popular and he recorded under his own name and also as Chris Hamalton and his Hammond Organ.

Robert Farnon (born 1917) — (see chapter on Service Bands) — A Canadian who came to England during the war and led his country's element of the AEF band (with Glenn Miller and George Melachrino running the American and British elements respectively). A world class arranger and composer, who eventually settled in Guernsey.

△ *Like both Billy Cotton, and Johnny Claes, Buddy Featherstonhaugh enjoyed racing cars!*

Buddy Featherstonhaugh (1909-1976) — Band leader, tenor saxophone player and motor racing star! After playing for Ronnie Munro, Jack Jackson, Carroll Gibbons, Spike Hughes, Jay Wilbur, Bert Firman, and Rudy Starita, he formed his own 1935 group called the Cosmopolitans. He also recorded pre-war with Benny Carter and Stanley Black before joining the RAF and fronting his Radio Rhythm Club Sextet, a group which recorded for HMV and included both Vic Lewis and Jack Parnell among its personnel.

Paul Fenoulhet (1906-1979) — (see chapter on Service Bands) — In the 1920s he led his own band called the Metro Five, but then played trombone and trumpet with Arthur Rosebery, Percival Mackey, Jack Hylton and Carroll Gibbons. During the war he led the famous RAF band called the Skyrockets, eventually taking them successfully into the theatre pit of the London Palladium. In 1947 he formed his own orchestra and toured until 1950, when he took over the reins of the BBC Variety Orchestra, staying with the Corporation for a further 20 years.

◁ *Two wartime band leaders. Robert Farnon (left) and Leslie Douglas, both of whom continued active music-making after hostilities ceased. Farnon, a Canadian, who settled in Guernsey, had a prolific orchestral output.*

George "Miff" Ferrie — Leader of the singing trio called the Jakdauz (with George Crow and Harry Parry — both *q.v.*), which performed with Jack Jackson at the Dorchester Hotel. Proficient on several instruments, he also played trombone with Stanelli, Roy Fox and Teddy Joyce, before forming his own band in the mid-Thirties. For several years after the war he led a band called the Ferrymen.

Peter Fielding (born 1907) — An Italian whose real name was Antonio Volpi, he ran away from home at the age of 11 and toured in several revues, including the "Mumming Birds" with Charlie Chaplin and Stan Laurel. Once in England he was advised to change his name, so he went out and looked at the two nearest adverts which said "Buy Peter's Chocolates" and "Fielding's Glass and China Stall". He never looked back and created his reputation via a long residency at the Oxford Galleries in Newcastle upon Tyne, interspersed with broadcasting from Edinburgh and the Midlands, and summer seasons at seaside resorts such as Eastbourne and Morecambe.

Len Fillis (1903-1953) — An excellent South African-born guitarist who made hundreds of records under no fewer than 30 different pseudonyms. He appeared with Fred Elizalde, Rudy Starita, Jack Hylton and Van Phillips, before fronting his own groups, including the Radio Rhythm Rascals.

Vic Filmer (1894-1973) — A real veteran, who led a touring band in the late 1920s and also doubled as a musical director. He moved to

Guernsey in 1938, but unfortunately lost everything when he was forced to flee the invading Germans soon afterwards, eventually ending up playing at Blackpool's Tower Ballroom. He continued band leading after the war and toured the world before finally returning to England in 1962.

Firman Brothers — The original musical Feureman family came from central Europe, but emigrated to London in the 1880s where their four famous sons changed their surname. **Bert** (1906-1999), and **John** (1904-74) made hundreds of records between them from 1924-1937. For commercial reasons, however, many were disguised under a variety of different pseudonyms, including the Arcadians, Eugene Brockman, Hal Christie, Newton Carlisle, Eddie Norman, the Rhythmic Eight, Midnight Follies, and even the Jazz Band del Gramofon! Bert eventually became the last surviving pre-war band leader from London's West End and, being a favourite of the Prince of Wales (later Edward VIII), had many interesting stories to tell. On one occasion, after playing at a royal garden party, he was given a 5am tour of Buckingham Palace where he chanced upon a somewhat bemused King George V wearing his nightshirt! **Sidney** (1896-1932), a violinist and leader of the London Radio Dance Band (*q.v.*), died prematurely, as did the oldest brother **Sammy** (1894-1941), a lead violinist at the Empire Theatre, Leicester Square.

George Fisher — Under his real name of George Fishberg he played piano with Art Hickman's New York London Five, and Teddy Brown at the Café de Paris, but changed it when he took his own band into the Kit-Cat Club in

▽ *The Jackdauz, who sang with Jack Jackson, all became band leaders themselves. Left to right: Miff Ferrie, Harry Parry and George Crow.*

1928. Post-war he was the piano accompanist to Marlene Dietrich during her world tours.

Michael Flome (1908-1944) — As an appropriate signature tune he chose *Midnight in Mayfair*, the time of day when he could be heard broadcasting from the hotel during an 18 month stay just before the war. He then joined the RAMC and toured with "Stars in Battledress", but was sadly killed when the Army lorry in which he was travelling over-turned in an accident.

Teddy Foster (1908-84) — A trumpet player who began his career in 1929 by leading a provincial band called the Collegians, after which he toured with Billy Cotton before forming a jazz oriented group called the Kings of Swing. Surprisingly, he continued as a band leader until 1960 when he became a theatrical manager.

Forces Bands — (see chapter on Service Bands).

Reginald Foresythe (1907-1958) — West Indian-born, he came to England in the 1920s and formed a studio band to record some of his many fine compositions. He then led a band at the Café de Paris before serving as an RAF intelligence officer during the war. He toured Europe after hostilities ceased, and was still active playing the piano when he died prematurely at his London home.

Dave Frost (1901-1989) — Originally a club pianist, he went on to play with both Alfredo and Jack Payne, before leading his own sextet at the Café de Paris and Café Anglais in the early Thirties. He then led the New Cumberland Dance Orchestra before emigrating to Australia after the war,. He continued to make music "down under" and, after a brief spell in Fiji, eventually retired to New Zealand.

△ *(Top) Drummer and vocalist Ray Ellington, also found fame performing in the "Goon Show".*

△ *(Above) Bert Firman, who died in 1999 — the last surviving pre-war West End band leader.*

◁ *(Far left) Peter Fielding, an Italian whose real name was Antonio Volpi, led a band in Newcastle.*

◁ *(Left) South African Len Fillis first appeared in this country with Fred Elizalde's orchestra.*

Michael Flome   Reginald Foresythe   Teddy Foster   Dave Frost

Harry Fryer (1896-1946) — Mainly a theatre and cinema orchestra band leader, Harry Fryer broadcast regularly from the Chiswick Empire and also appeared on the popular radio programme "Music While You Work". His appropriate signature tune was *I'm Just Wild About Harry*.

Wally Fryer — Not a regular band leader but more of a dance teacher whose Perfect Tempo Dance Orchestra made a number of records in the 1950s.

Freddy Gardner (1910-1950) — Although he recorded relatively few titles under his own name, mainly but not entirely while on wartime leave from the Royal Navy where he was a key component of the Blue Mariners band, Freddy Gardner — a self-taught expert on every type of saxophone — made nearly 2,000 different recordings. Appearing with numerous bands, including most of the top names, he was regarded as a colossus of the

dance band era and his early death, caused by a brain haemorrhage, was a great shock to fans and fellow musicians alike.

Ronnie Genarder (1910-1973) — A broken leg put paid to his career as a Scottish professional footballer, so he became a band leader instead! Starting off in Aberdeen he then moved to London, and played and sang with Joe Loss, Roy Fox, and Jack Payne. After the war, he became the kilted laird in Sid Millward's famous Nitwits, performing alternately in Paris and Las Vegas. Sid was frequently ill, however, and Ronnie used to deputise as leader, eventually taking over completely when Sid died in 1972. Sadly, Ronnie himself died a short time afterwards.

Billy Gerhardi — A cousin of Al Bowlly, and a native of South Africa, his real name was William Hardy, and he first came to England to play with the Ragpickers, opposite the famous Original Dixieland Jazz Band at the Hammersmith Palais in 1919. He soon formed his own band and enjoyed several London West End residencies, including the Piccadilly Hotel, as well as undertaking a number of successful tours.

Melville Gideon (1884-1933) — Another American import who became a member of the famous Co-Optimists concert party. In 1931 he was asked to form an all-star band for the opening of the prestigious Dorchester Hotel, where he stayed for six months, enjoying prime time radio broadcasts in the process.

Howard Godfrey (1903-1992) — A member of the famous musical Godfrey family, he spent 14 years at the Waldorf Hotel, only leaving to join the war effort via the RAF in 1940. His band was usually known as the Aldwych Players, or Waldorfians.

◁ *Freddy Gardner's early death at the age of only 39 robbed the music scene of a saxophone genius.*

△ *South African violinist Billy Gerhardi, was a cousin of the crooner Al Bowlly.*

Harry Gold (born 1907) — A highly experienced professional musician who played with many pre-war bands including Tolchard Evans, Roy Fox, Bert Firman, and Oscar Rabin. It was with the latter during the war that he put together his cleverly named Dixieland-style band, the "Pieces of Eight", which featured future band leaders Norrie Paramor on piano, Geoff Love on trombone, and Ron Goodwin on trumpet — quite a treasure trove! It was an immediate success and, with a few changes in personnel, its founder continued to perform with it well into old age. Only a mere 5 ft 2 ins, Harry was little bigger than his bass saxophone!

Ron Goodwin (born 1925) — A prolific composer, he formed his first dance band at the age of only 15, then turned professional and enjoyed a glittering musical career. Replacing Jan Ralfini at the Court Ballroom, Balham, in 1947, his strict-tempo orchestra soon gave way to light music arrangements and compositions, becoming widely known via the broadcasting media.

The Grahamophones — Formed in the mid-1980s by leader Graham Dalby, this nostalgia band of young musicians successfully recreated the 1930s heyday of the British dance band era.

Cyril Grantham (born 1910) — A popular pre-war singer with several bands, he served with distinction in the Royal Navy before rejoining Sydney Lipton and Geraldo as a singer and sax player. In 1950 he formed his own band and was resident at the Dorchester Hotel for ten years.

Stephane Grappelli (1908-1997) — This legendary French-born swing violinist came to England in the late-Thirties together with jazz guitarist Django Reinhardt, and played with Benny Carter, Coleman Hawkins, and Fats Waller. Unfortunately, war caused Django to scuttle back quickly to his beloved France, but Stephane stayed on in Britain and made a name playing in London's West End clubs during the Blitz. He later appeared with Glenn Miller's band and also toured with the blind pianist George Shearing. Popular wherever he went, Stephane went on to front many and varied groups, steadfastly refusing to entertain the idea of retirement and ending his playing days in a wheelchair shortly before his death.

Johnnie Gray (born 1920) — It was hard to miss this large man with a handlebar moustache. He played saxophone and sang with Lou Preager, Frank Weir, Hatchett's Quintet, Ted Heath and Sydney Lipton, before forming his own band in 1952. Initially London-based, his Band of the Day embarked on extensive tours and also played on the ocean liner *Queen Mary*.

Alan Green (1895-1956) — An extrovert who toured with considerable success in the 1920s when he appeared in London and all over the provinces. During the 1930s he spent most summer seasons in Hastings, with winter spots at such famous West End venues as the Dorchester, Grosvenor House, and Claridges. During the war he appeared regularly at the Brighton Dome and, when hostilities ceased, in various places including three seasons at Butlin's in Skegness. In a career which spanned five decades, he continued playing until ill-health forced him to retire in 1953.

▽ *Ron Goodwin eventually became a highly successful light music composer*

Phil Green (1911-1982) — After entering Trinity College of Music at the age of only 14, within two years he was appointed musical director of the Prince of Wales Theatre and in 1935 began a long recording career with Decca and EMI, during which time he was involved with every type of band from small ensemble to full concert orchestra. As a composer, arranger and conductor, he regularly encompassed radio, television, films and advertising jingles. A musical adviser to Rank Studios, he scored more than 200 films.

Stan Greening (1888-1971) — A guitarist who organised a vast number of recordings during the 20s and early 30s, many under the title Greening's Dance Orchestra,

Johnny Gregory (born 1928) — He first played in his father's band which was resident at what was left of a bombed-out restaurant in Leicester Square, but in the 1950s he branched out on his own, specifically with a Latin American flavour. His recording pseudonyms included Chaquito, Nino Rico, and the Cascading Strings.

Eddie Grossbart (1900-1985) — Another American import in 1920 who later led his own band at several London night spots and restaurants, including the Ambassador, Café Anglais, and Café de Paris, eventually buying the club in which he was playing.

Jack Harris (1901-1976) — An American who arrived in London in 1927 and made many stylish recordings. By 1939 he was leading a band at the London Palladium which the *Melody Maker* described as the finest in England. When war broke out, however, he went back to the USA, never to return.

Jimmy Harris (1908-1986) — Born in Sheffield and extremely competent as a young pianist, he played with various pre-war bands and formed his own orchestra in 1945, opening at the Kingston Ballroom in Portsmouth. He soon attracted attention from the BBC and broadcast in "Saturday Night at the Palais". In 1949 he moved to the Royal Court Hotel, Southampton and, after a further 18 months, became resident at the Solent Hotel, Southsea.

Jack Hart (1910-1973) — While still only 21, and for his first band, he tried to "borrow" the name Savoy Orpheans, but the Savoy Hotel heard about it and stopped him, quickly reviving it themselves under Carroll Gibbons. For three years he then played at the Royal Mount Hotel before setting out on tour with Hughie Green's youthful troupe of entertainers in 1934. Like many others, however, he gradually faded from the limelight during the war.

Fred Hartley (1905-1980) — Hailing from Dundee, he was a fine solo pianist before he reached his majority, first broadcasting at the age of only 19. After playing in Jack Hylton's original Kit-Cat band he formed his own famous Quintet in 1931 (later a Sextet and Septet) and, built around his rhythmical piano playing, gained a huge radio following. He later became BBC's Head of Light Music.

Harry Hayes (born 1908) — An alto saxophonist who played in many top pre-war groups, and made history in 1941 by performing for three different bands (George Evans, Geraldo and Johnny Claes), during the same international Jazz Jamboree. He formed his own recording group in 1945 and played at several London West End venues during the next two years. He then joined Ambrose but, after losing top spot to Johnny Dankworth in the *Melody Maker* top saxophone player poll in 1949, left to concentrate mainly on his music and record shops. He later re-formed his band, however, and between 1957 and 1965, played at both the Haymarket Theatre and Winston's Club in Bond Street.

Ted Heath (1900-1969) A fine trombonist who, after cutting his teeth with Jack Hylton, Bert Firman, Ambrose, Sydney Lipton and Geraldo, formed his own orchestra during the war. Loosely modelled on Glenn Miller, the band became famous throughout the land, and also in America, partly via radio appearances but also through touring concerts. He had a hit record in the mid-50s with *Swinging Shepherd Blues* and

△ *Jack Harris wanted to return from America to England during the war, but was unable to secure a passage.*

the band played successfully right up until his death. Among his well-known vocalists were Dickie Valentine, Lita Rosa and Dennis Lotis.

Fred Hedley (born 1906) — Unusually for a well-respected band leader, he refused to turn fully professional, despite appearing regularly at most top venues in the London area, including the Hammersmith, Wimbledon and Ilford Palais; the Savoy, Dorchester, Mayfair, and Grosvenor House hotels; and many other ballrooms all over the south of England. The measure of his quality meant that his band always broadcast without the need to import any professional sidesmen, many members later graduating to their ranks anyway. When he finally retired in 1980 many of Fred's loyal team had been with him for more than 20 years.

▽ *Ted Heath's post-war band was famous throughout both Britain and America.*

△ *The legendary Heralds of Swing. Back Row (left to right) Bert Barnes, Tommy McQuater, George Firestone, Dave Shand, George Chisholm, Norman Maloney. Front Row (left to right) Tiny Winters, Benny Winestone, Sid Colin, Archie Craig.*

Heralds of Swing — An outstanding but short-lived pre-Second World War group featuring, among others, George Chisholm, Tommy McQuater, Tiny Winters, and Dave Shand.

Bobbie Hind (1888-1950) — The first dance band to play on the London stage and the first to appear in a Royal Variety Performance, at the London Coliseum in 1923. During the war he entertained with ENSA and continued with summer seasons after hostilities ended.

Harry Hines (1911-1971) — Another instrumentalist turned band leader — but with a big difference. In 1947 he formed a comedy group called Dr. Crock and his Crackpots, playing zany music similar to Sid Millward and his Nitwits (*q.v.*). Taking the part of a pathetic looking clown, Harry led it with great professionalism, a clever part of the act being taken by down-trodden midget Charlie Rossi (Little Charlie) who pulled funny faces and tried to perform solos — but was always restrained from doing so by other members of the band.

Jerry Hoey (1895-1979) — He began as leader at the Piccadilly Grill Room in 1929 and stayed there, without a contract, until war intervened. Featuring a performance called Piccadilly Playtime, he then toured with ENSA, and carried on playing the halls until 1949.

Stanley Holt — (see 2LO Orchestra).

Jack Howard — An American tenor sax player who came to London with Art Hickman's New York London Five in October 1920. He soon formed his own group, and by the mid-Twenties was enjoying late night radio broadcasts, as well as attracting 12,000 dancers a week to the Olympia Ballroom at Earl's Court — quite a feat! He also played at Covent Garden, but disappeared in 1927 after a summer season at Douglas, on the Isle of Man.

▽ *Fred Hartley and his Quintet, a ubiquitous feature of the 1930s musical landscape.*

Johnny Howard — He led a band which included a variety of popular modern tunes, before reverting to strict tempo music.

Bobby Howell (1900-1962) — Leading mainly a variety orchestra, which also played jazz and classical music, he broadcast on radio and accompanied many famous stars in the 1930s.

Harry Hudson (1898-1969) — Latterly more famous as the pianist in Wilfred Pickles's radio show "Have a Go", Hudson recorded an enormous amount of dance music under more than 20 different names, including the Blue Jays, Deauville Dance Band, Radio Melody Boys, Beltona Methodists, Scala Dance Band, and the Palm Beach Players.

Spike Hughes (1908-1987) — Although almost entirely a studio recording band, Patrick "Spike" Hughes made a major contribution to the early swing era between 1930-33. He later became a respected music critic.

Leslie 'Jiver' Hutchinson (1906-1959) — Came to London from Jamaica to join Ken 'Snakehips' Johnson in 1936, and was with him during the wartime Café de Paris bomb explosion. He then played with Geraldo, Lew Stone, Ambrose, and Sid Phillips, before forming his own touring band. Not to be confused with the pianist and entertainer of the same name, better known as "Hutch".

Walford Hyden — (see Café Colette Orchestra)

Mrs. Jack Hylton (1894-1957) — Between 1933 and 1937, Jack Hylton's ex-wife Ennis (née Parkes), ran her own band which recorded for Crown, the cheap Woolworth label. When she retired through ill-health, Billy Ternent, her husband's talented deputy, took over the reins.

Roberto Inglez (1919-1978) — A Scot, whose real name was Bob Ingle, but playing piano for Edmundo Ros caused him to make a slight, but significant, alteration to it! Much of his early post-war band leading career was spent at the Savoy Hotel, before a lucrative offer tempted him to tour South America. He was so impressed with the continent that he made it his home, eventually dying in Chile.

Howard Jacobs (1900-1977) — Yet another American import who, between 1922 and 1938, played at several posh London hotels, including the Savoy, Berkeley, Carlton, and Claridges. Initially with the Savoy Havana Band, he eventually became leader of the Savoy Orpheans and, in 1931, persuaded Carroll Gibbons to return to England from Hollywood to assist him. Gibbons eventually took over as leader, and Jacobs moved on to the Café Anglais and Café de Paris. In 1936 he went "down under" and formed a dance band for Australian radio, but was quickly forgotten during his 12 months absence, so returned home to the USA where he changed his name to Howard Jones.

Arthur Jacobson (1895-1988) — Born in Newcastle upon Tyne he was taken to America as a child, but returned to the north east of England after the Great War, running various bands before moving south to play at Lyon's Corner House in London's West End. He recorded several times as a vocalist and fronted the resident orchestra at the Floral Hall, Southport, from 1935-1949.

▷ *Mrs. Jack Hylton and Her Boys.*

Edgar Jackson (1895-1967) — Real name Edgar Cohen, he was the founder and first editor of *The Melody Maker* and a respected music critic who managed bands for both Jack Hylton and Howard Jacobs. He also found time to lead a band at the Gargoyle Club in London, and at the Spiders Web at Bushey in Hertfordshire, recording several tracks in 1932.

Max Jaffa (1911-1991) — Prior to finding fame as leader of the BBC Palm Court Orchestra — which broadcast from the fictitious "Grand Hotel" in a London studio — Max Jaffa played pre-war with Jack Harris. He then led his own post-war dance bands at Lyon's

△ *Howard Jacobs was originally a well-known band leader but, surprisingly, became a forgotten figure after touring Australia in 1936.*

Corner House, the Trocadero, Piccadilly Hotel and Ciro's Club until switching musical styles in 1950. He was also famous for his legendary trio, with himself on violin, Reginald Kilbey on cello and Jack Byfield on piano. Such was his musical status that he was awarded the OBE in 1982.

Leslie Jefferies (1898-1960) — An early post-First World War dance band leader, who moved from Edinburgh to the Rialto Ballroom in London during the mid-Twenties. He then

◁ *Far left — Harry Hudson*

◁ *Centre — Spike Hughes*

◁ *Left — Edgar Jackson*

recorded numerous titles under no fewer than 50 different pseudonyms, before finally turning his hand to more serious music, broadcasting regularly from the Grand Hotel, Eastbourne.

Sydney Jerome — First broadcast as a piano accompanist from 2LO in the early Twenties. He then formed his own band in 1926, which went on to the airwaves four year later. Latterly he became a musical director for both Jack Hylton and Arthur Askey, and also appeared with Stanelli in his radio comedy programmes.

Ken "Snakehips" Johnson (1911-41) — A native of British Guiana, the highly-educated Johnson fronted an all-coloured band playing mainly swing music. His swift, dramatic and untimely end, however, came just as he was making a name for himself when, during an air raid on 8th March, 1941, a direct hit destroyed the Café de Paris during a live performance, killing him, his tenor-sax player, Dave Williams, and more than 30 members of the audience. The club was situated near the Rialto cinema in Coventry Street, Piccadilly, and like many other basement buildings was thought to be fairly bomb-proof. In reality, however, there were only two ceilings between it and the sky but, had a supporting bomb exploded instead of just breaking apart, then the destruction would have been even more severe.

Laurie Johnson (born 1927) — One of the finest orchestral arrangers in the country, who began his career with Ambrose. He then fronted his own band before moving on to work in television where he orchestrated many famous scores, including "The Avengers". Latterly he formed another big band which made several recordings.

Archibald Joyce (1873-1963) — Known as "The English Waltz King" or "The English Waldteufel" he was one of the first genuine British dance bands. Extremely well-known before the First World War, he played at all big society functions, and was also patronised by Royalty, on one occasion finding himself being accompanied on his piano by two small boys, one at each end — the future Kings, Edward VIII and George VI. He recorded from 1912 onwards, but did not adapt very well to the new post-war craze of more syncopated jazz rhythms, unlike his contemporary light music composer Albert Ketèlbey. He still remained popular on the dance floor for many years, however, and his most famous piece, *Dreaming*, is one of those tunes which everybody recognises but nobody can put a name to.

Teddy Joyce (1904-1941) — Nicknamed "The Stick of Dynamite" because of his boundless energy and enthusiasm, he was a Canadian import who fronted a successful band at the Kit-Cat restaurant in the mid-1930s but, while on-stage in Glasgow during the war, collapsed and died from a brain haemorrhage at the age of only 37.

Eric Jupp (born 1922) — A native of Brighton in Sussex, he formed his first band when only 15 years old. After wartime service in the RAF, he worked with Ronnie Munro, Oscar Rabin, Ambrose, and Cyril Stapleton, before again forming his own orchestra. He then moved to Australia in 1960, where he continued active music-making for more than three decades.

Alan Kane (1913-1996) — Born the son of a Jewish cantor in London's East End, Arthur Keizelman became a drummer-vocalist called Alan Kaye, but was then renamed again, by Lew Stone, the first of the 38 bands he sang with between 1933 and 1950. He then branched out with his own band, pursuing an active career in London clubs and summer holiday camps, especially Skegness, the final 23 years being at the Wellington Club, Knightsbridge, from where he retired in 1983.

Joe Kaye — Violinist-leader at London's Ritz ballroom, until it closed in 1938, following

▷ *Far Right — Teddy Joyce*

▷ *Centre — Sydney Jerome*

▷ *Right — Leslie Jefferies*

△ Walford Hyden's Café Colette Orchestra purported to play in Paris but actually broadcast from a London studio.

△ Reginald King and his orchestra, at the Floral Hall, Bridlington.

which he moved to Paris where he was boycotted by French musicians and forced to return to England.

Johnny Keating — Played with the Ted Heath band before becoming its chief arranger. He then had his own recording band, and also conducted the London Symphony and Royal Philharmonic Orchestras in his own compositions. A well-known arranger for television.

Albert Ketèlbey (1875-1959) — Better known as a light music composer he also made several dance band records between 1912 and the early 1920s, many of them as director of the Regal Dance Orchestra. Although classically trained, he adapted well to changing fashions and many of his compositions remained popular on the dance floor until the Second World War.

Felix King (1912-1982) — He began his career at the Grand Hotel, Eastbourne, before moving to London in 1932. He later took his band on tour to Norway and Italy, only escaping from the latter six days before war broke out. After wartime service in the RAF, and using his own composition *The Night and the Nightingale* as his signature tune, he appeared post-war at the Nightingale Club in Berkeley Square, and broadcast regularly on "Music While You Work".

Reginald King (1904-1991) — A well-known light music pianist whose groups also played popular dance tunes, both pre- and post-war.

Tommy Kinsman (1901-1984) — Another versatile band leader who could play several instruments, and first came to prominence in 1928 with his London Frivolities Band, from

Weston-super-Mare! Later recordings included pseudonyms such as Eddie Harding and his Night Club Boys, the Florida Band, the Ballroom Monarchs, and the Fifteen Crimson Dominoes!

Ivor Kirchin (born 1905) — Among his early discoveries were Geraldo and Maurice Winnick, and later, Steve Race. After starting as a 16-year-old band leader in London, he quickly relocated to Blackpool, before moving to Manchester where he joined the Mecca company who retained his services until he retired in 1967, almost 40 years later! During that time he travelled all over the country, from Belfast to Brighton, and Edinburgh to Eastbourne, playing for several generations of dancers along the way. Of his many London venues the most memorable was a wartime performance at the Covent Garden Opera House, when a bomb blew the roof off in mid-performance! He then returned to the comparative safety of the Paramount Dance Hall in Tottenham Court Road which, being situated underneath the cinema, was one of many perceived similar "safe" venues for patrons who danced the night away while air raids continued overhead.

Basil Kirchin (born 1929) — Ivor's son who continued in his father's footsteps. Both drummers, they made sure that the Kirchin sound was heard across the country from the Thirties through till the Sixties. After playing with Teddy Foster, Jack Nathan, and Ted Heath, Basil teamed up with his father to lead the "Biggest Little Big Band in the World". He later toured extensively at home and throughout Europe.

John Kirkham — A pre-war and post-war favourite at the Palace Ballroom, Douglas, Isle of Man, he spent much of the intervening period either at the Tower Ballroom, Blackpool, or touring the north of England.

Kit-Cat Band — This was largely synonymous with Al Starita's band, although others also used the name when they played at the Kit-Cat Club.

Arthur Lally (1901-1940) — For many years a saxophonist with Ambrose, Lally directed a large number of recordings between 1929-1932, many under other names, including Fenton's Rainbows, the Million-Airs, Rhythm Maniacs and Savana Players. He also led bands at the Café de Paris, and at both the Savoy and Dorchester Hotels. An increasingly hectic lifestyle began to take its toll on his health, however, and when the War Office refused him permission to personally fly a bomb-laden plane to kill Hitler at Berchtesgarden, he took his own life.

Harry Landau (1909-1992) — Starting out as a drummer in the Boys' Brigade he moved on to professional band leading and, via his friendship with Syd Roy, was in charge of musical proceedings at the 1935 Mayfair Hotel reception when brother Harry married Princess Pearl of Sarawak. He later twice-led Syd and Harry's Lyricals band, and also fronted his own group at the Pier Ballroom, Eastbourne, from 1947-1952. In between times he played with

△ *Felix King began his career at the famous Grand Hotel, Eastbourne.*

several famous names, including Sydney Lipton, Jack Jackson, Teddy Foster, and George Elrick — as well as enlisting with "Geraldo's Navy" when he led a band on the Canadian Pacific liner *Empress of Canada*.

Brian Lawrance (1908-83) — Arriving from Australia in 1927, he quickly made his mark as a fine singer with Fred Hartley's Quintet, before fronting his own band in London between 1935-40, initially at the

▽ *A unique photograph of eight famous band leaders playing together. Back row (left to right): Bert Ambrose, Joe Loss, Maurice Winnick, Sydney Lipton (violins). Front row (left to right): Roy Fox (trumpet), Harry Roy (clarinet), Billy Ternent (saxophone), Lew Stone (piano).*

△ *Alan Kane's real name was Arthur Keizelman.*

Showboat on the River Thames. As a violinist, he guested with George Scott-Wood's Six Swingers, and also sang with Carroll Gibbons. His new-found fame did not go unnoticed elsewhere, however, and in 1941 he was invited to return home to take up residence at a newly-opened night club in Sydney. The pull of the warmer Antipodes over grey, war-torn England was just too great and, after a 13-day trip by flying boat, he arrived back "down-under" where he remained an active musician until his death.

Syd Lawrence (1923-1998) — A trumpet-playing former member of the wartime Middle East Command Dance Orchestra, and the post-war BBC Northern Dance Orchestra. In between times he also played for Teddy Foster, Sydney Lipton, Ken Mackintosh, and Geraldo, before forming his own band in 1967. Similar in style to Glenn Miller, it quickly gained a huge following and, so well-known had it become, that it retained his name when ill-health forced him to stand down a few months before his death.

Dare Lea (died c. 1946) — Something of an enigma. Little is known about this band leader who flared brightly and then, after an accident with a "live" microphone, ceased his musical activities altogether. As his name is also an anagram of "a leader", and he was previously an actor, could it have been someone else in disguise? What is certain, however, is that he went straight to the top in 1934, his picture appear-

ing in musical magazines alongside all the other top band leaders resident in London's West End.

Jimmy Leach (1905-1975) — A pianist and organist who made 1930s recordings with Jack Wilson, and then went on to become famous with the Northern Dance Orchestra (*q.v.*), and his own group called the Organolians, often broadcasting on the radio.

Harry Leader (1906-1987) — A successful, and aptly-named band leader for over 40 years, although his real name was Henry Lebys, a fact which he kept secret, together with his age, right up until his death. During his long career, he helped and encouraged many budding musicians and singers to climb the ladder of fame, including Freddy Gardner, Chick Henderson, Matt Monro and Steve Race. For his first broadcast in 1933 he chose *I'm Just Wild About Harry* as his signature tune, but in 1943 changed it to *Music, Maestro, Please* — with its perfect chorus line "Please Mr. Leader, play that lilting melody". After performing at the Charing Cross Astoria for nearly 15 years, he went on tour from 1955-67, after which he retired to composing and teaching.

Jack Leon (1906-1967) — A recording band leader who made several tracks in the Thirties, and ended his career as conductor of the Scottish Variety Orchestra.

Louis Levy (1893-1957) — As both a composer-arranger, and director of the Gaumont-British Symphony Orchestra, Louis Levy's name is credited on countless numbers of films in the

▽ *Dare Lea's flame burned brightly in 1934 but was quickly extinguished by an accident with a live microphone.*

1930s and 40s. He also led the Gaumont-British Dance Band, with whom he made many recordings.

Philip Lewis (1892-1931) — A musical director of Decca, but his named bands were actually directed by Arthur Lally.

Vic Lewis (born 1919) — After forming a wartime joint jazz group with Jack Parnell, Vic Lewis fronted a big band modelled on Stan Kenton, which was active until the mid-Fifties when financial constraints forced him to reduce its personnel. Thereafter he concentrated on smaller groups before withdrawing from the circuit in 1960. He did reappear for later studio recordings, however.

Terry Lightfoot (born 1935) — Forming his first band in 1955, he was in the vanguard of the traditional jazz revival, which had young people dancing new steps all over the country. He continued band leading, on and off, right up to the present day.

Monia Liter (1905-1988) — Born at Odessa on the Black Sea, his family escaped to China during the Russian Revolution of 1917, where he trained as a classical pianist. He then switched to jazz and made his way to England with the aid of his helpful friend, Al Bowlly. He made outstanding contributions to several top bands as both player and arranger, and led various groups of his own, including the 20th Century Serenaders. He and his wife were fortuitously away during the air raid which killed Al Bowlly in a neighbouring flat.

Benny Loban (1902-1993) — Together with his brother Maurice, Benny arrived from Canada in 1929 to play with the New Savoy Orpheans, becoming leader the following year.

△ *Harry Leader had two appropriate signature tunes.*

When he took the band away with him, however, the Savoy made him rename it. As the Music Weavers they stayed together for another 12 months. Benny then joined Debroy Somers, but reformed his band in 1937, playing for a further five years.

London Radio Dance Band — (see BBC Bands).

Mario 'Harp' Lorenzi (1894-1967) — One of very few harp players to make a name in dance music. An Italian who hailed from Florence, he played with both Fred Elizalde and Jay Whidden before forming his own band for the Madame Tussaud's Restaurant. His later Rhythmics, formed and scored by George Scott-Wood, recorded for Columbia in the mid-Thirties, after which he toured extensively during the early war years.

Geoff Love (1917-1991) — Born at Todmorden, an isolated outpost in the Yorkshire Pennines, he cut his musical teeth in nearby Rochdale, Lancashire. After wartime service, when he helped to re-form the dance band of the Royal Green Jackets, he played with Harry Gold, Lew Stone and Stanley Black, also running his own sextet. By the 1950s he was a top arranger and musical director for EMI. The rest of his career was given over to hugely successful theme and mood music, netting him many prestigious awards, including no fewer than 15 gold discs. His theme tune, *Love Walked In*, was mirrored in his 49-year marriage to his wife, Joy.

◁ *Louis Levy was a musical giant of the cinema screen but still found time to lead the Gaumont-British Dance Band.*

△ *Bram Martin, who chose his signature tune after his daughter asked him a searching question.*

Howard Lucraft (born 1916) — In 1943 he formed a small RAF band which included Steve Race on piano, later making recordings for Forces' radio stations overseas, as well as the BBC. With his wife, well-known swimmer Phyllis Turnbull, he emigrated to the USA during the Fifties.

Don Lusher — A fine trombonist who played with many famous post-war names, eventually becoming quite a media celebrity and fronting the Ted Heath band after its leader's death.

Humphrey Lyttelton (born 1921) — Educated at Eton, following which he served in the Grenadier Guards, Humphrey Lyttelton was perhaps the first important British jazz musician to come to wider public attention after the war. By the late 1940s fans were flocking to hear his Dixieland style, and jiving to his hot rhythm in London clubs. He went on to become a popular and accomplished broadcaster and raconteur.

Percival Mackey (1894-1950) — Competent pianist, arranger and band leader from the early 1920s, his recordings spanned almost 20 years, many under his own name but also as the Riviera Club, and Kit-Cat Band. On the departure of Ray Noble, he also directed the HMV house band, the New Mayfair Dance Orchestra. He was married to the singer and dancer, Monti Ryan.

Madame Tussaud's Dance Orchestra — (see Stan Barnett, Mario "Harp Lorenzi, and Maxwell Stewart).

Bram Martin (1901-1984) — Making his first appearance at the Holborn Restaurant in 1936, he went on to run a popular showband for many years. Once when listening to the radio, his daughter Naomi asked where the music was coming from — "Out of the blue, blue sky" replied her father. When the next piece of music to arrive from his publishers turned out to be *Out of the Clear Blue Sky*, Bram immediately adopted it as his signature tune!

Ray Martin (1918-1988) — Austrian-born, he came to England in 1938 when he was "discovered" by Carroll Levis. A successful career as an arranger eventually led to him fronting his own orchestra which had a number of hits, the most enduring being *Marching Strings*, the theme tune for the BBC Radio schools quiz, "Top of the Form".

Billy Mason (died 1960) — A Scotsman who came to London to play with Fred Elizalde, and thereafter led bands at the Café de Paris and Florida Club. His band also backed Louis Armstrong in 1932. Returning to Scotland he led a band at Glasgow's Empire Exhibition in 1938, before vanishing from view during the war.

Mayfair/Peerless Dance Orchestra — (see also New Mayfair Dance Orchestra) — This was the Gramophone Company's own early house orchestra — as Mayfair on HMV and Peerless on Zonophone — beginning in 1913 and lasting until 1928, when it became the New Mayfair Dance Orchestra (*q.v.*)

Ken Mackintosh (born 1921) — After spells as a saxophonist with both Oscar Rabin and Frank Weir, Mackintosh branched out on

▽ *Mario "Harp" Lorenzi*

his own in 1948, from which time his large-sounding big band could be heard throughout the length and breadth of the country. Popular for many years, his signature tune was Ray Noble's *The Very Thought of You*. Regular television and radio appearances in the Fifties were considerably reduced in the Swinging Sixties, when popular music switched to smaller sounding electronic groups. He remained popular, however, and performed regularly at the Empire Ballroom, Leicester Square; the Hammersmith Palais for seven years; and the Lyceum Ballroom in the Strand. He later played aboard the cruise liner *QE2*, before retiring in the Eighties.

Billy Mayerl (1902-1959) — Although now best-remembered for his piano compositions, (which included more than 60 named after garden flowers), he was an early member of the Savoy Havana Band and led a number of mid-1920s recordings with his own studio dance band.

Jock McDermott (1895-1946) — A Scot who during the early 1930s played at, and also broadcast from, the Royal Opera House, Covent Garden.

Bill McGuffie (1927-1987) — Amazingly for a piano player, he had only nine fingers, the result of a childhood accident in a phone box, which prevented him from becoming a classical concert pianist. Opting for dance music instead, he played with Teddy Foster, Joe Loss, Maurice Winnick, Sidney Lipton, and Cyril Stapleton's show band, eventually leaving the latter in 1954 to go freelance and run his own assorted musical groups, which ranged from a quartet to a big band recording group. He seemed to pop up everywhere on radio, supporting such popular programmes as the "Goon Show" and "Round the Horne". Unfortunately, ill-health suddenly overwhelmed him and he died at the age of only 59.

Ray McVay — Led a strictly functional band for championship contests.

George Melachrino (1909-1965) — A child prodigy who could play several instruments, he was accepted at Trinity College of Music when only 14 years old, and appeared with many famous bands, including Ambrose and Carroll Gibbons, before forming his own orchestra in 1938. Following successful spells at the BBC, and London's Café de Paris, he went on tour with the wartime show "Stars in Battledress". He was then promoted to Sergeant-Major and, at the request of the War Office, formed the British band of the AEF (Allied

△ *Pianist Billy Mason, a Scotsman who played with Louis Armstrong.*

Expeditionary Force), which was in friendly competition with Major Glenn Miller's equivalent American band and Captain Robert Farnon's Canadian band. This group of around 50 musicians formed the basis of his own world-famous post-war orchestra which spawned several smaller ensembles, all famous for their string sound. For 20 years George was a household name but then, tragically, drowned in his bath at the peak of his powers, aged only 56.

Jimmy Miller — (see Service Bands).

Sid Millward (1909-1972) — Formerly a clarinettist with several famous bands, he formed his own group in 1937 which soon

▽ *Billy Mayerl was a gardening enthusiast and composed more than 60 clever tunes named after cultivated flowers. His signature tune was "Marigold".*

evolved into a madcap comedy group called Sid Millward and the Nitwits. As the "Professor", and dressing rather like an unkempt Charlie Chaplin, he fronted all kinds of crazy stage-acts which brought him fame around the world, particularly in Paris and Latin America. He died while performing in Puerto Rico.

Mick Mulligan — Another splendid post-war traditional jazz band which had young people flocking to hear it in the 50s and 60s.

Billy Munn (born 1911) — A Glaswegian pianist with Jack Hylton who finally became a band leader in 1946, playing at the Ocean Hotel, Sandown on the Isle of Wight, following which he spent almost 30 years at Torquay's Imperial Hotel.

Ronnie Munro (1897-1989) — A successful early arranger for Ambrose and other leading bands, London-born Ronnie Munro recorded regularly from 1926 to the outbreak of war, when he went to work for the BBC. Most of his early records were made under his own name, plus pseudonyms such as Buddy Rose, Mel Rose, and George West. After the war he was a household name for many years, being associated especially with the radio programme "Sunday Serenade". He also provided the music for several famous show-business stars, including

△ Sid Millward, originally a clarinettist with several bands, changed his image to zany madcap humour.

▽ The Nitwits, the creation of Sid Millward in 1937, brought smiles to the faces of many with their crazy antics. The kilted laird is Ronnie Genarder.

Dancing Attractions in Blackpool

△ A typical pre-war New Year's dance at Blackpool Tower Ballroom. The band was led by Norman Newman (pictured right).

◁ (Top) Horace Finch played music for dancing at the Empress Ballroom in the Winter Gardens.
(Centre) Syd Seymour's Mad Hatters were always a popular act.
(Bottom) Norman Newman's was one of a number of resident Blackpool bands in the 1930s.

Syd Seymour (left) star of "On With the Show." (Below) Norman Newman and his Tower Ballroom band

△ *The band which started it all. The Original Dixieland Jazz Band (ODJB) at the Hammersmith Palais in 1919. Left to right: Billy Jones, Larry Shields, Nick la Rocca, Emile Christian and Tony Spargo.*

Al Read, Jimmy Edwards, and the Crazy Gang. After working solo on the Union Castle ships to South Africa, he settled in Johannesburg, where he made several broadcasts with a string orchestra before blindness finally forced him to hang up his baton in 1975.

Jack Nathan (1910-1990) — A pre-war pianist and arranger with Roy Fox, he led an efficient post-war band with the appropriate signature tune *Happy Listening*, with which he always began his radio broadcasts, including "Bright and Early" and "Music While You Work". His career lasted until the early-1980s, and included lengthy spells at the Edmundo Ros Club, Churchill's, and the Stork Club.

New Mayfair Dance Orchestra — Unrelated to the Mayfair Hotel, this was the HMV house recording band which, between 1929 and 1934 was synonymous with Ray Noble (*q.v.*). Other leaders and arrangers included Percival Mackey, Carroll Gibbons, Debroy Somers, Harry Leader, Ronnie Munro, George Scott-Wood, and Phil Green.

Norman Newman (born 1907) — First-class drummer, saxophonist, and arranger, Norman first came under the influence of Al Starita before setting sail as a musician on several ocean liners, including the *Berengaria* and *Majestic*. After dropping anchor back in England he played with Ambrose, Roy Fox, and Jack Jackson before forming his own band, succeeding Bertini at Blackpool's Tower Ballroom.

Cyril Ramon Newton (1892-1965) — Born in Malvern, Worcestershire, he emigrated to Canada at the age of 17, just after his father died. He returned to the UK when he was offered the chance to join the Savoy Havana Band, with whom he probably became the first dance band singer to broadcast on radio. He led the group as a violinist and vocalist for some time and also appeared with the Savoy Orpheans. He later played at Ciro's Club and toured with his New Havana Band.

Cecil Norman (1897-1989) — A prolific pianist and arranger who with his brother Leslie (1901-1994) directed several recordings in the late-1920s, many under different names. For a brief spell in 1928 he led a band in America, but returned the following year having become worried about the prohibition era of gangster-related crime. During the 1930s he freelanced with a large number of famous bands including Bert Firman in Monte Carlo, Ray Noble in Holland, and Howard Jacobs in Australia. Back home he appeared with Jack Jackson, Ray Noble, Maurice Winnick, Jay Wilbur, Nat Gonella and Jack Payne, and continued to make music in wartime London, regularly running the gauntlet during the Blitz. On the night the Café de Paris was destroyed he was due to accompany singer Inga Anderson there, but she rang to say she was ill. Instead of sitting in his usual seat overlooking the stage, Cecil decided to take the night off — which was just as well because the balcony was completely destroyed by the bomb which killed band leader Ken Johnson, and a large number of others. In 1945 Cecil formed his own band again, the Rhythm Players making more than 1,000 post-war broadcasts, of which more than 500 were on "Music While You Work". They also appeared in "Play It Again; Piano Playtime; Workers' Playtime" and "Bright and Early", which began live at 6.30 am! Cecil eventually moved away from London and retired with his wife to Bexhill-on-Sea in East Sussex.

Northern Dance Orchestra (see also Alyn Ainsworth, and BBC Bands) — In 1948 the Manchester-based BBC Northern Variety Orchestra was formed, but when the strings

△ *Ramon Newton (top) in later life as a singer and (bottom) as he appeared when performing with the Savoy Havana Band.*

△ *Harry Pell managed to juggle several different musical balls at the same time.*

and woodwind were disbanded in 1956, with the addition of organist Jimmy Leach, it was renamed the Northern Dance Orchestra fronted by Alyn Ainsworth, who also used it for his own commercial recordings. When he left after four years he was succeeded, firstly by Tommy Watt and then by Bernard Hermann, at which point the band became popularly known as the NDO. It lasted until 1981 when the sharpened BBC economic axe split it asunder.

ODJB (Original Dixieland Jazz Band) — A group of white American musicians who played a popular form of jazz and set England alight when they toured here just after the First World War, especially with their performances to huge crowds at the newly-opened Hammersmith Palais. With their new rhythms they were arguably the biggest influence on 20th century British dance band music.

Organists — see separate entries on Harry Davidson, Reginald Dixon, Harry Farmer, Jimmy Leach, Harold Ramsay, Robin Richmond, and

Fela Sowande. — As early as December 1928 London's newly rebuilt Leicester Square theatre opened with cine variety, featuring a 35-piece band led by organists Sandy MacPherson and Reginald Foort but, by 1930, the talkies had caused 65 smaller London cinemas to dispense with their bands, putting more than 600 musicians out of work. Nevertheless during the inter-war period, especially during the 1930s when the mighty Wurlitzer was enjoying its heyday, organists continued to perform alongside dance bands in many larger cinemas and theatres. Typical of the period was Harry Davidson (*q.v.*) pre-war leader of the Commodore Cinema Orchestra, Hammersmith, who also doubled on organ and piano, both of which he managed to play at the same time! Although Reginald Dixon ("Mr. Blackpool") was the doyen of them all, many other organists were famous for their catchy dance rhythms, including Sidney Torch, Quentin Maclean, Reginald New, Edward O'Henry, Donald Thorne, Reginald Porter-Brown, Robinson Cleaver (see chapter on Billy Thorburn), Stanley Tudor, Horace Finch (Empress Ballroom, Winter Gardens, Blackpool), Charles Smart and his son, Harold Smart, Al Bollington, Dudley Beaven, Douglas Reeve (who enjoyed a 50-year relationship with the Brighton Dome), Ernest Broadbent (formerly

△ *Reginald Foort was a household name in the Thirties, broadcasting from the Regal Cinema, Kingston-on-Thames.*

accompanist to the singer Josef Locke, and Reginald Dixon's successor at the Blackpool Tower Ballroom in 1970), and Sydney Gustard. Later rhythmic organists included Phil Kelsall (who succeeded Ernest Broadbent at Blackpool in 1975), Robert Wolfe, Nicholas Martin, and Nigel Ogden.

◁ *Quentin Maclean was training as a classical organist in Leipzig when the First World War broke out and, as a consequence, was arrested and interned for the next four years. Returning to England after hostilties ceased, he initially became assistant organist at Westminster Cathedral but then switched moods and, in 1920, became the first person to broadcast on a cinema organ. During the 1930s he broadcast regularly on the biggest Wurlitzer in Europe, at the Trocadero Cinema, near the Elephant and Castle in south London.*

Edward
O'Henry

Reginald
Dixon

Reginald
New

Harold
Ramsay

Four famous organists from the Dance Band era. Above left, Dudley Beaven; above right, Donald Thorne; below left, Harry Farmer, and below right, Reginald Porter-Brown.

△ *Canadian Sandy MacPherson was a popular and regular broadcaster in this country, but initially was a band leader with fellow organist Reginald Foort.*

▽ *Charles Smart appeared in the Arthur Askey and Richard Murdoch wartime programme "Band Waggon". His son, Harold, was also a swing organist.*

△ One of the most prolific and talented musicians of the 20th century, Sidney Torch was equally at home on the organ, composing light music, or conducting his own orchestra. This 1930s publicity photo shows him standing by a barrel organ, but he could create virtually any sound on the real thing.

▷ Stanley Tudor, a church organist at 10 years of age, was playing professionally at the Hippodrome in Stoke by the time he was 16. In 1932 he moved to London and was appointed to the newly opened Gaumont Palace in Hammersmith, from where, in 1935, he transferred north to the huge 4-manual Wurlitzer of the Gaumont Cinema, Manchester (pictured here). He regularly recorded the background music for the weekly Gaumont Cinema Newsreels and was the first person allowed to play swing music on the massive, but stately, organ at Manchester Town Hall.

▽ Sydney Gustard (left) and Robin Richmond, were extremely popular figures, both before and after the Second World War, with the latter founding the long-running radio programme "The Organist Entertains".

△ *Sid Phillips was one of a large musical family.*

Joe Orlando (died 1991) — One of the successors to Henry Hall at the prestigious pre-war LMS railway hotel at Gleneagles in Scotland, from where he recorded in the late-Thirties.

Tony Osborne — Formerly a trumpeter with Cyril Stapleton, he later became a successful pianist, conductor and arranger.

Jack Padbury (1892-1989) — When the London Radio Dance Band was succeeded by Jack Payne in 1928, Jack took most of it under his own wing and formed a new band. Thereafter he played at venues in London, Nottingham and Eastbourne, before war curtailed his musical activities.

Norrie Paramor (1914-79) — Another hugely popular post-war band leader, Norrie first played pre-war with Harry Leader, Maurice Winnick, Sydney Kyte and Jack Harris. During the war he ran Ralph Reader's "Gang Show" and then teamed up with Harry Gold before joining Columbia in 1952, eventually taking over the whole record label. A prolific and broad musical career then unfolded, his own orchestra appearing regularly on TV and in films.

Don Parker (1899-1936) — After recording with the Original Dixieland Jazz Band in the US, he came to England in the mid-Twenties and played at the Piccadilly Hotel and Kit-Cat Club, before leaving to tour Europe with his Lido Orchestra. He eventually returned to America.

Jack Parnell (born 1923) — After uniting in the RAF with fellow enthusiast Vic Lewis to form a joint-Dixieland jazz group, he joined Ted Heath's band where his strong drumming underpinned the powerful rhythm section. He eventually formed his own band in 1951, and its great success eventually led to him taking charge of music at ATV, a top independent television company which featured weekend musical spectaculars, especially from the London Palladium.

Harry Parry (1912-56) — Initially a member of Percival Mackey's band, Harry Parry became a regular broadcaster during the war years, and his Radio Rhythm Club Sextet first brought jazz to the ears of a truly nationwide audience. Using his own composition, *Champagne*, as a signature tune, with its appropriately sounding "plop" to signal the opening of a bottle, his lively music brought pleasure to a great many people. Sometime members included the blind pianist George Shearing and singer Benny Lee, while Steve Race joined him for a time after the war. With changing musical fashions, however, he eventually moved into a new avenue of entertainment, becoming the compere of "BBC Jazz Club" in 1947. He also presented "Housewives' Choice" and the children's television show "Crackerjack", before his early death from a heart attack.

Pasadena Roof Orchestra — An unashamedly nostalgia group formed in 1970, specifically to recreate dance band music of the Twenties and Thirties. Brainchild of amateur musician John Arthy, and dressed in period costume, they brought a breath of fresh air to a popular music scene suffering from the excesses of the Swinging Sixties. Even though they followed original scores to the note, they quickly gained cult status and an international following, proving that tuneful music still had a place in the pop scene of the late 20th century.

Roland Peachey (born 1912) — Arriving in England from Canada in 1938, his skill on the guitar was soon evident and he became leader of Felix Mendelssohn's Hawaiian Serenaders, with whom he toured extensively. He formed his own band towards the end of the war, before eventually moving back home

Sir Robert Peel (1898-1934) — A brief sortie into the field of dance band recordings was made by this hereditary peer in 1930, with Cavan O'Connor as one of his vocalists! He was married to the film star Beatrice Lillie who enjoyed being addressed as Lady Peel. Unfortunately the title died with their son Robert, who was killed during the Second World War.

Peerless Dance Orchestra — (see Mayfair/Peerless Dance Orchestra).

Harry Pell — A Geordie by upbringing, Harry was an extremely versatile musician who managed to specialise in three different types of music. With his Syncopators, he was the first dance band to broadcast regularly from the Newcastle studio, and later went on to broadcast light music from the Birmingham

△ *Sydney Phasey at the New Victoria Cinema, Bradford.*

Hippodrome every Wednesday afternoon on National radio. Concurrently, he also managed to run several different Midlands dance bands, and keep his hand in on the brass band scene, having previously been an expert BBC adjudicator in the north east!

Sydney Phasey — Leader of a large mid-Thirties orchestra at the New Victoria Cinema, Bradford.

Sid Phillips (1907-73) — One of eight children in a musical family brought up in London, he had several early successes in conjunction with his three brothers, Harry, Ralph and Woolf — the first two as musicians in his band called the Melodians, and the latter as a musical arranger and copyist. After joining Ambrose, Sid became well-known as a quality arranger and composer, and was regarded as the musical brains behind much of the success of this outstanding band. Resisting several lucrative post-war offers whilst on tour in America, he was irresistibly drawn back to his native country where he formed a bright and breezy Dixieland jazz group, featuring his own up-tempo clarinet playing. His instantly recognisable signature tune, *Hors D'oeuvres*, became a best-seller.

Van Phillips (1905-92) — American-born, he was invited to England by Carroll Gibbons, and began his career as a 20-year-old with the Savoy Havana Band in 1925. He soon became indispensable as its arranger, and the band subsequently collapsed after he departed to join the Lawrence Wright music publishing company. It was not long before he was in charge of his own recording orchestra, and quickly became an integral part of London's musical montage,

eventually graduating to become president of the Musicians' Union. He also wrote his own signature tune *The Two Of Us*, which he regularly used until hanging up his baton in the early 1970s, when he moved back to the US and became a successful professional photographer.

Woolf Phillips (born 1919) — The youngest of four musical brothers, he began as a music copyist for famous brother Sid, before emerging as a fine trombonist with Teddy Joyce, Ambrose, Joe Loss and Jack Hylton. During the war he became a successful arranger and soon formed his own band which, because of its success, led to him being asked to succeed Paul Fenoulhet as leader of the Skyrockets at the London Palladium. From there he became a celebrated international band leader and, in 1967, moved permanently to California where he renewed working relationships with many Hollywood stars.

▽ *Van Phillips's career spanned more than half a century.*

Piccadilly Dance Band — The house band for recordings on Piccadilly, being a pseudonym for, among others, Billy Cotton, George Fisher and Allan Selby.

Piccadilly Dance Orchestra — Formed in 1988 by leader, pianist and vocalist Michael Law, this band of young musicians was dedicated to reviving the great traditions of English dance band music.

Piccadilly Players — A famous band directed by Al Starita (*q.v.*).

Piccadilly Revels Band — A famous band directed by Ray Starita (*q.v.*).

Piccadilly Hotel Dance Band — (see David de Groot).

Murray Pilcer (born 1892) — An early American import who arrived in 1916, leading a band which played at several London theatres, clubs, hotels and restaurants. In the days of acoustic recordings his percussion set included wood blocks, bells and klaxon horns. In the 1930s he enjoyed considerable publicity by playing non-stop for 12 hours in Margate.

Ronnie Pleydell (1913-1994) — After cutting his pre-war musical teeth with various bands, he became a post-war West End band leader of some status, especially at the Trocadero and Embassy Club. He eventually scaled down his band to a trio, but was still musically active right up until his death.

Sid Plummer (1901-1967) — A drummer and xylophone player who recorded with Bram Martin in the mid-Thirties, having previously run his own band called the College Boys, which played at Selfridge's department store in Oxford Street.

Danny Polo (1901-1949) — An American who came to Europe in the late Twenties, and moved to London from Paris in May, 1929, making records under his own name and with Ambrose and Jay Wilbur's bands. An outstanding clarinet and saxophone player, he returned to the USA before the outbreak of war.

Reginald Pursglove (born 1902) — After playing with the Savoy Orpheans, Howard Jacobs and Ray Starita, he formed his own band in 1930 and, as a competent arranger and freelance, later appeared on many pre-war recordings with several top bands. Post-war he regularly appeared on "Music While You Work".

Harry Rabinowitz (born 1916) — A native of South Africa, he came to England after the war in 1946. Within a couple of years he was conducting theatre orchestras and musical spectaculars, before being appointed conductor of the BBC Revue Orchestra in 1953. He moved to BBC television in 1960 and ITV in 1968.

Steve Race (born 1921) — A remarkably versatile pianist, composer, arranger and broadcaster, who appeared with many different bands and also led his own quintet. So busy was his lifestyle that he suffered a premature heart attack which forced him to slow down somewhat, although few would have noticed. Extremely popular as the chairman of the Radio 4 quiz show "My Music".

RAF Dance Orchestra — (see Service Bands and Squadronaires).

Archie Ralfini — Brother of Jan, with whose band he used to alternate at cinemas in north London during the Thirties, eventually renaming his group André and his Band. A good supporting orchestra which played in between films and variety acts.

Jan Ralfini (1898-1976) — Real name Ralph Goodliffe, he adopted the Italian sounding *nom-de-plume* to fit the contemporary fashion. Leading a musical variety act and various bands, he toured the country for more than 50 years, beginning during the First World War and ending in 1972! Among his many musicians, before they became famous, were comedian Tommy Trinder (alto sax) and disc jockey Tony Blackburn (vocals).

Bert Ralton (1900-1927) — A talented American saxophonist who led the popular Havana Band at London's Savoy Hotel, before touring Australia and then embarking on an ill-fated game-hunting expedition to South Africa, during which he was accidentally shot dead in January 1927. Allegedly he strummed his guitar as he was dying! A real showman, he used to appear in diamond-studded boots which literally sparkled in the limelight.

Harold Ramsay (1900-1976) — A native of Great Yarmouth in Norfolk, he emigrated with his parents to Canada while still only young and, after schooling in Alberta, began his career as an organist in the USA. A trained pilot in the early years of aviation, he flew everywhere to give recitals and also led a dance orchestra before deciding to move back to England. He became the organist at the Granada, Tooting, and when he took charge of a piece called the *Eight Piano Symphony* was immediately commissioned to form the Rhythm Symphony Orchestra. Playing a cross between dance band and classical music, it toured with some success during the mid-Thirties. He also led a swing band at the Union Cinema, Kingston-on-Thames.

△ Harold Ramsay was an extrovert with a great sense of timing, but his elaborate plans came unstuck when some friends cunningly played a practical joke on him. A pioneer of aviation, before returning to England he often flew solo to engagements throughout America, but was totally unprepared for events on arriving at an unusually small rural airfield. When he asked the way to the dance hall, he was informed he was hundreds of miles from his true destination! Only then did he realise his charts had been changed without his knowledge.

◁ Harold Ramsay and his swing band at the Union Cinema, Kingston-on-Thames.

Freddy Randall (1921-1999) — Another example of the early post-war jazz revival, he toured all round the country, his band proving extremely popular with a new generation of dances and dancers.

Ken Rattenbury (born 1920) — Played in various Midlands dance bands after the war before being discovered by Steve Race. He then led his own traditional jazz band which broadcast regularly during the Fifties.

Frank Rea — By the age of 15 he was leading a pit orchestra at the Royal Avenue Picture House in Belfast, before forming his own Romany gypsy orchestra. He later broadcast regularly on the Northern Ireland radio network from the Orpheus Restaurant, Belfast, with a band, unsurprisingly, called the Orpheans.

Billy Reid — (see Chapter on Accordion Bands)

Roy Richards — A band leader who made a number of recordings under his own name in the mid-Thirties, also appearing as Dick Roy.

Robin Richmond (1912-1998) — Well-known as the founder-presenter of the BBC radio programme "The Organist Entertains", he was a regular rhythmic organist for many years, including a spell with his Organ Grinders Swing at the Hammersmith Palais.

Hugo Rignold (1905-1976) — Emigrated to Canada at the age of four, returning in 1923 to study at the Royal Academy of Music. Originally a violinist with Jack Hylton, Howard Jacobs and Eddie Carroll, he first broadcast as the original leader of the Fred Hartley Quintet. He formed his own band in 1939, before founding the Cairo Symphony Orchestra during wartime service in the RAF. He also conducted the Palestine Symphony Orchestra and, after returning home, became conductor of the Liverpool Philharmonic.

Eric Robinson (1909-1974) — A highly respected and gifted musician (and younger brother of Stanford Robinson) who started out life playing for the BBC. When war came he quickly made a name as leader of the RAOC

133

dance band called the Blue Rockets, paving the way for a glittering post-war career which included much radio and television work with his own orchestra. In 1969 he was awarded the OBE for services to music.

Harry Roche (died 1988) — Formerly a trombone player with Ted Heath, he organised his own recording band called Harry Roche's Constellation, and also led the Billy Ternent band after Billy died in 1977.

Charles (Buddy) Rogers (1904-1999) — A silent film star with Paramount, he appeared in England in a 1935 film called "Dance Band" in which he played the band leader. The following year he conducted the Jack Hylton Orchestra while Jack himself was in the USA. In between films Charles also led his California Cavaliers and Famous Swing Band. In 1937, following her divorce from Douglas Fairbanks Snr., he married the "World's Sweetheart" — film actress Mary Pickford.

Buddy Rose — A pseudonym for Ronnie Munro when he recorded on the Imperial label.

Mel Rose — A pseudonym for several bands recording on Regal Zonophone, including Ronnie Munro, Joe Loss and Harry Leader.

Arthur Rosebery (1905-86) — While still only 16 he formed a small band with his school friends, among whom was a young drummer called Billy Cotton! By 1928 he was leading his own Kit-Cat band, broadcasting and recording under his own name, but also as Vincent Howard, Bert Maddison, Bernie Blake and Barry Bryan. A true extrovert, he continued to play during the war, appearing on Radio Luxembourg and also briefly, in Iceland.

Johnny Rosen (1898-1943) — A violinist with Jack Hylton for many years, he then led an extremely popular 1930s Lancashire-based band, mainly at Lewis's store in Manchester, but also in Liverpool.

△ *Syd Roy, seated on the piano, with some of his Lyricals.*

Val Rosing (1910-1969) — Son of the distinguished Russian operatic tenor, Vladimir Rosing, he was himself better known as a singer, and will always be remembered as the vocalist on Henry Hall's classic recording of *Teddy Bears' Picnic*, which for many years was used as a test piece by BBC sound engineers because of the high range of notes between the high xylophone and low bass-sax. He did, however, record and broadcast with his own band in 1936, before eventually emigrating to Hollywood where he enjoyed a successful career in opera and the concert hall, also appearing in some films.

Andy Ross — For more than 20 years the genial resident band leader of BBC Television's long-running series "Come Dancing", playing every conceivable type of dance band music, from old time to Latin American. The show began as an inter-regional British affair but eventually branched out on to the international scene, attracting all the world's top ballroom dancers. Among the many hosts were David Jacobs, Peter West and Angela Rippon.

Johnny Rosen

Hugo Rignold

134

Dick Roy — (see Roy Richards).

Syd Roy (1895-1981) — Pianist, and older brother of famous band leader Harry, Syd Roy was nevertheless a force in his own right. With a band called The Lyricals, he performed lively jazz tunes at London's Café de Paris in 1924 and, for the opening of the RKO Theatre in Leicester Square in 1931, formed a new group called the RKOlians. Thereafter he concentrated mainly on promoting his more famous brother's career.

Peter Rush — (see Blue Lyres).

Brian Rust (born 1922) — Perhaps the greatest ever expert and authority on British dance band music who, with the help of his friends, actually formed his own band called the Original Barnstormers, which played on both radio and television, as well as appearing at the Royal Festival Hall.

Arthur Salisbury (born 1883) — Violin playing band leader who broadcast every Monday afternoon during the early Thirties from the Savoy Hotel. Unlike the resident late evening bands at the hotel, Arthur's orchestra was mainly string orientated, but he played true dance music and made several records.

Tommy Sampson (born 1919) — Edinburgh-born, he organised and led a highly impressive big band from 1947 to 1950 but, despite appearances at the prestigious Hammersmith Palais, post-war austerity unfortunately forced him to abandon the project.

△ Arthur Rosebery formed his own band when only 16.

Albert Sandler (1906-1948) — A world-class violinist and founder of the long-running radio programme "Grand Hotel" which was first broadcast from the Grand Hotel, Eastbourne, in 1925. Two years later he moved to the West End of London, where he consolidated his new-found fame. In 1943, as leader of the Palm Court Orchestra, he revived "Grand Hotel" from a London studio, but died prematurely soon afterwards.

▽ Debroy Somers was a Radio Luxembourg favourite, and is seen here with an enormous orchestra in the film "Stars on Parade". (See page 37).

△ *Reginald Batten (standing) with a publicity photo of the Savoy Havana Band in the mid-Twenties.*

Savoy Havana Bands, The — Before the Musicians' Union put a stop to it, American bands regularly visited Britain, and London's Savoy Hotel saw early performances from Joe Wilbur and the Savoy Quartet, 1916-19; Bert Ralton's New York Havana Band (with Billy Mayerl on piano), 1920-23; Frank Guarente's Georgians, 1923; and Reg Batten, (1901-1973) who directed the officially-styled Savoy Havana Band (alongside the Savoy Orpheans) from 1923-27. One of his saxophonists was Rudy Vallee who had been specially imported from America, together with his friend, Carroll Gibbons.

Savoy Orpheans, The — London's most famous hotel was something of a Mecca for early dance band music and from 1923-1927 the resident group was the Savoy Orpheans, led by Debroy Somers. There then followed brief spells by Cyril Ramon Newton, Carroll Gibbons, Fred Elizalde, Al Collins and Geraldo, before Gibbons — a lilting rhythmical American pianist — returned in 1931 to lead the slightly renamed Savoy Hotel Orpheans, staying until his early death in 1954. He was succeeded by his former assistant pianist, Ian Stewart, who retired in 1978 and died in 1989.

▽ *Carroll Gibbons conducting the Savoy Hotel Orpheans, with Howard Jacobs (standing) playing lead saxophone.*

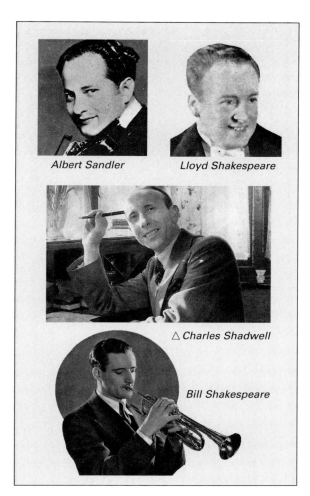

Albert Sandler   Lloyd Shakespeare

△ Charles Shadwell

Bill Shakespeare

◁ *Four very different dance band personalities of the Thirties and Forties. Cousins Bill and Lloyd Shakespeare were often confused by the media.*

Service Bands (see also separate Chapter) — Many top-class musicians were called up in 1939, some of whom got together to form various bands. The best-known was the RAF No. 1 Dance Band, alias the **Squadronaires**, boasting such names as Jimmy Miller, Ronnie Aldrich, George Chisholm and Tommy McQuater. Its main rival was the **Skyrockets**, formed from a collection of musicians undergoing training at Blackpool as barrage-balloon rigger fabric workers! Led initially by George Beaumont, it was taken over by Paul Fenoulhet, later to find fame as the conductor of the post-war BBC Variety Orchestra, who was in turn, succeeded by Woolf Phillips. The Army's contribution was the **Blue Rockets** founded by the hugely popular BBC favourite, Eric Robinson, and later led by Eric Tann and Benny Daniels — while the Navy chipped in with the **Blue Mariners**, led by pianist George Crow, featuring Freddy Gardner on saxophone. Sergeant-Major **George Melachrino** (*q.v.*) ran a rather larger AEF band for the Army, with Major **Glenn Miller** and Captain **Robert Farnon** (*q.v.*) fronting the American and Canadian equivalents, both on tour in this country.

Syd Seymour (1906-1958) — Together with Dr. Crock and his Crackpots, and Sid Millward and his Nitwits, Syd Seymour and his Mad Hatters completed a trio of outrageous comedy bands which had their audiences roaring with laughter at their crazy antics. Touring, both at home and abroad for nearly 20 years, the Mad Hatter (Syd himself), used to twiddle his grey bowler hat which he wore with an outsize checked suit. He also performed several successful seasons at Blackpool.

Charles Shadwell (1898-1979) — A household name in the Thirties, especially with the Coventry Hippodrome Orchestra (*q.v.*) and the BBC Variety Orchestra, which he led with tremendous success as a raconteur, as well as a musician. A regular broadcaster with an infectious laugh that rattled the studio, his tall, thin, bald appearance caused ITMA star Tommy Handley to dub him "The Human Hairpin", a joke which Charles thoroughly enjoyed. After leaving the BBC towards the end of the war, he travelled widely and conducted shows by the dozen.

Bill Shakespeare (1900-1982) — Never actually a band leader himself (although he claimed to have played trumpet for everybody

Primo Scala — (see Harry Bidgood, and chapter on Accordion Bands).

George Scott-Wood (1903-78) — Glasgow-born and classically trained, he moved into popular music in the 1920s and, after first appearing with Jay Whidden, became recognised as a fine composer and arranger. With his Six Swingers he displayed a lively jazz style throughout the 1930s, during which time he was also Director of Light Music for Parlophone Records. One of his best-known atmospheric compositions was *Flying Scotsman*, popularised as an organ solo by Sidney Torch.

Ronnie Scott (1929-1997) — After playing with Jack Jackson, Ambrose, Ted Heath and Jack Parnell, he formed his own band and later founded the Ronnie Scott Jazz Club, which quickly became a mecca for jazz enthusiasts in London.

Allan Selby — Active in the late-Twenties and early-Thirties, he made several recordings as the Frascatians and Piccadilly Dance Band, and also played with his Sussex Serenaders at the Regent Dance Hall in Brighton.

△ *Simone performed at the Café de Paris.*

famous, except Henry Hall), but is included here to distinguish him from his cousin Lloyd, with whom he was regularly confused, even by connoisseurs.

Lloyd Shakespeare (1895-1963) — With a band referred to as his Merrie Men, he toured extensively during the Twenties and appeared on radio in the Thirties. During the war he worked for ENSA before retiring to the Essex coast. He claimed to have been the first band to use a female vocalist (Florence Oldham in 1928), the first to use amplifiers on stage, and the first to use a regular signature tune, *Hunting Horn*.

Dave Shand — A saxophone player from Dundee who played with George Elrick in Aberdeen, before following the latter south to London, where he played with Jack Hylton, Sydney Lipton, Jack Payne and Maurice Winnick. Immediately pre-war he played with the famous Heralds of Swing, and also with Teddy Joyce. Post-war he played with Ted Heath before forming his own band in the Fifties, later appearing at Rhyl, Wembley, the Wimbledon Palais and Savoy Hotel. He also worked with Cyril Stapleton and led his band in a considerable amount of film work.

Sir Jimmy Shand (born 1908) — Synonymous with Scottish dance music, accordionist Jimmy Shand and his Band seemed to be everywhere after the war, both at home and throughout the Commonwealth. After working for four years as a coal miner, he became a professional musician after the general strike of 1926, eventually becoming a regular and prolific broadcaster, especially on the BBC television show "The White Heather Club". He was knighted for his services to music at the age of 91!

Bob Sharples (died 1987) — Originally with Teddy Foster's big band, he came into his own after the war and made many recordings for Decca during the Sixties. He also appeared regularly on television.

Bill Shuttleworth (born 1919) — Already a band leader by the age of 17, Bill operated all over Lancashire, including Blackpool, Fleetwood and Southport, but especially in his home town of Preston. After the war he played opposite all the top bands, and carried on making music until the demise of the dance band era in the mid-Sixties.

Sid Simone Usually known simply as "Simone", he led the band which Ambrose formed to play at the Café de Paris, where he occasionally accompanied regular diner, and star entertainer, Noel Coward. He also led a broadcasting band at the Potomac Restaurant, before forming a Soho band-booking agency with former rival Alf Van Straten.

Jack Simpson (1905-1977) — Drummer and xylophone player with Sydney Kyte, Sydney Lipton, Jack Payne, and Ambrose, he then formed his own Hawaiian and tango bands. His best-known outfit, however, was the Jack Simpson Sextet which he formed in 1940, evolving from the Five Jacks (consisting of Messrs. Simpson, Cooper, Collier, Penn, and Miranda — all named Jack!). He successfully led this group until the post-war closure of music halls forced its demise after which, in 1958, he emigrated to California.

Skyrockets — (see Chapter on Service Bands).

Don Smith — Formerly a trumpeter with Oscar Rabin, who appointed him to his first band leading job in Norwich in 1948. Thereafter he played at Lowestoft and Brighton before appearing as leader of the Stardusters at Nottingham in 1950. As one of Mecca's most popular contract bands, his later residencies included the Wimbledon Palais, Purley, Luton and Oxford.

Fela Sowande (1905-1987) — Born in Nigeria, his musical church background soon found him installed as organist and choirmaster at Lagos Cathedral but, after he became hooked on British dance band music, in 1935 he decided to come to England as a student. Quickly switching from engineering to music, his bouncy Hammond organ playing subsequently gained him appearances on both radio and television. Also a serious composer, he managed to successfully combine all musical aspects of organ playing.

△ *The unmistakable monocled figure of J.H. Squire.*

Michael Sparks — Pianist for many years with Stan Atkins's band, when war ceased, he took over the reins of Atkins's second-string band called the Ambassadors, whom he led until 1947 on several one-night stands across London, including the occasional spot at Stan's resident venue, the plush Embassy Ballroom in Welling, Kent.

Fred Spinelly — He made a number of recordings as the Lido Venice Band between 1927-1931, which included Harry Hudson as vocalist.

Squadronaires — (see Chapter on Service Bands).

J.H. (John Henry) Squire (1880-1956) — Although better remembered as an exponent of light music, this stylishly monocled band leader also made a few dance band recordings after the First World War with his Karsino Orchestra, and also occasionally during the Twenties with his famous Celeste Octet.

Stanelli — Initially just a band leader, Edward Stanley de Groot became famous for his largely solo comedy act involving a "hornchestra", a collection of motor car horns suitably arranged to play popular music. He also made a handful of dance band records, and hosted two radio comedy shows which featured several popular musical turns of the Thirties, including the Three Ginx, Sydney Jerome, Judy Shirley, and Charles Shadwell.

Cyril Stapleton (1915-1974) — Before entering the RAF, Stapleton was a violinist with both Henry Hall and Jack Payne. After demob he formed his own orchestra before conducting the BBC Show Band from 1952-57. He then reformed his own extremely successful group, finally becoming a record producer. His son, Robin, followed in his father's footsteps and made regular radio broadcasts.

Charles "Nat" Star (1887-1950) — A prolific band leader who made hundreds of recordings between 1924 and 1935. In addition to being musical director of Sterno Records he was also much in demand as an instrumentalist. Among his many different pseudonyms were Lester Conn, Jack Falkland and Wallace McIntyre, with at least as many different named bands!

The Stardusters — A relatively short-lived, but exceptionally fine post-war late-Forties dance band led by tenor sax player, George Birch and trumpeter Don Smith (*q.v.*).

Al, Ray & Rudy Starita — Three American brothers who charmed London in the 1920s and early 30s. Al first came to prominence at the Kit-Cat Club, and Ray at the Piccadilly Hotel, where Rudy starred on drums and vibraphone. When Al and Ray returned to the States in the mid-30s, Rudy stayed on as a popular virtuoso soloist before briefly flirting with an all-girls band. Al died in 1963, Ray in 1967 and Rudy in 1978.

Victor Sterling — A pseudonym of Nat Star, used while he was recording for the Pathe record label in the 1920s — and also for Wag Abbey.

Ian Stewart (1908-1989) — Classically trained, and a former pupil of the composer Herbert Howells, he also had a love of dance music, becoming assistant pianist to Carroll Gibbons at the Savoy Hotel from 1935-40. Following distinguished wartime service in the Army — when he was awarded the MBE — he led a band at the Berkeley Hotel from 1946 until 1955, at which point, on the death of his mentor, he returned to the Savoy, where he remained until his retirement in 1978.

△ *Ian Stewart enjoyed both a distinguished musical and military career.*

△ *Ray Starita (seated) and his Ambassadors Club Band. Rudy Starita, standing behind his brother, stayed on in Britain after Al and Ray returned to America.*

Al Starita

Rudy Starita

Maxwell Stewart — A band which played at Madame Tussauds and operated under the title of Ballroom Melody immediately prior to the last war, featuring Freddy Gardner on saxophone and Sam Costa as vocalist.

Monty Sunshine — Another product of the post-war trad-jazz revival, he became famous as Chris Barber's clarinettist before branching out with his own band.

Hal Swain (1894-1966) — Born in Yorkshire he left to work in Canada where he formed a band in 1921, returning to England three years later with a group which played opposite Alfredo at London's New Princes' Restaurant, styling itself the Toronto Band. Although Hal Swain officially fronted the eight-piece outfit, his co-leader was Les Allen who went on to find fame as Henry Hall's vocalist. During the next 15 years Hal toured all over the country with considerable success, both with a large band and also with smaller groups.

Al Tabor (1898-1983) — A Londoner who went to America as a 16-year-old where he formed his own band. He returned post-First World War and within a short time was leading a new band which played at several London venues, including the Hammersmith Palais, and Royal Opera House, Covent Garden.

Eric Tann (1911-1988) — Sometime leader of the Army band, the Blue Rockets, whose close association with the Charlie Chester radio programmes is best-remembered for their opening sequence — "Ring that bell (ding, ding), bang that drum (bang, bang), sound that horn (honk, honk), shoot that gun (bang)." He later worked for George Melachrino before emigrating to Australia.

Phil Tate (born 1922) — Formed his first band in the RAF and kept it together to become a firm favourite on the post-war radio programme "Music While You Work". He broadcast from both Folkestone and London before becoming a band leader at the Hammersmith Palais, from where he branched out into television, including championship playing.

Ted Taylor (1927-1992) — After working with ENSA during the war, he toured with Syd Seymour and his Mad Hatters before forming his own Ted Taylor Four which played all over the country for Mecca and also at various West End clubs in London. He later became a record and television producer.

Temperance Seven, The — Formed in 1955, this nostalgia band was made up of students from the Royal College of Art who imitated dance music from the Roaring Twenties, modelling themselves on the original Savoy Havana band. Brilliantly successful for more than a decade, they are best-remembered for their hit record of *Pasadena*, which had feet tapping all over the country.

Nat Temple (born 1910) — After cutting his musical teeth as a saxophone and clarinet player with Ambrose, Geraldo, Harry Roy and Lew Stone, Temple formed his own band in 1944 which eventually found its way on to radio, becoming famous as the resident musical background support to two lively comedy programmes featuring the extrovert Canadian entertainer Bernard Braden and his wife Barbara Kelly, plus the singers Pearl Carr and Benny Lee. He also appeared in a children's programme called "Jack in the Box", for which he wrote the musical script. In 1992 he and his wife Freda celebrated their Golden Wedding.

Revell Terry (1913-1995) — Turning professional at only 16 years of age, his piano

△ *Stanelli and his "Hornchestra".*

playing was much in demand and he first broadcast from Edinburgh just before the war. After enlisting in the Army he accompanied many entertainers in "Stars in Battledress", including Charlie Chester, and then formed his own band after fighting ceased. He broadcast again, from various London West End clubs, had a spell in India during 1951, and then alternated between winters in London and summers at a holiday camp in Selsey, the southernmost point of Sussex.

Emlyn Thomas — Recording under the name of the London Band, his mid-Twenties group included Nat Star, Ronnie Munro and Debroy Somers.

Sydney Thompson — An undisputed master of old time dancing, eventually forming his own record label.

Pasquale Troise (1893-1957) — Born in Naples, he came to England in 1926 and became an original member of the London Radio Dance Band. In 1932 he formed his first group which, as Troise and his Mandoliers, became world famous. In their silk gypsy costumes they cut a dashing image and enjoyed considerable popularity until well after the war ended, often appearing on radio. He later led a successful group called the Banjoliers, which had a distinctive sound and played regularly on "Music While You Work", also recording for Decca.

Van Straten Brothers — Of Dutch descent, Alf (1905-1988), together with his brothers Leon and Joe, played at several London venues in the 1920s, including Claridges, before embarking on a 10-year tenure at Quaglino's Restaurant in 1933. He then played for three years at the Piccadilly Hotel before going on tour, after which he set up a Soho band-booking agency with former rival Sid Simone. Leon recorded between 1926 and 1939.

△ *Troise was a Neopolitan who played in the London Radio Dance Band before forming his famous Mandoliers.*

Ray Ventura (1908-1979) — Leading a nominally French show band called the Collegians, Ray Ventura was a regular visitor to both Britain and America, and was effectively a clone of Jack Hylton and Paul Whiteman. His success can be measured against the fact that he survived into the 1950s.

Lord Vivian (1906-1991) — As Tony Vivian he led a 1931 dance band at both the Café Anglais and the Ritz Hotel.

Waldini — (see Wally Bishop).

Bob Wallis — With his Storyville Jazzmen, during the Fifties he kept to the true traditions of early 20th century New Orleans jazz.

Abe Walters (1913-1993) — An Australian piano and trombone player who came to England in 1936 and later met with considerable success as a band leader — but not under his own name. Initially he played with Tommy Kinsman, Harry Roy, Lew Stone, Benny Carter, Maurice Winnick, Eddie Carroll, Al Collins, Carroll Gibbons and Sid Phillips — quite a list. Then, under the influence of theatrical band agent Howard Baker (*q.v.*), he became a top post-war West End Latin American band leader, under the unlikely pseudonym of **Don Carlos** and his Samba Orchestra. Although he employed no foreign musicians the band was a great success, broadcasting and recording until the early-Sixties. In 1969 Abe returned home to Perth, Western Australia, where he continued playing until shortly before his death.

Hilda Ward — A 1920s lady band leader who claimed that women could also successfully tackle the new syncopated music, an unusual claim for the period.

Tommy Watt — (see Northern Dance Orchestra).

Hal Swain

Eric Tann

Ray Ventura

Phil Tate

George Webb (born 1917) An important pioneering British traditional jazz revival group, George Webb and his Dixielanders were active only from 1942 to 1948, but spawned a whole new range of similar bands, including that of former member, Humphrey Lyttelton. They also helped to change the dancing patterns of post-war young people.

Frank Weir (1911-1981) — After working for Jack Hylton and Howard Jacobs, during the war he became a leader himself and toured afterwards with a big band which included George Shearing on piano.

Alex Welsh (1929-1982) — Another highly successful post-war traditional jazz band which did much to enhance the genre in the Fifties and Sixties.

Jay Whidden (died 1968) — Another American import, who made a big impact in England between 1926-1932 playing at the Metropole and Carlton hotels. He made many fine recordings and also claimed to be the first band leader to utilise guest nights. Considering his father had once been forced to amputate the fingertips of his young son's left hand after frostbite had set in (there was no doctor on hand in the remote part of the western USA where they lived), it was remarkable that Jay was such a good violinist! When he returned home he briefly organised bands for Hollywood films, and then took his own band on a tour of Australia before disappearing abruptly from the musical map.

Jack White (1905-1988) — With his brothers Tom and Jay, Jack ran a pre-war band called the Collegians, but he only turned professional after being advised against continuing his football career with Everton by no less a playing partner than the legendary Dixie Dean. Dixie felt that band leading would be more profitable, and he was subsequently proved right! Starting at the Liverpool Rialto, Jack progressed via Manchester, Birmingham, Shanklin (Isle of Wight) and Brighton before arriving in London at the Hammersmith Palais. From there he graduated to playing opposite Joe Loss at the Astoria dance hall in Charing Cross Road where, after wartime service in the RAF, he continued to play for a further 10 years.

Jay Wilbur (1898-1969) — Born in Bournemouth, he made over 1,000 recordings, mainly under his own name but also as the Aldwych Players, Connecticut Collegians, Hottentots, Radio Serenaders and Victory Dance Orchestra. In 1940 he became the first band leader to broadcast on a Sunday and also

△ *Jack White once played football with Everton.*

fitted easily into the wartime radio show "Hi Gang", with Bebe Daniels, Ben Lyon and Vic Oliver. He then emigrated, firstly to Australia, where he regularly broadcast with his own orchestra, and later to South Africa.

Eric Wild (died 1989) — A Canadian trumpet player who came to England with Billy Bissett in 1936, and quickly became famous with his Tea-Timers, probably the first regular dance band to appear on the small screen. Made up mainly from the parent BBC Television Orchestra, among its ranks was Eric Robinson on guitar, with vocals by Anne Lenner. Eric saw wartime service with the Canadian Navy and then became the well-respected conductor of the Winnipeg Symphony Orchestra.

Reginald Williams (1914-1988) — After working with Teddy Foster and Philip Brown, he formed his own successful group called the Futurists, signing up a young George Shearing on the strength of an accordion solo played down the phone! In 1939 he was awarded the coveted summer season spot at the Grand Spa, Scarborough, and was appearing in Bristol when war intervened — at which point he joined the Merchant Navy as a wireless operator. When hostilities ceased he was offered a band leading job at the Savoy Hotel, but eventually returned home to the West Country where he toured seaside resorts during the summer seasons. He finally moved into management in the mid-Fifties, but remained musically active and went on a musical study tour of the world in 1970. In total he made more than 1,000 BBC radio broadcasts, mainly late night dance music.

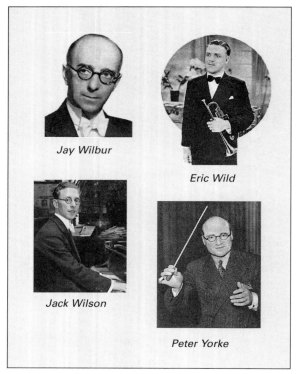

Jay Wilbur

Eric Wild

Jack Wilson

Peter Yorke

Jack Wilson (born 1907) — A pianist with Charles Shadwell's Coventry Hippodrome Orchestra (*q.v.*), he later made several recordings with his own Versatile Five, numbered among whom was the famous violinist Jan Berenska, with Sam Browne as a regular vocalist.

Anona Winn (1904-1994) — Australian-born, her real name was Anona Wilkins, but this was changed by Dame Nellie Melba when Anona first auditioned with her. After moving to England she became well-known as a post-war radio and television star, but during the 1930s was more famous as a singer — and also fronted her own broadcasting band called Anona Winn and her Winners.

Eric Winstone (1915-74) — Leading his first band as a 20-year-old at London's Spanish Club, Winstone was an accomplished accordion player who later moved into bigger-sounding music after hostilities ceased. A firm favourite at post-war Butlin's, he appeared at every camp between the summers of 1946 and 1969, most commonly at Bognor Regis. A genial person, his lively approach to dance band music meant he was popular with everyone. During the winter season he enjoyed engagements at various ballrooms and theatres, and had hit-tunes with *Stagecoach*, *Oasis* (which he wrote in an underground shelter during the London Blitz) and *Pony Express*, all of which fitted his larger-than-life approach.

Marius B. Winter (1898-1956) — The first band to broadcast on the BBC in 1923, and on commercial airwaves from Radio Paris in 1930, Winter also claimed to have been the first to use a regular signature tune. He played until 1938 when he switched to running a music agency instead.

Richard Winter — Leader of the Mayfair Dance Orchestra, a late 20th century recreation of its 1930s counterpart.

Peter Yorke (1902-1966) — Educated at Trinity College, London, he pursued his early career with Percival Mackey and Jack Hylton, before founding his own dance band, and then in 1937 the Peter Yorke Concert Orchestra. He later moved into light music, part of which was a brilliant but all too brief spell with Freddy Gardner. Thereafter, Yorke's magnificent scores reflected his pre-war jazz grounding. A prolific composer, arranger and broadcaster, he wrote many fine tunes including *Silks and Satins*, the theme for the television programme "Emergency Ward 10". His musical philosophy was simple — "I visualise an entire arrangement before I write it, and try to present dance music which is pleasing, by visualising my public as being above the age of 25!"

Arthur Young (1904-1965) — A pianist and arranger with Jack Hylton in the 1920s, Young spent a short time in Germany before returning to play with Freddy Gardner and George Scott-Wood's Six Swingers, also fronting his own Paradise Club Music and Strict Tempo orchestra. During the early stages of the war he led Hatchett's Swingtette, which included both Stephane Grappelli and Chappie d'Amato, but was badly injured in an air raid on London, in September 1940. He emigrated to Australia in 1950, where he became a musical director and toured as an accompanist to the well-known harmonica player, Larry Adler.

△ *Australian Anona Winn had her name changed by Dame Nellie Melba.*

A contemporary 1930s cartoon by the artist "Sherriffs".
Extreme left, Joe Crossman; top row (left to right) Brian Lawrance, Elsie Carlisle and Sam
Costa; middle row, Gerry Fitzgerald, Les Allen, Harry Bentley and George Barclay; front row,
Sam Browne, Harry Roy (with sax), Peggy Dell, Nat Gonella (with trumpet), and Phyllis
Robins; Girvan Douglas stands behind the microphone; extreme right, Perry Cochrane.

Other Band Leaders — A large number of other dance bands broadcast on the radio, especially during the heyday of the 1930s. Included below are some of those not already mentioned who are known to have appeared either on the National network transmitted from London, or on one of the Regional networks based on major cities throughout the country, including Bristol, Birmingham, Plymouth, Cardiff, Manchester, Newcastle, Glasgow, Aberdeen and Belfast.

Roy Allan, Jack Ansell, Tommy Arnold, Don Bamford, Al Berlin, Colin Biggin, Frank Biffo, James Bullock, Sidney Chasid, Jack Chapman, Arthur Clark, Norman Collins, Len Colvin, Reg Conroy, Gerald Crossman, Evered Davies, Wally Dewar, Teddy Dobbs, Al Durrant, Reg Edwards, Dick Escott, Harry Evans, Tommy Finnigan, Hugh Forrosard, Louis Freeman, Sim Grossman, Mr. and Mrs. Wilf Hamer, Ord Hamilton, Roland Hyatt, Jimmy Jack, Yascha Krein, Eddie Ladbroke, Al Lever, Jack McCormick, Tommy Matthews, Lionel Millard, Peter Mills, Alex Monaghan, Norman Nankervis, Max Newman, Vincent Norman, Ronnie O'Dell, Ben Oakley, Neville Oppenheim, Stan Paynter, Roland Powell, Henry Reed, Phil Richardson, T.W. Robinson, Charles Rowe, Harry Saville, Al Saxon, Les Seager, Eddie Shaw, Jack Sheehan, Leon Shortt, Charlie Steel, Doug Swallow, Conri Tait, Leslie Taylor, Bert Thomas, Archie Todd, Sibbald Treacy, Austin Treliving, Richard Valery, Di Vanni, Vince Vaughan, Shirley Waldron, and **George Weldon.**

Jimmy Jack

Al Durrant

Ben Oakley

Al Lever

Al Saxon

Harry Saville

Bert Thomas

Jack Sheehan

Teddy Dobbs

Don Bamford

▽ Al Berlin

Shirley Waldron

▷ Benny Loban and his Music Weavers. Originally called the New Savoy Orpheans, the Savoy Hotel made them change their name!

◁ Al Durrant and His Blue Boys. Like many lesser-known professional bands, Al toured the country giving one-night stands.

▷ Rudolph Dunbar and his Orchestra. A native of British Guiana, Rudolph played at London's Prince's Restaurant, and was also a composer.

Billy Amstell

Dave Shand

Stanley Barnett

Nat Temple

George Melachrino

△ *Although there was considerable rivalry between the top bands, there was also great camaraderie and friendship. Among those celebrating Henry Hall's 70th birthday in 1968 were the nine famous band leaders pictured here:- left to right, Harry Roy, Billy Ternent, Joe Loss, Sydney Lipton, Edmundo Ros, Geraldo, Ambrose, Lew Stone and, seated at the piano, Henry Hall himself.*

▽ *Dance bands featured prominently in many pre-war films, some of which were simply a showcase for their talents. Al Saxon is seen here conducting his Murray's Club Orchestra in a scene from the 1935 Lupino Lane movie "The Deputy Drummer". Singing on the dance floor is Phyllis Clare.*

Top left: *A scene from the Henry Hall picture "Music Hath Charms".*

Top right: *Two young singers with Roy Fox's band were Mary Lee and Bobby Joy, both of whom made several records.*

Above: *Hold Up! A shot from the Jack Hylton picture "She Shall Have Music". Perhaps it was a request number?*

Left: *An unusual publicity photo of Buddy Rogers taken in 1935. A star of silent movies and a fine band leader, he married Mary Pickford in 1937, a marriage which survived until she died in 1979. Buddy himself lived for a further 20 years.*

Gerry Fitzgerald

Peggy Dell

Evelyn Dall

Pat Hyde

Chick Henderson

Paula Green

Some well-known singers of the Dance Band Days

Kitty Masters

Dinah Miller

Fred Latham

Phyllis Robins

July Shirley

Jack Plant

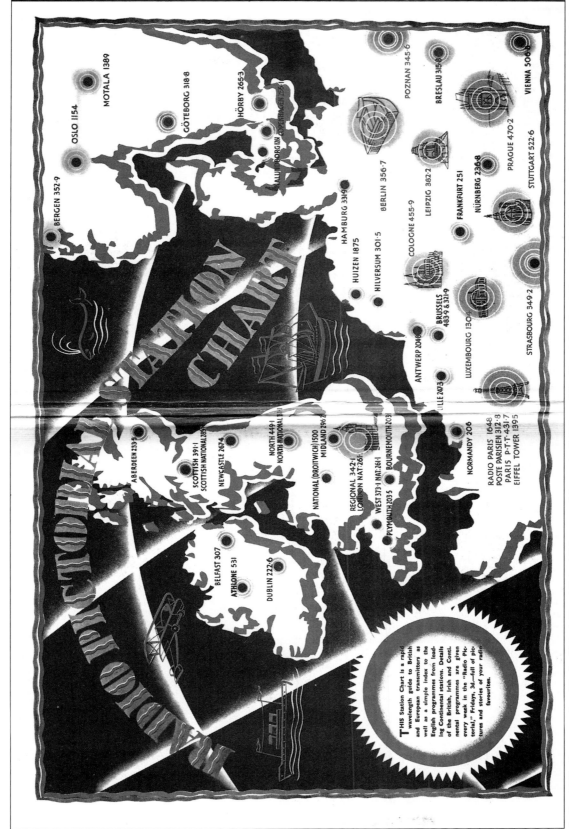

In the 1930s the magazine "Radio Pictorial" published this map of the main British and Continental radio stations, all of which played dance music at some time during their transmissions.

Top Tunes

Ten for each year, from the Twenties to the Fifties

1920

After You've Gone
Alice Blue Gown
Avalon
I'm Forever Blowing Bubbles
Indian Summer
Japanese Sandman
Let the Rest of the World
  Go By
Someday Sweetheart
The World is Waiting for the
  Sunrise
Whispering

1921

Ain't We Got Fun?
All By Myself
I Never Knew
I'm Nobody's Baby
Look for the Silver Lining
Margie
Ours Is a Nice 'Ouse Ours Is
Playthings
Sweet and Low
Twelfth Street Rag

1922

A Kiss in the Dark
April Showers
I'm Just Wild About Harry
Limehouse Blues
Ma! He's Making Eyes at Me
Peggy O'Neil
Say It With Music
Second Hand Rose
The Sheik of Araby
Three O'clock in the Morning

1923

Carolina in the Morning
Estrellita
I Cried For You
I Wish I Could Shimmy Like My
  Sister Kate
Marchéta
My Buddy
Toot Toot Tootsie Goodbye
Way Down Yonder in New
  Orleans
Who's Sorry Now?
Wonderful One

1924

Bugle Call Rag
California Here I Come
It Had To Be You
Nobody's Sweetheart
Riviera Rose
Romany Rose
Somebody Loves Me
Somebody Stole My Gal
The One I Love Belongs to
  Somebody Else
What'll I Do?

1925

Alabamy Bound
Always
Charleston
I'll See You in My Dreams
Indian Love Call
Mexicali Rose
Rhapsody in Blue
Show Me the Way To Go
  Home
Sweet Georgia Brown
Tea For Two

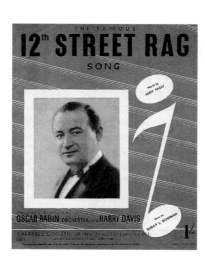

1926

Am I Wasting My Time
    On You?
Brown Eyes, Why Are You
    Blue?
Dinah
Drifting and Dreaming
Fascinating Rhythm
Five Foot Two, Eyes of Blue
I Found a New Baby
Moonlight and Roses
Rolling Round the World
Sleepy Time Gal

1927

Ain't She Sweet?
Among My Souvenirs
Blue Skies
Charmaine
Jealousy
My Blue Heaven
Shepherd of the Hills
Side by Side
Someone To Watch Over Me
The Desert Song

1928

Are You Lonesome Tonight?
Girl of My Dreams
Miss Annabelle Lee
Mistakes
Ol' Man River
Sweet Sue — Just You
That's My Weakness Now
The Man I Love
Together
When Day is Done

1929

Ain't Misbehavin'
Carolina Moon
I'll Always Be In Love With You
I'll Get By
Marie
My Mother's Eyes
She's Funny That Way
Singin' in the Rain
When You're Smiling
You Were Meant For Me

1930

Amy, Wonderful Amy
Basin Street Blues
Beyond the Blue Horizon
Body and Soul
Bye Bye Blues
Dancing With Tears in My Eyes
Falling in Love Again
Happy Days Are Here Again
Honeysuckle Rose
Tip-Toe Through the Tulips

1931

Goodnight Sweetheart
Just One More Chance
Lady of Spain
Love Letters in the Sand
Memories of You
On the Sunny Side of the
    Street
Sally
Stardust
Sweet and Lovely
When Your Hair Has Turned To
    Silver

1932

As Time Goes By
By the Fireside
Chinese Laundry Blues
Embraceable You
Georgia on My Mind
In a Shanty in Old Shanty Town
Love is the Sweetest Thing
Marta
The Clouds Will Soon Roll By
Underneath the Arches

1933

Don't Blame Me
Have You Ever Been Lonely?
I Cover the Waterfront
I'm Getting Sentimental
    Over You
Lazybones
Let Bygones be Bygones
Stormy Weather
The Man on the Flying Trapeze
The Teddy Bear's Picnic
Try a Little Tenderness

1934

All I Do Is Dream of You
Did You Ever See a Dream
    Walking?
I'll String Along With You
Little Man You've Had a Busy Day
Love's Last Word is Spoken
Play To Me Gipsy
Smoke Gets in Your Eyes
The Last Roundup
The Very Thought of You
When You've Got a Little
    Springtime in Your Heart

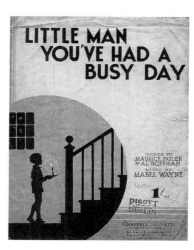

1935

Back to Those Happy Days
Blue Moon
Dancing With My Shadow
I Only Have Eyes For You
I'm in the Mood for Love
Lovely to Look At
Red Sails in the Sunset
The Lady in Red
The Song of the Trees
When I Grow Too Old to
    Dream

1936

Did Your Mother Come From
    Ireland?
It's a Sin to Tell a Lie
Poor Little Angeline
Shoe Shine Boy
The Music Goes 'Round and
    'Round
The Way You Look Tonight
These Foolish Things
When Somebody Thinks You're
    Wonderful
When the Poppies Bloom
    Again
Would You?

1937

A Foggy Day
Boo Hoo!
Harbour Lights
Home Town
Ida, Sweet as Apple Cider
Pennies From Heaven
September in the Rain
She's My Lovely
That Old Feeling
The First Time I Saw You

1938

A-tisket A-tasket
Hear My Song, Violetta
I Double Dare You
Love Walked In
Music Maestro Please
Remember Me
Rose of England
The Donkey Serenade
The Girl in the Alice Blue
    Gown
The Lambeth Walk

1939

Boomps-a-Daisy
Deep Purple
Jeepers Creepers
Little Sir Echo
Moonlight Serenade
Run Rabbit Run
South of the Border
There'll Always be an England
We'll Meet Again
You Must Have Been a
    Beautiful Baby

1940

A Nightingale Sang in
    Berkeley Square
I'll Never Smile Again
In the Mood
Over the Rainbow
Sierra Sue
The Nearness of You
The Sailor With the Navy Blue
    Eyes
Tuxedo Junction
When You Wish Upon a Star
Who's Taking You Home
    Tonight?

1941

Amapola
Beneath the Lights of Home
Bless 'em All
Down Forget-Me-Not Lane
I Don't Want to Set the World
    on Fire
Maria Elena
My Sister and I
The Hut Sut Song
Tumbling Tumbleweeds
Yours

1942

Blues in the Night
Chattanooga Choo Choo
Deep in the Heart of Texas
Moonlight Becomes You
Someone's Rocking My
    Dreamboat
The Anniversary Waltz
The White Cliffs of Dover
When the Lights Go On Again
White Christmas
You Are My Sunshine

1943

Coming in On a Wing and a
    Prayer
Constantly
Dearly Beloved
I'm Thinking Tonight of My
    Blue Eyes
My Devotion
Pedro the Fisherman
Sunday, Monday or Always
That Old Black Magic
You'd Be So Nice To Come
    Home To
You'll Never Know

1944

Don't Sweetheart Me
I Couldn't Sleep a Wink Last Night
I'll Be Seeing You
I'll Walk Alone
I'm Making Believe
Lilli Marlene
Long Ago and Far Away
Mairzy Doats and Dozy Doats
Roll Me Over
Shoo Shoo Baby

1945

Ac-cent-chu-ate the Positive
Don't Fence Me In
I'm Beginning to See the Light
Let Him Go, Let Him Tarry
Saturday Night is the Loneliest Night of the Week
Sentimental Journey
The Hokey Cokey
There Goes That Song Again
There I've Said It Again
We'll Gather Lilacs

1946

Ashby de la Zouch
Bless You
Cruising Down the River
I Can't Begin to Tell You
I'll Buy That Dream
In the Land of Beginning Again
Nancy (with the laughing face)
September Song
The Old Lamplighter
You're Nobody 'Till Somebody Loves You

1947

Five Minutes More
Guilty
I Was Never Kissed Before
Now Is the Hour
Oh What a Beautiful Morning
Open The Door Richard
People Will Say We're in Love
The Girl That I Marry
This is My Lovely Day
Zip-a-Dee-Doo-Dah

1948

A Tree in the Meadow
Cool Water
Count Your Blessings
Galway Bay
My Happiness
On a Slow Boat To China
Rambling Rose
So Tired
Take Me To Your Heart Again
The Dream of Olwen

1949

A - You're Adorable
Baby It's Cold Outside
Confidentially
Far Away Places
It's Magic
Lavender Blue
Maybe It's Because I'm a Londoner
Powder Your Face With Sunshine
Put Your Shoes On Lucy
Red Roses for a Blue Lady

1950

A Dream is a Wish Your Heart Makes
Ashes of Roses
Autumn Leaves
C'est Si Bon
Daddy's Little Girl
Dear Hearts and Gentle People
Goodnight Irene
Mona Lisa
Mule Train
My Foolish Heart

1951

A Beggar in Love
Because of You
Good Luck, Good Health, God Bless You
I Love the Sunshine of Your Smile
Mocking Bird Hill
Rose, Rose, I Love You
The Roving Kind
The Tennessee Waltz
Too Young
Unforgettable

1952

Auf Wiederseh'n Sweetheart
Because You're Mine
Half as Much
High Noon
Love is Here to Stay
Lullaby of Birdland
Why Worry?
Wimoweh
Wonderful Copenhagen
You Belong to Me

General Index

157

Bibliography

And the Bands Played On —
   Sid Colin, (Elm Tree 1977)
Ballad Years, The 1945-1960 —
   Don Wicks, (published privately)
British Dance Bands on Record, 1911-1945 —
   Brian Rust & Sandy Forbes, (Gramophone Publications 1987)
Dance Band Era, The —
   Albert McCarthy, (Hamlyn, 1974)
Directory of Popular Music —
   Leslie Low, (Peterson 1975)
Fascinating Rhythm —
   Peter Cliffe, (Egon 1990)
Golden Age of Radio, The —
   Dennis Gifford, (Batsford, 1985)
Oxford Companion to Popular Music, The —
   Peter Gammond, (Oxford, 1991)
Radio & Television Who's Who —
   Cyrus Andrews, (George Young, 3rd edition, 1954)
Signature Tunes —
   Chris Hayes, (published privately in 1989)
World of Big Bands, The —
   Arthur Jackson, (David & Charles, 1977)

The following periodicals were also of great assistance:-

Journey into Melody —
   magazine of the Robert Farnon Society
Memory Lane —
   PO Box 1939, Leigh-on-Sea, Essex, SS9 3UH
Melody Maker —
   a long-running popular music journal
Radio Pictorial —
   a weekly magazine popular throughout the 1930s
Radio Magazine —
   a monthly magazine first published in 1934